Everyday Life in the Modern World

Everyday Life in the Modern World

Henri Lefebvre

Translated by Sacha Rabinovitch

With a New Introduction by

Philip Wander

Transaction Publishers

New Brunswick (U.S.A.) and London (U.K.)

Fourth printing 1999
New material this edition © 1984 by Transaction Publishers
New Brunswick, New Jersey 08903. Original edition copyright © 1971
by Sacha Rabinovitch.

Library of Congress Catalog Number: 84-8653
ISBN: 0-87855-972-8 (paper)
Printed in the United States of America

Library of Congress Cataloging in Publication Data

Lefebvre, Henri, 1905-
      Everyday life in the modern world.

      (Classics in communications series)
      Translation of: La vie quotidienne dans le monde moderne.
      Reprint. Previously published: New York : Harper & Row, c1971.
(Harper torchbooks ; TB1608).
      Includes bibliographical references.
      I. Civilization, Modern—1950-   I. Title. II. Series.
CB427.L413   1984   909.82   84-8653
ISBN 0-87855-972-8 (pbk.)

Contents

Introduction to the Transaction Edition

Philip Wander

> Everyday life is a crust of earth over the tunnels and caves of the unconscious and against a skyline of uncertainty and illusion that we call Modernity, while overhead stretch the Heavens of Permanence; among the greater planets are Scientificness, clear, cold and somewhat shadowy, and the twin planets Virility and Femininity; there are stars, constellations and nebulae; high over the polar horizon we have Technology and elsewhere Youthfulness; there are *novae* such as reliability, frozen, extinct stars like Beauty and the strange signs of Eroticism; among the fixed stars of the first magnitude we might place Urbanism and Urbanization (so long as we do not omit Naturalness, Rationality and a few others); and then the sub-lunar planets, Fashion (or "fashionability") locatable in the vicinity of Femininity, and Sportiveness, etc.
>
> —Henri Lefebvre

The question underlying *Everyday Life in the Modern World* is what gives a society devoted to the all-consuming transitory, and to accelerated change, the illusion of stability. It is a profound question, leading to a radical reassessment of ourselves as products of this world and of our society which, along with other modern societies, is now poised on the brink of unredeemable catastrophe. It is odd to associate all this with everyday life, but this is crucial if we are to follow Lefebvre's critique. "Everyday life" refers to dull routine, the ongoing go-to-work, pay-the-bills, homeward trudge of daily existence. It indicates a sense of being in the world beyond philosophy, virtually beyond the

vii

capacity of language to desribe, that we know simply as the grey reality enveloping all we do. In this sphere of nonwork relations we live out our lives with our acquisitions, compulsions, and fears. The way time and space are made up in the urban areas—which during the nineteenth and twentieth centuries have grown up around the great factories to house the workers—and what this means for the individual is the focus of Lefebvre's work and the meaning of what he calls the "quotidian."

The "modern world" refers to the products of industrialization and the controls necessary to socialize workers and regulate consumption. It is a society whose rational character is defined through and has its limits set by highly organized groups (bureaucracies) operating through the state and/or the corporate state; whose purpose lies less in production than in consumption; whose level of operation takes place on and is aimed at influencing everyday life. In this way Lefebvre joins together technological, consumer, affluent, and leisure societies emphasized by other social theorists, into what he calls a society of bureaucratically controlled consumption. Its poetry is found in advertising; its persona is the consumer; and its mechanism for insuring individual conformity lies in the communication of fear—fear of being out of fashion, of not being young and attractive, being odd, out of it, the subtle terrors through which advertising motivates.

The intellectual significance of Lefebvre's critique is that it identifies an undeniable body of experience—our own in relation to the society in which we live—and challenges its naturalness. Neither nature nor fate, science, or technology determines what is. The shape and content of our lives is the product of a number of decisions in which we do not participate and about which we may or may not be aware. The building in which I live is the product of negotiations between builders, environmentalists, and bankers: its cost, which is a product of interest rates, a depressed construction industry, and the efforts made by unions to preserve jobs, as well as its shape—the kind of building materials used, where it sits on the lot, its relation to the sun at mid-day. The nature surrounding me? Every shrub is planned, its selection influenced by what is planted on the freeways and in front of office buildings (this establishes a fashion and lowers the cost of the plants involved). The sky, the azure blue of romantic poems, is laced with wires the telephone company, electric utilities, and lumber interests did not wish to bury. The sunset, the fiery orb dropping through dark clouds, is a product of automobile and industrial emissions and the efforts of ecology groups to establishing smog controls. The water, the crystal springs gushing forth, its clarity and taste are the result of a struggle between petro-chemical corporations, high-tech industries (that use chemical baths to sterilize the microchips), and groups seeking to improve public health and to promote clean water.

It is not that Lefebvre politicizes everyday life; rather he unveils its ideological structure. He reverses the notion that home is a haven, that although depression, famine, and war are beyond us, we can manage our own lives. In place of this duality between everyday life and public affairs enshrined in the evening news, Lefebvre points to a dialectical relationship between where we live, how we live, what we consider natural, and decisions which have been and are being made (or not being made) by people operating in government and the corporate state.

But beyond the bleakness of an everyday life regulated by the needs of consumption, Lefebvre points to the cracks in the concrete made by that which cannot be wholly repressed: The awakening of sexual desire and love; the undeniable delights of play; and the allure of the festival, the bursting of work-time and prefabricated leisure experienced in celebration. "What scope has an 'industrial society' if it fails to produce a fruitful *urban life?*" he asks. "None, unless it *be to produce for the sake of producing.*" The failure of modern society lies in our alienation —a sense of powerlessness in trying to influence the world in which we live; of meaninglessness in our search for guides to conduct and belief; of isolation from others; of estrangement from one's self. For modern society to have meaning, to convey a sense of coherence, it must find some purpose beyond consumption. Lefebvre argues that it ought to be the production of autonomous, thinking, feeling individuals able to experience their own desires and develop their own style.

Utopia? Of course, replies Lefebvre. We are all utopians, as soon as we wish for something different and stop our role playing, gamesmanship, and watchdogging. It is, however, utopian thinking grounded in the modern world and the way ordinary people experience it. That we should consider the great contribution of industrialism to human life, namely urban society, and wish to make it a wonderful place to live, though radical in its implications, certainly has the virtue of settling on common ground.

The content of *Everyday Life in the Modern World* is intellectually significant and so is its form. It is not a book in the classical sense. It is aphoristic, episodic, the transitions unclear. A key to understanding Lefebvre's style may be found in his critique of writing. Writing fixes the word. Fixed, it may be appealed to as Holy Writ or statute law to legitimize the use of force. Writing kills the living moment of creative exchange. That sharing of the commons we know as communication dies for lack of dialogue between real people. Spontaneity, creativity, dialogue, the unrestrained movement and compenetration of speech, the poetic moment, all this is buried in the written word. Bureaucracies thrive on writing. They create and interpret the text. The text may intimidate through abstruseness or through dissociation from historical context, and this leaves ordinary people with a feeling of ignorance and reluctance to speak.

Even as Lefebvre denounces an eternal world of ideas in favor of the living moment, he embraces Plato's scorn for writing: "No intelligent person," notes Plato in one of his letters, "will ever be so bold as to put into language those things which his or her reason has contemplated, especially not into a form that is unalterable, such as writing." The problem is complicated in the modern world. The muses speak through a medium fashioned by those who determine what language is permitted, what texts are reproduced. Language itself is therefore tainted by the established order—educational, governmental, mass media. Not only writing that embalms the living moment but also language shaped by an established order confront the poet of change, who would reveal the hidden beauty of the world, make familiar objects unfamiliar, purge from our inward sight the film of familiarity which obscures us from the wonder of our being, and would create anew the universe, after it has been annihilated in our minds by the recurrence of images and ideals blunted by endless reiteration in modern society.

Lefebvre, like Marcuse in the *Aesthetic Dimension,* treats art as a harbinger of an alternative world. In creative expression we glimpse not only the springs of creativity but also a form appropriate to content in opposition to what is. But while writing may confront us with alternatives, who gets to write, who can read, and who can afford the "text" represent political barriers to deliberation. Further, when one is calling for cooperative activity, when one is committed to collective deliberation so that action will not only be purposefully but also theoretically informed, the written word becomes an obstacle. Lefebvre, through what he says and how he says it, calls for dialogue, face-to-face communication over ways of improving the quality of life for ordinary people. His vision of a radically reformed urban environment contains within it both space and time for conversation.

Where does Lefebvre stand in relation to our intellectual landscape? He is of course a Marxist. Along with the young Lukács, Karl Korsch, and Sartre, he attacks the suppression of the individual and opposes bureaucratization in both corporate capitalism and authoritarian socialism. Along with the Frankfurt School (Marcuse, Adorno, Horkheimer, and Fromm) and the Praxis group in Yugoslavia (Marković), Lefebvre anchors his critique in the young Marx who envisioned a revolution dedicated to producing human beings. When workers control the means of production and participate in making decisions about their lives (safety conditions, work time, work relations) they are no longer slaves.

Some of the concerns shared by this group and which orient their critique of both theory and practice include: hierarchy—the rigid stratification of society and the channeling of the masses into levels assigned according to race, sex, age, IQ, etc.; alienation—the estrangement of the individual from society, politics, the other, and ultimately from him or herself; and subjectivity—the alternatives open to the individual through existing arrangements and made possible by radically changing existing arrangements with the aim of overcoming alienation.

The full force of Lefebvre's critique reveals itself in relation to the work of others. Fromm, for example, offers an analysis of alienation that amplifies Lefebvre's work. Fromm stresses the importance of work in shaping an individual personality in the modern world. The "I" who is born into and learns to function in the "quotidian" is to a large extent fashioned in response to the routines of everyday life. The "I" I encounter as a fact here and now is most visible in the workplace. Except for the privileged few, we are expected to work for a living. In the United States this has largely come to an eight-hour day, five-day week job in the corporate state or state bureaucracies. Travel to and from the job (given our urban environment), worrying over it, gossiping about it, take-home work—take all this into account and the amount of time devoted to job-related concerns consumes half of our waking hours. If we work forty years, we sell twenty to the workplace. Consider further the time spent getting ahead or just surviving on the job, and how this influences our dress, reading, conversation, relationships, and how we organize our leisure time. That such intense, ongoing, and unrelenting activity should influence our "personalities," that what we do with half of our waking hours should shape our awareness of things (our "consciousness"), that it carries with it a set of values disguised as "real life," is hardly surprising.

While real life may now seem natural, it has not always been so. The workplace has changed over the last hundred years. It now values a different type of personality. It has been only recently, notes Fromm,

> that the package, the label, the brand name have become important, in people as well as in commodities. The gospel of working loses weight an the gospel of selling becomes paramount. In feudal times, social mobility was exceedingly limited and one could not use one's personality to get ahead. In the days of the competitive market, social mobility was relatively great, especially in the United States; if one "delivered the goods" one could get ahead. Today, the opportunities for the lone individual who can make a fortune all by him [or her] self are, in comparison with the previous period, greatly diminished. He [or she] who wants to get ahead has to fit into large organizations, and his [or her] ability to play the expected roles is one of his [or her] main assets.[1]

Encountering our selves requires us to encounter the type of personality valued in the workplace.

In contrast to a self-employed people living in villages (shop-owners, shipowners, the small family farmers at the heart of Jeffersonian democracy) where independence and integrity are necessary, modern society with its bureaucratic organizations values the ability to "fit in," to "get along." In a marketing economy the valued personality is not independent, eccentric, or outspoken. The modern mass market is impersonal. It depends on calculations of supply and demand and the ability to motivate demand for even useless and potentially damaging commodities. The worth of a product no longer depends on its use (the purpose it serves for either the individual or society) but on its exchange value (how much one can get for it).

In anonymous urban centers, serving faceless masses, workers depend for success not only on their skills but also on the willingness of the other to employ them or buy their goods and services. Clerks, salespersons, business executives, doctors, lawyers, assembly-line workers—all must cultivate "winning" personalities. In a lifelone sequence of encounters with anonymous others, each of us must be able to "put ourselves across," to "sell ourselves" to the other.

In this kind of relationship, our worth depends on conditions beyond our control, thus any setback in the drive for success may cause a severe threat to self-esteem. Helplessness, insecurity, and inferiority threaten when the other does not respond in the appropriate manner. This undermines a sense of autonomy and independence. The feeling that "I am whatever you want me to be," that when the boss tells me to jump my response is to ask "how high?" takes over. Since it is not production skills that are valued in the marketplace (more and more skill requirements are broken down into specialized or "mindless" work) but instead our attractiveness, we are led to see ourselves and others as commodities. The other becomes a button to be pushed, a link to be forged, a "contact." We rank the other according to officially sanctioned values, according to his or her intelligence, attractiveness, influence, or success. The other is not unique; his or her peculiarities are not valued. The other is measured against some other like-thing; the other is someone who is better or worse, is superior to or subordinate to me. Relationships become superficial. Wit becomes one-up, one-down exchanges between competitors. We search for "meaningful" relationships. The media communicate a frenzy of love stories, locating them farther and farther away from adult life and the workplace. Young love is the real thing. Old love is a prayer, and naturally so in a society where being attractive is equated with youth.

In the marketing orientation, according to Fromm, reason must conform to the changing expectations of others. What is valued is not the probing, thoughtful question, but the swift retrieval of data and rapid and accurate calculations. The model for thinking is not the sage but the computer. The fruit of thought becomes not wisdom but success. In order to be successful in the modern world, concludes Fromm, one must be adaptable, responsive, saleable, free of individuality or subjectivity, objective and empty.

The modern world fosters a childlike personality, a person who constantly seeks and needs approval, who is not hung up on the past and is not committed to a future apart from becoming a success. It fosters a person who enters into the here and now of adjustment demanded by bosses and customers, who has no principles to speak of, who remains ever alert for opportunities knowing that they may never knock again. Aimless, overreactive, inconsistent, face aching at the end of the day from the ever-present and required smile, the marketing persona is of a piece with the modern world.

Because it is valued in and rewarded by the real world, the marketing orientation is a part of each of us. It is a way, an all-too-familiar way of being-in-the-world. We may develop a different persona away from work, find solace in our hobbies, have others serve us, travel to other parts of the world in search of nature or exciting relationships, but we know the value of a "winning smile." To be sure, there are positive aspects to the marketing orientation. It encourages us to be open-minded, social, undogmatic, efficient, curious, and tolerant. But freedom from prejudice does not build anything. Being open-minded does not tell us what is worthwhile.

Lefebvre carries Fromm's diagnosis into leisure time. We divide the quotidian between work and leisure, between the "salt mine," "jungle," the "rat race," and free time. The other side of a market economy for those who suffer in the workplace—for whom "thank God it's Friday" has become an acronym—is consumption. People must be brought to the point of purchasing what is being marketed. Thus leisure time is invaded by the same economic arrangements dominating the workplace. It too fashions a persona. It is a persona geared to the needs of the marketplace. The consumer orientation sends us seeking after those things eroded by the workplace. We buy love, joy, fulfillment, security, a sense of identity, the compensatory aura enveloping products and services. This aura is the product of a multibillion-dollar motivation industry. Advertising is the poetry of the modern world; and what it promises is freedom from fear.

Lefebvre calls the modern world a "terrorist" world. He stresses the motivating element in consumerism as internalized terror. This may seem an overstatement. Terror tactics by the police or the army are obvious enough, but advertising? Yet we must recall Lefebvre's project: an exploration of what makes modern society appear coherent to the individual. What he is talking about is internalized terror, terror so fundamental to modern life that it has become second nature. We may appreciate his argument more by referring it back to everyday life, life as we experience it. Consider our concerns about how we appear. Through advertising we are daily persuaded to become self-conscious about our bodies. Our bodies should be slim, clean, unblemished (women's hands should be "baby soft" to be attractive). We must beware of our teeth (are they white enough?), our mouths (are they kissable?), our armpits (do they stink?), our feet (are they dry?). Our bodies become attractive through the use of powders, chemicals, and sprays. All this sounds funny, until we consider the operations performed to remove fatty tissue, alter noses, etc., and the neuroses about being ugly, misshapen, unattractive. Through it all is the suspicion that beyond race, sex, and age, important decisions about one's life are also made on the basis of attractiveness—from grades in school to hiring and promotions—a situation exploited for its profitability by a marketing economy and registered in the inner recesses of the individual in heightened self-consciousness about appearance.

Trained in a market economy to look upon ourselves as commodities and to worry over whether or not we are sufficiently pleasing and attractive, we confront an enormous corporate complex accentuating our insecurities and, in effect, selling us back to ourselves. Painted over, sprayed, powdered, covered in ways that are fashionable and therefore attractive, we purchase the ability to feel good about ourselves.

Alienation growing out of the workplace and exploited

through bureaucratically regulated patterns of consumption is a pivotal theme. Subjectivity is another. It is tempting to leave the definition of subjectivity up to the "observations" of social scientists or to dismiss it altogether as something anarchic and unreliable. But observing individual behavior in the modern world would most likely reveal people lost in routines, feeling helpless, estranged from themselves and others, experiencing anger and despair (even "crises" at mid-life) about their jobs and future. However objective such findings might be, they cannot address the question of potential, of human capabilities not called upon or actually suppressed in everyday life. We must therefore rescue subjectivity from what is and enter the realm of what is not, namely the world of possibilities.

Lefebvre does not blush at utopianism. Yet when it comes to outlining real possibilities, both he and Fromm, like Marx, draw a great deal from village life (the "community" to be retrieved out of urban civilization), artisanship (the "productive" orientation in Fromm, the implicit model for "creativity" in Lefebvre), and the individual within entrepreneural capitalism. Claims about individual potential may of course be grounded in a collective past and serve as precedents for what we might create in the future. Such claims may also be grounded in individual history—Marcuse's emphasis on the awakening of sexual desire and love within our own experience. They may also be grounded in the experience of people during the course of collective activity—the antiwar movement in this country, the resistance movements in Europe during World War II, the courage and resourcefulness displayed during the American and French revolutions.

An argument for improving the quality of life presupposes some vision of and belief in individual potential. Throughout *Everyday Life in the Modern World* Lefebvre hints at such potential. He does so primarily by identifying forces that distort and blunt individual sensibility. "Everyday life should be a work of art," he declares firm in his faith that each person is a potential artist, and that the creative impulse can be encouraged through a radical reorganization of modern life.

Yet it is difficult to see just what Lefebvre believes to be individual capabilities in this matter. Again it is useful to amplify his position. Thus while Lefebvre is content to hint at their existence and realization, Mihailo Marković tries to spell them out. He considers the following faculties fundamental:

1. *Unlimited Development of the Senses.* Man [and woman] can have an increasingly rich and manifold experience of the world. Our sensory powers may be magnified by the creation of suitable instruments. On the other hand, they can be refined by progressive cultivation and they can be liberated to the extent to which our surroundings become dereified. There is hardly any limit to the increase of our ability to see, to select, to interpret, to concentrate on one interesting dimension of our perceptive field, and to associate what we immediately perceive with a whole world of former experiences and thoughts.

2. *Reason.* Descartes believed that there is nothing else in the world which is so well distributed among human individuals as reason. Even if it is granted that there are considerable differences in intellectual capacities of various persons, the fact remains that every sane human individual is able to analyze objects and situations, to grasp regularities, to discover order in constant change, to derive conclusions, and to solve problems. Unfortunately, in modern production, modern political life, and mass culture, man does not have sufficient motivation to develop this faculty.

3. *Imagination.* The given world is always a small, narrow world for man. In the most primitive communities, in the earliest phases of individual development, there is already manifest a capacity to transcend in thought the limits of the given, an ability to project idealized objects, human beings, and situations. In modern production and public life this capacity is redundant and is being wasted.

4. *A Capacity for Communication,* not only in the sense of learning a language, but also in the sense of an increasing ability to understand the thoughts, feelings, desires, and motives of other persons who belong to other nations, classes, races, and cultures. Under favorable social conditions all forms of narrow-mindedness may be transcended and the level of a universal social consciousness may be reached.

5. *A Capacity for Creative Activity,* one which does not invariably repeat the same form but introduces novelties. Modern industrial society is inconceivable without this faculty; however, it favors its one-sided

actualization toward increasing efficiency and success at the market. In modern industrial production of commodities, the producers are condemned to a complete uniformity and a renunciation of all creative impulses.

6. *The Ability to Harmonize Interests, Drives, and Aspirations with Those of Other Individuals.* Without it men would not be able to live in a social community. Nevertheless, this faculty is very much blocked in social conditions favoring competition and struggle, and the survival of the fittest.

7. *Discrimination, Assessment, and Choice among Alternative Possibilities.* This faculty is the ground of human freedom. It can be actualized in a distorted way if an external authority (church, state, party) succeeds in imposing upon human individuals its own criteria of evaluation, its own conception of who they are and what they can be. That is why genuine human freedom coincides with the actualization of the capacity of *Self-Identification* and *Self-Consciousness.*

8. *Man's Ability to Develop a Clear Critical Consciousness about Himself.* This is the ability to distinguish between what he actually is and what he potentially could be. Owing to this capacity, man can decide to change his style, his social role, his relationship toward other human beings. This faculty accounts for sudden, discontinuous, consciously directed changes in human behavior which make human history so much more open and unpredictable a process than the history of physical nature.[2]

These capabilities grounded in history, experience, and the imagination point to the potential of the individual as an autonomous, creative force to draw together with others to change reality, just as what has become reality now is the product of efforts to change what was reality in the past.

What have we learned in the twenty years since the publication of *Everyday Life in the Modern World* which bears on our interpetation of its message? Two things come to mind. One is the link between the quality of life in the modern world and the policies of modern, industrialized societies toward Third World countries. And the other is the subtlety and pervasiveness of the ideology of modernism in mass media.

Improving the quality of life in the modern world costs

money, takes energy, requires vast amounts of natural resources. Programs to improve everyday life in the modern world are therefore joined with life in the Third World through the availability of raw materials, markets, the cost of labor, and through the impact of change in the Third World on domestic politics. Lefebvre concerns himself for the most part with French society. When his book first appeared, French losses in Indo-China and the catastrophe in Algeria were still fresh. The connection between everyday life and foreign policy in France may have been clear, especially so because the French governments had long identified their "sphere of influence" as an empire, and justified it on, among other things, its economic benefits.

If anything, the link between everyday life and foreign affairs needs to be made even more explicit today. Beyond the quandary advocates of radical and expensive reforms in modern societies face when they examine what such programs mean for people living in Third World countries (when oil was two dollars a barrel, the "affluent society" was a term that had some substance to it), there is the problem of resource exhaustion. Oil, tungsten, chromium, tin, and bauxite are some of the resources essential to the functioning of modern industrial societies that may be all but mined out by the end of the century. Growing demand by modern and would-be modern societies, dwindling supply, and rising costs will lead to increased competition for raw materials between nations. Increased competition over essentials increases the likelihood of confrontation and war. In a world fueled by gasoline, lightened by aluminum and titanium, and illuminated by tungsten we discover links between modern and primitive, underdeveloped, or Third World societies, which bring foreign policy closer to home.

Another aspect of the modern world we have come to appreciate since Lefebvre's book appeared, and in part because of it, is the subtlety with which the ideology of modernism insinuates itself into the media. A program of cultural criticism has emerged since the late 1960s in American society and has found some support in the academy. Film, TV, popular music, science fiction, romance novels—every medium and mode of communication have been subjected to a critique based on the world view commended to the mass audience. What characterizes the best of *Everyday Life in the Modern World* is its avoidance of the notion that some small, conspiratorial group is demanding that popular culture convey a particular world view. The alternative is to acknowledge that there is, in Marcuse's phrase, an official "reality principle," that it is widely if uncritically held, that it is functional up to a point for particular groups, but that it is not the totality. The test of such a critique is its ability to acknowledge the existence of that which does not conform to the official reality principle and to explain the alternative it represents.

Though it probably would not occur to us on reading Lefebvre's book to identify a popular prime-time TV program of the late 1960s as an objective correlative of modernism, I cannot think of any clearer exemplar than "Star Trek": science, technology, youth, virility, femininity, reliability—all play a part. The future takes place in a womblike environment fashioned out of the miracles of science and technology. There are no concerns about food, clothing, shelter, unemployment—they have been taken care of through a socialist society. It is a militarized society though; therefore it maintains a rigidly defined hierarchical order. Those at the top are the most intelligent and resourceful people on board. They deserve to be on top. They are also the best fitted for engaging in a free and open deliberation of problems facing the ship. They are the best and the brightest a technically advanced society could send into outer space.

Their purpose is twofold: to go "where no man has gone before," that is, to explore uncharted regions, and to search for raw materials needed by the "federation." This effort includes establishing colonies on unpopulated planets—enrolling "animals" living there to help in the mining; working out trade agreements with the natives on populated planets; and, when necessary, violating the "prime directive" of nonintervention to bring progress or to protect a people from the Klingon menace.

In this way—through the danger of attack, economic necessity, and vast differences in intelligence and ability to reason, we come to accept a caste society, one where only those at the top are allowed spontaneous, "human" relationships. The rest of the crew stand guard, bring food, work communications, fire lasers. Burned, boiled, and frozen, they occasionally gasp for dramatic effect. In a positive universe all this is legitimized through the joking, pleasant, artful relationships portrayed among the officer corps. In a negative universe superiors work their will on subordinates for personal gain, sexual favor, or for revenge.

What made "Star Trek" stand out at the time, and this was a period of growing dissatisfaction with American policy in Vietnam, was much richer and more subtle than the weekly moonwalk it provided in the face of the bombing of Hanoi, the invasion of Cambodia, and the ghetto riots. "Star Trek" explored the tensions between playful egalitarianism and formal hierarchy, free-world agreements and totalitarian force, trade and exploitation, and between defensive weapons and genocidal force. As for the individual, it explored the tensions between reason and emotion, spontaneity and calculation, humanity and the machine, creativity and technical expertise.

The "Star Trek" film series continues to address important conflicts in modern societies, and despite its popular, if not critical, success, it reveals the limits of scientism even as it celebrates its future triumphs. One film in the series focuses on the threat of dehumanizing technology, which can envelop everything and stand poised for the destruction of Earth. It is deterred from doing so through the mystical insertion of a man and a woman into the center of purposiveness within the machine. All that was destructive about technology before stemmed from a lack of understanding of the direction it should take. Because there were no vested interests that stood to lose from changing the course of existing technology, all it took was the absorption of two brilliant, loving, technically trained, and dutiful young people into it to stay the prospect of total annihilation.

In another film, genocidal technology is captured by barbarians—irrational, undisciplined, mad geniuses. They are the product of genetic experiments on Earth centuries earlier. They threaten to use a new invention for purposes of massive destruction. Its use in the right place however can produce an Edenic environment. Thus the promise of new life or of more advanced forms of life in the centuries after an atomic war—the promise on which "Star Trek" is based—is compressed into a few seconds as science takes on the role of prime mover in the "Genesis Project."

Committed to solutions based on scientific expertise and the heroic efforts of those in power, "Star Trek" breaks down precisely at the point it addresses the question of human survival posed by science and technology. The products of science and technology are a given. When they are destructive, it is merely a matter of using technical knowledge and creative thinking to avoid destruction. That ordinary people could or should participate in deciding what kind of life they would like to lead and the place of technical innovation in that life; that ordinary people should join together to deliberate and influence the course of modern society, especially in its commitment to the production of genocidal weapons or its exploitation of primitive, underdeveloped, or Third World countries; that the natural resources necessary to support modern life may be exhausted in the next twenty years—all of this remains opaque in the romance of science fiction, and for that matter, in the reality that is everyday life in the modern world.

However insightful or "correct," cultural criticism is not the aim of Lefebvre's book. In the act of denouncing writing he writes a book, but in the act of reading we are confronted with a need to respond. What he says argues actively and explicitly against passive acceptance or reception. Lefebvre envisions praxis. His theoretical position is worked out in such a way that it can orient those who would deliberate and act to influence public policy (people who historically were known as "citizens" in democratic societies). He does not, however, map out a program—that should be worked out by people speaking to each other in a here and now that writing cannot touch. Lefebvre tries to get at the conditions operating against the individual and diminishing his or her quality of life.

Fixing on the quality of life, Lefebvre's critique affirms the importance of love, independent and creative thought, free time, and of meaningful work and human survival; yet it also inquires into the conditions necessary for their realization. It therefore embraces utopian visions animating a variety of social movements while transcending the religious, ethnic, gender, class, and national barriers erected around particular coalitions. There is no party, faction, or movement at this time offering a critique that can lead a society faced with declining markets and resources away from violent solutions to the twin problems of external opposition and internal rebellion.

Lefebvre begins with a subjectivity necessary for coping with a miserable reality, a subjectivity embracing the critical consciousness necessary to resist and to alter the reality principle of a bureaucratically directed economy and its underlying structure. He argues for the freedom to understand existing conditions and the need to submit these conditions to the principle of enhancing human life. Such an awakening is necessary for a more integrated opposition. He marks off a vantage point transcending Left and Right, capitalism and socialism, dualities subsumed in "everyday life" and embraced by the "modern world."

Notes

1. Erich Fromm, *Man for Himself* (New York: Rinehart, 1947, pp. 81-82.
2. Mihahilo Markovic, *From Affluence to Praxis* (Ann Arbor: The University of Michigan Press, 1974), pp. 13-14.

1   An Inquiry, and Some Discoveries

In the past fifty years . . .

Imagine that you have before you a complete set of calendars dating from 1900, of which you select one at random that happens to represent a year towards the beginning of the century. Pencil poised, you then close your eyes and make a cross beside a day in this year; you open your eyes and you find that it is the sixteenth of June you have marked. Now you try to discover what took place on this particular day among so many others in a relatively peaceful and prosperous year – for this continent and country at least. You go to the public library and consult the national press for this date; you are confronted with news items, accidents, the sayings of contemporary personalities, a clutter of dusty reports and stale information and some unconvincing revelations concerning the wars and upheavals of the time; but there is practically nothing that might enable you to foretell (or to suppose that a reasonably perceptive person living in those days could have foretold) any of the events about to take place, those occurrences that must have been silently developing in the hidden depths of time; on the other hand, neither will you find much information as to the manner in which ordinary men and women spent that day, their occupations, preoccupations, labours or leisure. Publicity (still in its infancy), news items and a few marginal reports are all that is now available to reconstruct the everyday life of those twenty-four hours.

2 Everyday Life in the Modern World

Having perused papers and periodicals from this not-so-distant past – noting the familiarity of headlines and the out-of-date typography – you can now give rein to your fancy: might not something have happened on that sixteenth of June which the press has omitted to report ? You are indeed free to imagine that it is precisely then that a certain Mr Einstein – of whom nobody at the time had ever heard – had his first perception of relativity in the Zurich room where he inspected patents and toed the narrow lonely path between reason and delirium. Nor can anyone prove that you are wrong if you choose to believe it was that day and no other that an imperceptible but irreversible action (the apparently insignificant decision of a bank manager or a Cabinet minister) accelerated the passage from competitive capitalism to a different form of capitalism thus initiating the first cycle of world wars and revolutions. You might further select this early summer's day with the sun in its solstice, dominated by the sign of Gemini, for the birth in some quiet village or town of children who, for no obvious reason, would grow up gifted with an exceptional awareness of the times and events.

Thus it is by chance and not by chance that this particular day – a sixteenth of June at the beginning of the twentieth century – was significant in the lives of a certain Bloom, his wife Molly and his friend Stephen Dedalus, and as such was narrated in every detail to become, according to Hermann Broch, a symbol of 'universal everyday life', a life elusive in its finitude and its infinity and one that reflects the spirit of the age, its 'already almost inconceivable physiognomy', as Joyce's narrative rescues, one after the other, each facet of the quotidian from anonymity.*

The momentous eruption of everyday life into literature should not be overlooked. It might, however, be more exact to say that readers were suddenly made aware of everyday life through the medium of literature or the written word. But was this revelation as sensational then as it seems now, so many years after the author's death, the book's publication and those twenty-four hours that were its subject matter ? And was it not foreshadowed already in Balzac, Flaubert, Zola and perhaps others ?

* Hermann Broch, *Dichten und Erkennen*, Zurich, 1955, pp. 183–210, 237.

The answers to these questions may contain a lot that is unexpected, but before attempting them we would like to point out some of the main features of one of the most controversial and enigmatic works of its time. *Ulysses* is diametrically opposed both to novels presenting stereotyped protagonists and to the traditional novel recounting the story of the hero's progress, the rise and fall of a dynasty or the fate of some social group. Here, with all the trappings of an epic – masks, costumes, scenery – the quotidian steals the show. In his endeavour to portray the wealth and poverty of everyday life Joyce exploited language to the farthest limits of its resources, including its purely musical potentialities. Enigmatic powers preside. Bloom's overwhelming triviality is encompassed by the City (Dublin), the metaphysical speculations of 'amazed' man (Stephen Dedalus), and the spontaneity of instinctive impulses (Molly); here is the world, history, man; here are the imaginary, the symbolic and the prophetic. But in making use of all the potentialities of speech a twofold disruption of language, both literary and general, was inevitable; the inventory of everyday life implies the negation of everyday life through dreams, images and symbols even if such a negation presupposes a certain amount of irony towards symbol and imagery; the classical object and subject of philosophy are found here in concrete form; that is to say, things and people in the narrative are conceived in terms of the object and subject of classical philosophy. But they are not static, they change, expand, contract; the seemingly simple object before us dissolves when subjected to the influence of acts and events from a totally different order; objects are super-objects, Dublin, the City, becomes all Cities, the River stands for all rivers and waters, including the fluids of womanhood; as to the truly protean subject, it is a complex of metamorphoses, of substitutions, it has discarded the substantial immanence–transcendence of the philosophers, the 'I think that I think that I think . . .' and unfurls through the medium of interior monologue. During these epic twenty-four hours in the history of Ulysses (Odysseus, Otis-Zeus, man-God, essential common man, the anonymous and the divine made one) the I merges with Man and Man is engulfed in mediocrity.

This subjectivity which unfurls is time in its dual aspect of man and divinity, the everyday and the cosmic, here and elsewhere; or in the triple form of the man, the woman and the other, waking, sleeping and dreaming, the trivial, the heroic and the divine, the quotidian, the historical and the cosmic. Sometimes 'they' are four: four wayfarers who are also the four Old Men, the four Evangelists, the four Corners of the Earth, the four Horsemen of the Apocalypse. Time is the time of change – not localized or particular change but the change of transition and the transitory, of conflict, of dialectics and of tragedy; the River is the symbol in which reality and dream are one and which is without form. The writing captures the world of desire and the narrative is dreamlike in its matter-of-factness (precisely in its matter-of-factness); in no way contrived, it reproduces the flowing image of a cosmic day, leading the reader into the turmoil of a linguistic carnival, a festival of language, a delirium of words.

Time – the time of the narrative, flowing, uninterrupted, slow, full of surprises and sighs, strife and silence, rich, monotonous and varied, tedious and fascinating – is the Heraclitean flux, engulfing and uniting the cosmic (objective) and the subjective in its continuity. The history of a single day includes the history of the world and of civilization; time, its source unrevealed, is symbolized over and over again in womanhood and in the river; Anna Livia Plurabelle, the flowing Liffey, Molly and her impetuous dream-desires in the boundless, unpunctuated realm between sleeping and waking, merge, converge and mingle.

Before pursuing our investigation let us summarize the preceding observations:

a) This narrative has a referential or 'place', a complex that is topical, toponymical and topographical: Dublin, the city with its river and its bay – not merely a distinctive setting, the scene of action, but a mystical presence, material city and image of the City, Heaven, Hell, Ithaca, Atlantis, dream and reality ceaselessly merging but with reality giving the tone; a city cut to the size of the citizens: the people of Dublin have moulded their surroundings which mould them in turn. Drifting through the streets of Dublin the wanderer gathers together the scattered fragments of this reciprocal assimilation.

b) Meanings proliferate, literal, proper and figurative, analogical, symbolical, mythic or mystic, not to mention the ultimate unfathomable meaning (related perhaps to enigmas of wandering, death, absence), as well as the different levels of meaning familiar, historical, kindred, foreign and so forth. And these meanings coexist. Joyce excels in the art of weaving them together, composing fugues with his themes; his linguistic resources seem truly inexhaustible. It has been suggested that one could write out the meanings on musical staves, superimposed as in an orchestral score. Joyce works on a substance, the written word, and in his hands it acquires polyphony, gathering and receiving speech till the reader hears the subject's voice emerge from the page with all the connotations of subjectivity. Musicality always prevails over the purely literal; melodic line and harmonic progression determine the phrasing with necessary transitions (recurrence of the key-note, which may be a symbol or simply a specific sound). The writing tries to capture the enigmatic depth, the inherent musicality of language – or rather of speech – the polyphony pertaining normally only to orchestral music. Connotations play the part of harmonics; though he works in his own medium, the writer does not hesitate to borrow polyrhythmics, polyvalence, polyphony from the musician so that we find here writing, language and speech organically merged and redefined by the methods of musical composition.

c) Yet duration is not entirely structureless. There is in Joyce – and not only in *Ulysses* – a symbolic system with coherent cross-references (though it must be admitted that in the glare of linguistic fireworks the coherence is not always self-evident). Where for others the relation signifier–signified is purely formal, for Joyce it is essentially dialectical; the signifier becomes signified and vice versa; the accent is continually being displaced, here the one predominates, there the other. Thus womanhood is signified by fluidity, rivers and waters but when two washerwomen at dusk evoke the legend of the river, from being signifier it becomes signified; all the rivers of the world are its tributaries. We find symbolical systems of womanhood, of the city, of metaphysical thought (the maze), of ordinary objects (a lighted cigar in the dark recalls the Cyclops' eye). It would be interesting to construct a science of everyday life starting from these symbols, though such a 'science' belongs to another age than our own, an age where symbolism was in its prime; with Joyce at the beginning of the century each group of symbols was thematically related, distinct but undistinguished, and man could be represented by the prophetic bird: 'Be my guide, dear bird; what birds have done in the past men will do tomorrow, fly, sing and agree in their little nests.' Alas, an optimistic symbolism reflecting a youthful century!

d) For Joyce – after Vico and perhaps Nietzsche – cyclical time underlies all quotidian and cosmic duration. Everyday life is composed of cycles within wider cycles; beginnings are recapitulations and rebirths. The great river of Heraclitean becoming has many a surprise in store: it is linear; symbols, words and their repetitions reveal ontological correspondences that are fused with Being; hours, days, months, years, epochs and centuries intermingle; repetition, recollection, resurrection are categories of magic and of the imaginary but also of reality concealed within the visible; Ulysses is Bloom, and Bloom re-enacts Ulysses and the Odyssey; quotidian and epic merge like Same and Other in the vision of Perpetual Recurrence. As the mystic or the metaphysician – and because he is a poet – Joyce challenges the incidental; with everyday life as mediator he passes from the relative to the absolute.

'Why must you go and choose an author whose work meanders through an impenetrable atmosphere of supreme boredom? There are others besides his Molly who are reduced to drowsiness by those endless pages. . . . And how can you have the cheek to quote an untranslatable author into the bargain? All you say is completely meaningless to those who are not well versed in the English language. Furthermore Joyce is dated, as dated as nineteenth-century music in an epoch of atonality, concrete music and random constructions. He made writing unpredictable by the incessant intervention of a hero who is always just ahead or trailing behind the narrative. The works of Joyce and his contemporaries elude the strictures of dimension by subjecting words to musicality and thus making them indeterminate. The dichotomy "word-writing" (reminiscent of those other dichotomies "melody–harmony" and "harmony–rhythm", from which it is none the less distinct) was fully exploited by Joyce; there is not a subterfuge, trick or contrivance that he spares us: hints (with a wink and a nudge), puns, *trompe-l'oreille*, every gap in coherent speech is filled with something; yes, but with what? What? The language of *Zarathustra*, however, truly soars on the wings of harmony instead of being reduced and limited by syntactical strictures, so that Nietzsche is always present while Joyce recedes . . .'

Maybe; yet are not intelligibility and 'translatability' insured by Joyce's symbolical constructions carried as they are on the tide of Heraclitean time? Coherent groups of symbols are easily transferred from one language to another and from one 'culture' to another (in so far as 'cultures' exist . . .); such groups play the part of 'universals'. Is there not clearly perceptible in Joyce's writing a sort of tonal system conveyed precisely by its fluidity, continuity and transitoriness? Clear phrasing, return to the key-note, tension followed by the resolution of a cadence, startings and endings, punctuation in depth . . .; are none of these still intelligible? Could Beethoven be lapsing into folk-lore? Or Wagner? What neo-dogmatism! Nietzsche? How the times have changed! A little, a lot, vastly, not at all? We shall see. Joyce's *Ulysses* is everyday life transfigured not by a blaze of supernatural light and song but by the words of man, or perhaps simply by literature. If the authorized questioner who has just intervened is right, all the more reason to define what has changed in half a century, whether it is everyday life or the art of representing it through metamorphosis, or both, and what the consequences are.

What has changed after roughly half a century? That the subject has become blurred is news to no one; it has lost its outline, it doesn't well up or flow any longer, and with it the characters, roles, persons have slid into the background. Now it is the object that plays the lead, not in its objectivity (which had meaning only in relation to the subject) but as a thing, almost a pure form. If I want to write today – that is write fiction – I will start from an ordinary object, a mug, an orange, a fly of which I shall attempt a detailed description; never departing from the perceptible – presented as the concrete – I shall proceed to make inventories and catalogues. And why should I not choose that raindrop sliding down the windowpane? I could write a whole page, ten pages, on that raindrop; for me it will become the symbol of everyday life whilst avoiding everyday life; it will stand for time and space, or space within time; it will be the world and still only a vanishing raindrop.

There are many ways of interpreting what is still known as the 'new novel' (apart from considerations of success, failure, tediousness or interest). It can be seen as a methodical attempt to create a rational style that deliberately avoids tragedy, lyricism, confusion and controversy, aiming instead at a pure transparency of language that might almost be called spatial. This 'objective' clarity could be seen as a sort of projector isolating the object on a stage if one were to overlook the fact that objects must first be created; it is a product neither of the subject as creator nor of the object as creation, but only of language imitating 'reality'. Can one even say that a story is being told? A story is no longer a story when words are reduced to bare necessities. Time is cancelled out in the process of exploring it, when the quest for a perfect recurrence, a coming and going in time, is achieved by means of pure prose, of writing reduced to its essence. The simultaneity of past, present and future merges time with space and is more easily realized in a film than in literature, where 'novelistic' implications are always present. Moreover it is not every subject that can be submitted to such a formal elaboration: things, people, gestures, words. And can anyone be sure that time will not intervene and disrupt such permanence? Is everyday life's changelessness a guarantee? Films and literature use everyday life as their frame of reference but they conceal the fact, and only expose its 'objective' or spectacular aspects. Writing can only show an everyday life inscribed and prescribed; words are elusive and only that which is stipulated remains.

Let us take an example. Shall we select for our particular example of 'objective' writing, the writing of strict form, a distinguished scholar or a novelist? If a novelist, who shall it be? We have made the arbitrary choice of Claude Simon in his book *Flanders Road*,* because there is a certain affinity between this

---

* Claude Simon, *Flanders Road*, London, 1962.

book and *Ulysses* notwithstanding the differences that distinguish them; an affinity that makes comparison possible while enabling us to note the contrasts. In both works short periods of time expand, dream and remembrance recreate a universal everyday life; in both we find the eternal triangle, wife, husband and lover; symbols and word-play abound. In Claude Simon there is a Blum, in Joyce a Bloom, a coincidence that suggests a connection perhaps not wholly unintentional on the part of the later author.

'Oh yes! . . .' Blum said (now we were lying in the darkness in other words intertwined overlapping huddled together until we couldn't move an arm or a leg without touching or shifting another arm or leg, stifling, the sweat streaming over our chests gasping for breath like stranded fish, the wagon stopping once again in the dark and no sound audible except for the noise of breathing the lungs desperately sucking in that thick clamminess that stench of bodies mingled as if we were already deader than the dead since we were capable of realizing it as if the darkness the night. . . . And Blum: 'Bought drinks?', and I: 'Yes. It was . . . Listen: it was like one of those posters for some brand of English beer, you know? The courtyard of the old inn with the dark-red brick walls and the light-coloured mortar, and the leaded windows, the sashes painted white, and the girl carrying the copper mugs . . .'

Fine. Now let us compare this to what we had noted in *Ulysses*.

a) Here we find no acknowledged, pre-established referential; the place is a place of desolation, a landscape laid waste by war and rain where corpses rot in the mud and slime, a sinister collaboration of civilization and nature. The symbolism is spatial, the place being the only stable thing there is. We are never sure in what moment of time the story is situated, nor in which tense is the narrative; and we do not need to know. Memories are centred around the place, symbolized and actualized by it as they flow from the remote past. In the course of the narrative, which proceeds in cycles, men are the playthings of fate; they circle around the place and their circling leads to death or captivity at the hands of the enemy.

b) Man's fate is not enacted here against a backdrop of normal everyday life; we are in time of war. And yet it is the quotidian that is conjured up. The past, before tragedy took over, was controlled by logic and order, or so it seemed; in reality logic and order, and meaning too, were only paving the way to tragedy (eroticism, passion and love), with its sequel of disillusions. The extraordinary in everyday life was everyday life at last revealed: deception, disappointment. . . . Passionate love turned out to be terribly similar to love without passion, the passion only accentuating the void and the hunger it was supposed to satisfy but from which it really stemmed. Could this be the *cool* style unambiguously replacing the *hot* style of the preceding period? In a cold passionless voice the author tells of passion, its illusion and its disappointments; the quotidian is unavoidable, and even those who believe they have eluded it are its victims; married couples and lovers are alike frustrated and betrayed, the first in everyday life, the others in the life of tragedy. The cycle of betrayals and frustrations spirals down from remembered time, in fact through a century and a half as the narrative passes from generation to generation; remembrance negates temporality.

c) Language becomes the only referential, as the 'real' referential is abolished by truth; the author has fashioned a reality from speech where the sentence conveys similarities, disparities, the order and disorder of impressions, emotions, sensations, dialogues (that are not really dialogues), solitude, in fact everything that serves to build up a 'character'. The writing imitates speech in an attempt to purify or perhaps to exorcize it. The critic J. Ricardou calls it the 'verso of writing', but if he is right then this verso corresponds exactly to the recto. It is indeed the very essence of writing, a literature passed through the crucible of literalness and aiming at total precision. Though it simulates speech, speech has disappeared, the writing is a linear trajectory; and meaning too has vanished, whether proper, figurative, analogical or hermetic; everything is made explicit; signs are distinct in their difference and the difference is entirely revealed in the significance. A voice or voices? A toneless voice, a writing that is precise and pure as musical intervals fixed by pitch. Connotations? Harmonics? Yes, adjusted by pitch and thus eliminating fluidity, extensions of sound and boundlessness. Time is divided into similarities and disparities before it dissolves into memory and fate, which are almost identical. Even the word-play is exposed, stated and explained. This pure writing has attained freezing point in so far as this point is pure transparency. A comparison with atonality will perhaps make this clearer; there is no determining note (referential), therefore no repose; there are interruptions but no beginnings or endings; there are intermissions but nothing that really corresponds to an act or an event, only memories and sentences; the semantic theme has changed, it has lost the alternate tensions and easings corresponding to beginnings and endings, actions and happenings, situations that emerge and conclude. Significance, translated into an elaborate verbal form, replaces expression; the theme disintegrates and is recomposed around the literal, without ambiguity or polyphony (or polyrhythm or polyvalence). The writing aims at saying everything that can be written; the writer's ear is attuned to depth and he rejects all that is not perfectly clear; he does not attempt to entrap depth, it is there.

At one end of this skyline dominated by important works we observed the emergence of everyday life, the revelation of its hidden possibilities; at the opposite end everyday life reappears but in a different perspective. Now the writer unmasks, discovers, unveils; everyday life becomes less and less bearable, less and less interesting; yet the author manages to create an interest in this intolerable tediousness simply by telling it, by writing, by literature. Our investigation has thus exposed a definite change both in the things written about and in the way of writing. We are not concerned here with further ramifications such as the contemporary theatre (Ionesco, Beckett), poetry (Ponge), films (Resnais, Godard), etc.; nor with any attempt at generalization. We only wish to underline the metaphysical function of contemporary literature. We shall come across these problems again and again under different aspects. The 'world' is divided into the world of everyday life (real, empirical, practical) and the world of metaphor; metaphorical writing, or the metaphorical world of writing tends either towards artificial oppositions and illusory contradictions or towards self-destruction in the comedy of insanity (existentialism, Artaud); but this is not the place to analyse these sub-divisions.

Philosophy and everyday life

We shall now tackle everyday life from the new angle of philosophy. In the nineteenth century the axis of thought was redirected from speculation towards empirical practical realism, with the works of Karl Marx and the budding social sciences forming landmarks on the line of displacement. In the social framework of freely competitive capitalism Marx concentrated mainly on the everyday existence of the working classes from the dual viewpoint of productive power and illusions to overcome. Notwithstanding the assaults of positivism and pragmatism, philosophy still directs such inquiries and is alone capable of connecting fragmentary ideologies and specialized sciences; moreover it cannot be dispensed with if we want to understand the essence and existence, the real or imaginary responsibilities, the potentialities and limitations of mankind; and there is no method to equal it in linking and assessing disconnected material. This is because philosophy, through the wide range of its interests, projects the image of a ' complete human being ', free, accomplished, fully realized, rational yet real. This image – implicit already in Socrates' maieutic – has, for approximately twenty centuries, been refined, revised, opposed, developed and adorned with superfluities and hyperboles.

Everyday life is non-philosophical in relation to philosophy and represents reality in relation to ideality. Secluded, abstract and detached, the philosophical life is considered superior to everyday life, but when it attempts to solve the riddles of reality it only succeeds in proving the unreality, which is, indeed, implicit in its nature. It requires a realism it cannot achieve and aspires to transcend itself *qua* philosophical reality. Philosophical man and ordinary everyday man cannot coexist; from the philosopher's point of view, because for him 'all', the world and man, must be thought and then realized; from everyday man's point of view, because philosophy would endow him with a positive conscience and proof and act as censor, both superficial and basic, to everyday life.

The philosopher who sees himself *qua* philosopher as complete wisdom is living in the world of the imagination, and his weakness becomes evident when he tries to achieve what is humanly possible through his philosophy. Philosophy is self-contradictory and self-destructive when it claims its independence from the non-philosophical, and that it could be entirely self-sufficient.

Should philosophy be isolated for ever from the contamination of everyday life and detached from everyday contingencies? Is the quotidian an obstacle to the revelation of truth, an unavoidable triviality, the reverse of existence and the perversion of truth, and, as such, another facet of existence and of truth? Either philosophy is pointless or it is the starting point from which to undertake the transformation of non-philosophical reality, with all its triviality and its triteness.

The solution is then to attempt a philosophical inventory and analysis of everyday life that will expose its ambiguities – its baseness and exuberance, its poverty and fruitfulness – and by these unorthodox means release the creative energies that are an integral part of it.

We must try to overcome simultaneously the shortcomings of the philosopher and those of the non-philosopher (his lack of ideological clarity, his fumbling myopia and constricted outlook), borrowing for this purpose the terminology of philosophy and its more elaborate concepts, isolated here from speculative systematizations and directed towards the study of everyday life. The Quotidian is a philosophical concept that cannot be understood outside philosophy; it designates for and by philosophy the non-philosophical and is unthinkable in another context; it is a concept that neither belongs to nor reflects everyday life, but rather expresses its possible transfiguration in philosophical terms. Furthermore it is not the product of pure philosophy but comes of philosophical thought directed towards the non-philosophical, and its major achievement is in this self-surpassing.

Is it possible that everyday life is no more than a primitive stage in the development of thinking and living where such modes of experience are still undifferentiated, where all that is perceptible seems to be part of the universe and where the world is seen as the sum of all that is? Could it be only a rather low-brow interpretation of experience where 'world' or 'universe' appear to contain and enclose the only truth there is? Is it perhaps but a collection of trivia not worthy of being associated with the 'serious' preoccupations of modern philosophy such as Nature, Divinity, Humanity?

It is impossible to overstress our objection to this kind of philosophical traditionalism. Philosophy should not serve as a barrier nor should it oppose attempts at improving the world and perpetuate distinctions between triviality and seriousness by isolating on the one hand notions of Being, Depth and Substance and on the other events, appearances and manifestations.

As a compendium of seemingly unimportant activities and of products and exhibits other than natural, everyday life is more than something that eludes natural, divine and human myths. Could it represent a lower sphere of meaning, a place where creative energy is stored in readiness for new creations? A place that can be reduced neither to philosophical subjective definitions nor to objective representations of classified objects such as clothing, nourishment, furnishings, etc. because it is more and other than these? It is not a chasm, a barrier, or a buffer but a field and a half-way house, a halting place and a springboard, a moment made of moments (desires, labours, pleasures – products and achievements – passivity and creativity – means and ends – etc.), the dialectical interaction that is the inevitable starting point for the realization of the possible.

I address the philosopher in his own terms. The question is how far can a compendium of compulsions and determinisms (desires – specialized labour – fragments of understanding – biological, geographical and historical compulsions) assume the appearance of a freely created world, projection of something greater than freedom? Philosophers may ignore these compulsions and determinisms when laying down their laws, but in so doing they will not have solved the problem. The limitations of philosophy – truth without reality – always and ever counterbalance the limitations of everyday life – reality without truth.

Continuing our address to the philosopher, we formulate the problem in the clearest possible terms: we are faced with a dilemma, *either* to go beyond Hegel in identifying (philosophical) reason with (social) reality (in realizing philosophy), to refute the distinctions between philosophical and non-philosophical, superior and inferior, spiritual and material, theoretical and practical, culture and ignorance, and to undertake a radical transformation not only of the state and politics, economics, jurisdiction and sociology but also of everyday life; *or* to revert to metaphysics, Kierkegaardian anxiety and despair and the liberalism Nietzsche strove to overthrow, and to put our faith in mythologies with philosophy as the greatest cosmogonic and theological myth of all.

Is our attitude an answer to classical philosophy? Is it possible to use philosophy as a frame of reference for the study of what it terms non-philosophical – the definitions 'philosophical' and 'non-philosophical' indicating mutual recognition, reciprocal and simultaneous control? Does such a revolutionary attitude allow for the inherent rationality of history, society and all forms of specialized activity and labour? Where does it come from, this rationality explicated by philosophy and implicit in everyday life? Hegel's reply is unambiguous: rationality comes from Reason, the Idea and the Soul. Marx and the Marxists are still clear enough: rationality is the outcome of action, of labour and the organization of labour, of production and of the thought involved in all creative activity. But does the fact of giving a meaning (this meaning) to history and society not imply their responsibility in meaninglessness, violence, absurdities, deadlocks? Responsibility involves guilt, and who is to be held responsible? It would seem that to be innocent existence must lack meaning and direction. We cannot eliminate *a priori* the Nietzschean theory of nihilism as a rung in the ladder of progress. If we adopt the Hegelian and Marxist trend, that is, the realization of the rational through philosophy, a critical theory of everyday life must ensue; if we adopt the Nietzschean theory of values, of alignments and of a pre-established meaning behind the meaninglessness of events, a constructive theory of everyday life emerges. This is the first step.

But there are more dilemmas to come; *either* we exert all our energy (such energy as every individual *qua* social individual possesses) in consolidating existing institutions and ideologies – State, Church, philosophical systems or political organizations – whilst attempting to consolidate the quotidian on which these 'super-structures' are established and maintained; *or* we reduce these entities (state, church, culture, etc.) to their true proportions, we refuse to see them as the substance and hidden being of human reality, we devalue them and we revalue the mere residuum upon which they are built – everyday life; *either* we elect to serve 'causes' *or* we support the humble cause of everyday life.

We are not submitting here for the reader's approval or his scepticism an interpretation of Marx and Marxist thought; we are interpreting the history of philosophy, the philosophical and theoretical situation in the mid nineteenth century. The theory whereby philosophy is not content to philosophize, contemplation to contemplate and speculation to attain total abstraction, this theory of the realization of philosophy is to be found in Hegel; for him the coincidence (identity) of reality and the rational is neither accomplished, over and done with, nor ideal, indeterminate and yet to be; he intercepts history at the point where it brings about this union, seizes it in its dual and single character, rational and real, philosophical and political, theoretical and practical. But the theory, in fact, goes back much further and its beginnings can be traced to Cartesian rationalism. For Hegel philosophical reason was not a theory of pre-existing reality but was being realized in the state founded under his own eyes and with his own assistance. The politico-philosophical system puts an end to history as it discloses its meaning, which is not only a philosophical system but the practical (political) organization of Right and the State.

The writings of Marx on the *realization of philosophy* expand Hegel's theory while directing it against itself. If philosophy can be realized, why should Hegel's and not the whole of philosophy from Plato on be freed at last from accidents and redundancies? Why should his theories be restricted to a state governed by a constitutional monarchy, and the subject of such theories be only the middle classes and state bureaucracy? Are the working classes not involved in the continuation of history?

Such passages throw a certain light on the fate of Hegelianism and are themselves clear only in this context.* But they should not

* Cf. *Marx philosophie*, Paris, 1964.

be confused with those where Marx attributes to the proletariat
at one and the same time the refusal and the capacity to make a
fresh start from a fundamental break in history. These only add
a few superficial assertions to the first.

We have now reached a junction, a kind of crossroads, and we
could do worse than to examine the lie of the land before we proceed any further. Behind us, as we stand at their point of inter-
section, are the way of philosophy and the road of everyday life.
They are divided by a mountain range, but the path of philosophy
keeps to the heights, thus overlooking that of everyday life; ahead
the track winds, barely visible, through thickets, thornbushes and
swamps.

We have, then, asserted that everyday life is the object of philosophy precisely because it is non-philosophical. Thus we direct
the course of philosophy away from its traditional objectives. Confronted with these objectives we retain a certain philosophical outlook that is foreign to everyday man, who, in such a predicament,
finds himself completely bewildered, though he is capable, when required, of taking risks; the certainty that is the philosopher's quest
has nothing to do with everyday man's search for security, and
philosophical adventures are free from any but spiritual dangers.
The philosopher tries unsuccessfully to dwell in the seclusion of his
speculations, while everyday man, circumscribed by his possessions and his needs, often regrets his limitations; the latter is, or
seems, closer to nature; and this applies more specifically to the
female of the species; she is more easily moved to anger, joy, passion and action, more given to emotivity and sensuality, less
estranged from the mysteries of birth and death and all forms of
elemental spontaneous generosity.

In this sense the philosopher who has learnt and adopted the
attitudes of philosophy (contemplation and speculation) sees everyday life as the repository of mysteries and wonders that elude his
discipline; it surprises him more than anything else in nature, and
he cannot forget that the first professional philosopher, Socrates,
who never wrote his own philosophy, used only everyday objects
to illustrate his dialogues: pots with the potter, shoes with the
cobbler.

Would it be possible for philosophy to rediscover the innocent wonder of revelation while dealing with everyday life? Whatever the outcome of such a confrontation philosophy will always vacillate between scorn and admiration for what is non-philosophical.

Though we try to direct the course of philosophy and establish ourselves firmly in metaphilosophy we have no intention of doing away with our philosophical heritage. We are not setting positivism against speculation; we only wish to extend philosophy so as to realize philosophical reason and determine the unity of reality and reason. We may borrow for this purpose the philosopher's directions for the use of concepts, but we reserve all rights to change the rules and to introduce new concepts. We must not forget that we are practising a sort of maieutic in assisting the birth of everyday life's potential plenitude. Yet the situation has considerably changed since Socrates; a new man must now be produced and the notion of maieutic will have to stand up to that of change and revolution.

We will resist the temptation to use such resolutions as a cover for more unquiet if not more disquieting intentions; thus we assert our decision to explore *recurrence*. Everyday life is made of recurrences: gestures of labour and leisure, mechanical movements both human and properly mechanic, hours, days, weeks, months, years, linear and cyclical repetitions, natural and rational time, etc.; the study of creative activity (of *production*, in its widest sense) leads to the study of re-production or the conditions in which actions producing objects and labour are re-produced, re-commenced, and re-assume their component proportions or, on the contrary, undergo gradual or sudden modifications.

The riddle of recurrence intercepts the theory of becoming. Could a fundamental recurrence be concealed within Heraclitean time flowing through the cosmos, history, social and individual life, exhaustless temporality glimpsed only by some of the greatest philosophers? Images, imagination and the imaginary would seem to be involved in this temporal flow and to extend it; and yet is not the fabric of the imaginary woven from threads of remembrance and therefore of recurrence? Images would thus be akin to memories and imagination to memory as well as to cognition; which last philosophers have always associated with reminiscence and re-cognition (of the subject in reflection, of the object in conception and of being in truth). Could images, memory and knowledge thus recapture a fragmented unity, a lost convergence? It is common knowledge that psychoanalysis stresses the morbid effects of trau-matic repetitions as well as the therapeutic effects obtained from an elucidation of these. What then of repetition? Is everyday life one aspect or the meeting place of all repetitions? Does it answer one of the questions inherited from philosophy by meta-philo-sophy: how to collate Heraclitean, Hegelian and Marxist notions of becoming with the crucial fact of recurrence? How to conciliate the Heraclitean theory of perpetual Otherness – where recurrence is a stumbling-block – and Parmenides' theory of immutable iden-tity and sameness, which universal motion invalidates? Would it be possible to establish a dialogue between the followers of Hera-clitus, Hegel, Marx and those of that Eastern philosophy which culminated in Nietzsche and includes Heraclitus as well? Could everyday life be the occasion for such a confrontation and does it possess the key to the mystery or a clue to some higher truth?

Modern scholarship shows a particular interest in language, an interest that is a legacy from the age-old preoccupation with the Logos (connected to the nature of the Logos). The study of lan-guage, and of related activities such as reading and writing, has distracted the attention of scholars from a subject that was in the earliest days of philosophy a major preoccupation: music, whose understanding was a matter for reflection long before that of lan-guage. Music is movement, flow, time, and yet it is based on re-currence; all transmissible themes are potentially recurrent – the more so when transcribed; all music included in the sound con-tinuum is repeatable; all melodies tend towards an end (cadence) that may start a repeat – as the key-note at the end of an octave divided into intervals (a scale) marks the beginning of another octave. There can be recurrence of motif, of theme and of com-bined intervals in a melody. Emotions and feelings from the past are re-evoked and moments recalled by and through music (and by the imagination and art in general). The recurrence of octaves in a sequence of given sounds, unity in difference, the relation of number and quality are inherent to harmony; and harmony has become an art and a discipline through the theory of chords, their repetition and inversion and the recurrence of intervals and of series; such a discipline contributes a logic both specific and general, affording a syntax and controlling and containing becoming – until the source runs dry of classical and non-classical harmony, the tonal system and its dissolution, atonality.

If there is a relation between music on the one hand and, on the other, philosophy, art and language, is there not a certain connection between music and everyday life as well? Does music express the secret nature of everyday life, or compensate, on the contrary, for its triviality and superficiality? Does it serve as a link between 'inner' and 'outer' life, and, once such a link has been established, can it be forceful and meaningful, given the ever-increasing split – now practically 'structural' – dividing the quotidian and the non-quotidian, the growing pettiness of everyday life? Could the same questions be asked in connection with a number of other 'subjects', such as architecture, painting, dancing, poetry or games?

Since man first speculated on music and thought – indeed since Pythagoras – he has known that both comprised two facets or sides (such words have so completely lost their freshness, their depth of connotation that not even philosophical rhetoric can restore it): number and tragedy. The musician here could enlighten the philosopher, for music is nothing else but number and proportion (intervals, rhythm, timbres) and it is at the same time nothing else but lyricism, profusion and dream. It is all vitality, exuberance and sensuality and all analysis, precision and permanence; but only the greatest composers know how to reconcile the two facets. *Number:* everything is calculated and measured; are there limits to enumeration, boundaries to calculation, barriers to mathematics? No, there are none or they are expandable, fluctuating: set up a wall and the mathematician will scale it. But then *tragedy*? Number is confronted with something it cannot grasp, which it encircles but fails to reduce: the residuum; it is always there though it recedes, seems to be nothing much, nothing, 'nothingness'; but look again: it has grown infinite beside your finitude, ocean by a strip of sand. What have science and the scientist to say? 'It is nothing'; a polder reclaimed from the sea by dams, canals, ships and dredgers, all the paraphernalia for overcoming and mastering the tides; then comes the tidal wave. . . . Obstinately myopic, the scientist refuses to see anything in this residuum; yet it is the object of his conquest, the wisdom of the future; if it is not infinite and infinitely valuable what is to become of him? His fate and that of the poet are one, though he ignores it. *Tragedy*: all is tragedy: life, death, failure and victory. I can count the dying, time their agony, but the nature of non-existence and of suffering still eludes me. The residuum is where conquest and creation take place. The characteristic error of traditional philosophy and metaphysics is to deny the value of numbers and of science, but to assert that the residuum cannot be reduced and that the realm of word and of song is the prerogative of civilization and gives it meaning.

And what of everyday life? Everything here is calculated because everything is numbered: money, minutes, metres, kilogrammes, calories . . .; and not only objects but also living thinking creatures, for there exists a demography of animals and of people as well as of things. Yet people are born, live and die. They live well or ill; but they live in everyday life, where they make or fail to make a living either in the wider sense of surviving or not surviving, or just surviving or living their lives to the full. It is in everyday life that they rejoice and suffer; here and now.

At this point our objector will break in with a load of accumulated arguments (of which he will certainly find no shortage): 'Non-philosophical reality? Real life? And with what else have the so-called humanities and social sciences been dealing for the past century or so? Political economy, psychology, sociology, history, these specialized sciences have shared between them the part of reality that eludes philosophy; reality is their particular province, and thanks to them reality and the rational will regain their unity. What entitles you to set everyday life thus in the limelight? What is it after all? Whether economic, psychological or sociological it is the subject and the specific province of corresponding methods and disciplines. Everyday life is sustenance, clothing, furnishing, homes, neighbourhoods, environment. . . . Call it material culture if you like, but do not confuse the issue.

Your demographies and inventories are only one chapter of a much wider science; a thing's obsolescence and its chances of survival are only one stage in the process of ageing; however methodically you may study the meanings of these things you will not avoid the dramatic attitude and the lyrical tone because you choose to dispense with the assistance of competent scholars and sciences.'

Our objector's arguments are serious; they are the arguments of positivism and science. We shall therefore make a serious reply: 'Why indeed should not one or other of the specialized sciences (history or political economy) contribute to the study of everyday life? And why should not such a study become the province of a provisionally selected science, such as sociology for instance? Now, you appear to belong to the school of thought that denies scientific relativism and sees science as absolute; but you cannot, we believe, have overlooked the danger such an attitude presents for the specialized sciences you are defending. What is their status? It has never been clear whether they carve their subjects and provinces from a whole too vast to be encompassed by their specialities, or whether they project their individual light-rays on to global reality. As a consequence of scientificness you will be forced to deny this quality to certain specialities in favour of others; thus on behalf of linguistics, seen as a model for scientific precision, you must withdraw this advantage from psychology, history and sociology. You seem to forget that these so-called disciplines have only a relative existence, related as they are on the one hand to practical activities and on the other to ideologies – which last it is their task either to consolidate or eliminate. These sciences came into being when man – or "the mind" – attempted and hoped to overcome fate, master nature and control its laws; such rational ambitions are not entirely vain, as the specialized sciences aim at operativeness – and in this they succeed. Indeed, they have methods, concepts, objectives, fields and provinces. But how are these determined? We must not forget that man or "the mind" could not cover the distance from blind subjection to freedom at a single leap; with the Industrial Revolution social existence in the nineteenth century slowly emerged from millenary conditions of want and subjection to unpredictable natural powers; and such circumstances required a long period of transition before attaining the conditions to which reason aspired. Want cannot be overcome all at once; some products answering basic requirements may become available in certain industrial areas, but others, more precious, continue to be rare, and furthermore, unforeseen shortages arise: shortages of space, time, necessities and the necessary. Are the sciences of which you think so highly not responsible among other things for the maintenance of existing conditions and for the unequal – and often unfair – assessment, in the name of necessity, determinism, law, rationality and civilization, of goods in short supply? Is this inequality, formerly imputed to legislation, not the result today of science, rationality and the knowledge of facts? Let it be understood that short supply is not for us an illuminating feature of history, still less a theory of economics, but a phenomenon that accounts for behaviour. Are the objectives of these sciences entirely unselfish and are they as impartial as the experts would have us believe? Are the assertions of these experts absolutely reliable? The endeavours of the so-called humanities cannot easily be rid of their ideological coefficient, for they are compounded of ideologies. Thus for the sociologist Durkheim compulsion was identified with social reality, while he saw himself as an upholder of freedom. It is by means of such contradictions that the specialized sciences seek a greater rationality, though they cannot avoid the occasional clash with the restricted rationality of existing societies or with legalized and institutionalized absurdities. The study of everyday life affords a meeting place for specialized sciences and something more besides; it exposes the possibilities of conflict between the rational and the irrational in our society and our time, thus permitting the formulation of concrete problems of *production* (in its widest sense): how the social existence of human beings is *produced*, its transition from want to affluence and from appreciation to depreciation. Such a critical analysis corresponds to a study of compulsions and partial determinisms; it aims at a reversal of the upside-down world where determinism and compulsion are considered rational even though reason has always attempted to control determinism. If the potentialities of everyday life could be realized it would be possible for people to *adapt* to their existence once again – such a possibility being one of the requirements of creative activity, by which the products of nature and necessity are turned into creations and assets, into a form of human freedom. Rational understanding has always been directed towards existing conditions – though not in order to accept them and bow before their *scientificness*. The attitude which puts a value on compulsion involves an ideology disguised as rationalism and science which it is our intention to refute. And we conclude our exposition with two connected, correlated phenomena that are neither absolutes nor entities: everyday life and modernity, the one crowning and concealing the other, revealing and veiling it. Everyday life, a compound of insignificances united in this concept, responds and corresponds to modernity, a compound of signs by which our society expresses and justifies itself and which forms part of its ideology. Will you deny modernity in favour of scientificness? You would rather annex it and pass off your science as an incarnation of the modern. Our argument against such a pretension is the simultaneous appearance of these two inter-dependent "realities", the Quotidian and the Modern, both as forceful as they were unselfconscious before they were adopted by language and thought. For their definition and connection facts will have to be examined, including people and what they say. Are these realities essential, are they systems of implicit or explicit meaning, or are they compendia of facts specifically meaningless before their appropriation by language and thought? The main point is to stress here and now their simultaneity and their connection. The quotidian is what is humble and solid, what is taken for granted and that of which all the parts follow each other in such a regular, unvarying succession that those concerned have no call to question their sequence; thus it is undated and (apparently) insignificant; though it occupies and preoccupies it is practically untellable, and it is the ethics underlying routine and the aesthetics of familiar settings. At this point it encounters the modern. This word stands for what is novel, brilliant, paradoxical and bears the imprint of technicality and worldliness; it is (apparently) daring and transitory, proclaims its initiative and is acclaimed for it; it is art and aestheticism – not readily discernible in so-called modern spectacles or in the spectacle the modern world makes of itself to itself. The quotidian and the modern mark and mask, legitimate and counterbalance each other. Today the universal quotidian, according to Hermann Broch, is the verso of modernity, the spirit of our time. Its various aspects are as momentous in our opinion as the atomic threat or the conquest of space – with which they are surely interdependent. But are they? This question will be dealt with later. Here are the two sides of a reality more amazing than fiction: the society of which we are members. It is impossible to state once and for all which of the two is the signifier and which the signified; both sides signify each other reciprocally; each one in turn becomes signifier or signified according to the slant of the inquiry, and up to the moment of the inquiry there is nothing but aimless signifiers and disconnected signifieds. In this world you just do not know where you stand; you are led astray by mirages when you try to connect a signifier to a signified – declamation, declaration or propaganda by which what you should believe or be is signified. If you allow the swarms of signs to flow over you from television and radio sets, from films and newspapers and ratify the commentaries that determine their meanings, you will become a passive victim of the situation; but insert a distinction or two – for instance everyday life and modernity – and the situation is changed: you are now the active interpreter of signs.

'Reader, this is not a newfangled guide to a maze of moments, facts, dreams and satisfactions; it is not a treatise on the correct use of modernity and everyday life; nor is it a manual of instructions on the art of falling on one's feet. All these might well be written, but they are not our concern, especially as we are really more interested in transforming everyday life than in setting it out rationally. It would indeed be surprising if we were restricted to the diptych modernity and the quotidian, for already a third phenomenon is peeping over the horizon: the rational or the reasonable. What can reason have to do with everyday life and modernity? What connection can there be between the rational and the irrational? We are already familiar with such questions; they will lead to a further examination of the function and place of the imagination; and on the way we shall consider some new terms such as the City, for instance. (We purposely avoid the terms "urban" and "urbanism" for fear of multiplying words that qualify concepts but surreptitiously tend towards entities and essences.)'

All that remains now to end this introduction is to beg the reader's indulgence for its shortcomings. Our study centres mainly – and only too obviously – on everyday life in France and we can but ask if it is the same elsewhere or if here it is singular and typical. But are not present-day Frenchmen trying as best they can to emulate the Americans? What are the signs of insularity and specificity? Is there a world-scale tendency towards homogeneity in everyday life and 'modernism', or on the contrary towards their differentiation? These questions necessarily concern our problem and we shall try to answer them as pertinently as possible, though these answers cannot be entirely satisfactory; a comparative study would require a wide knowledge of different countries and languages if it is not to become a superficial race-psychology; but it is not unpleasant to scan the horizon even while knowing that it is out of reach. The important thing is to keep going and to discover what we can on the way.

First stage*

We are about to undertake a fairly important inquiry into facts that philosophy has hitherto overlooked and the social sciences have arbitrarily divided and distributed. Indeed the experts of specialized sciences tend to isolate facts to their own conveniences, classifying them according to categories that are both empirical and distinct and filing them away under such headings as family sociology, consumption-psychology, anthropology or ethnology of contemporary communities, or the study of costumes and be-

* The following section is a summary of the first three volumes of the *Critique de la vie quotidienne* (Paris). The first, published in 1946, was re-issued in 1959 and it is an introduction; the second was published in 1963. The present work is a 'digest' of the third volume that is still in progress; that is to say, it contains the main themes while discarding a number of facts, analyses and arguments.

haviour; while the task of extricating some kind of pattern from this jigsaw puzzle devolves to the practitioner (advertiser or town planner). Or they ignore everyday facts such as furniture, objects and the world of objects, time-tables, news items and advertisements and join the philosopher in his scorn for the quotidian.

In the initial stage of our inquiry we shall try to understand these apparently meaningless facts and organize them systematically according to a pattern and a method. The advancement of learning is often sparked off by 'salvages' (from and by reflection) of previously neglected or misinterpreted facts which are then appreciated according to certain 'values' – or debatable ideologies – such as labour for Marx and sex for Freud. Undertakings of this order give a meaning to apparent meaninglessness and insignificance – and what could be more meaningless than everyday life?

Such a project requires a critical attitude. If we accept the quotidian passively we cannot apprehend it *qua* quotidian; we have to step back and get it into perspective. Critical distancing, debating and collating go together; if there were a system (social, political or metaphysical) that we could accept, if the truth was a question of 'all or nothing', if the system though real and true forbade critical distancing, we would not be able even to grasp it; we would be completely involved, essence and existence, reason and language; neither awareness of it nor any awareness at all would then be possible; either from the beginning of knowledge we would know all there was to know or it would be beyond our reach for ever. Everyday life – as distinct from art, science and philosophy – is indeed the living proof that such a system does not exist, for either the system includes everyday life and there is no more to be said, or it does not and everything is still to be said. On the other hand if there is no such complete and perfect system it will not be easy to sift knowledge from ideology; a critical analysis of everyday life will discover ideologies and the understanding of everyday life must include an ideological analysis and, especially, an incessant self-analysis.

We do not believe that our undertaking should distinguish knowledge and analysis; it must be both polemical and theoretical. In addition theses and hypotheses concerning society as a whole must be part of our inquiry in so far as it is the analysis of a portion of the reality of social experience and holds this portion for significant. This applies to all theoretical inquiries; sooner or later they merge with a general conception of society, of 'man' or of the 'world', and if we do not start from the whole – which seems the correct method – we will get to it in the end, short of remaining entrenched arbitrarily in the particular and in theoretically disconnected facts and ideas. Thus the analysis of everyday life will involve conceptions and appreciations on the scale of social experience in general. That is where it leads; it cannot avoid connections with strategical variables or the strategy of knowledge and action. This does not mean, however, that such theoretical and practical inquiries will take no account of individualities; the author assumes full personal responsibility in this series of operations and implicates no other person in any of its risks – not even in the risk of error – but he cannot undertake to avoid humour and irony and to maintain throughout the gravity proper to all forms of scholarship. By challenging the position of others – their gravity or lack of gravity – he challenges his own.

A method that aims at a comprehensive view of society is naturally opposed to empiricism and the collation of endless facts or would-be facts. Social and human facts are no more distinct (conceptually, ideologically and theoretically) than are social communities related by certain affinities to form a whole. If we wish to define everyday life we must first define the society where it is lived, where the quotidian and modernity take root; we must define its changes and perspectives, distinguishing from an assortment of apparently insignificant phenomena those that are essential and co-ordinating them. The quotidian is not only a concept but one that may be used as a guide-line for an understanding of 'society'; this is done by inserting the quotidian into the general: state, technics and technicalities, culture (or what is left of it).* This seems the best way of tackling the problem, and the most rational pro-

* The critical theory of everyday life is thus radically distinct from the study of interpersonal relations from which arise psycho-sociological theories that claim to identify the 'specifically social' (Cf. *L'Homme et la société*, III, 1967, p. 63).

cedure for understanding society and defining it in depth. It is surely to be preferred to those long, circuitous meanderings of which the most remarkable and at the same time the most popular is ethnology, which would have us believe that, in order to understand the modern world, it is essential to know all about the Bororos or the Dogons and that we will discover the meaning of culture and civilization through studying the habits of these populations; though we are well aware of the interest and utility of such inquiries we cannot but question the probability of their leading to a better understanding of our own society; the long way round is sometimes only an excuse for escape. Nietzsche at least was more thorough than these ethnological romanticists when he went right back to the earliest sources of civilization beyond Judeo-Christianity to pre-Socratic Greece and the East with Zarathustra.

The present inquiry should not be confused with those forming part of a popular series: Everyday life in different ages and civilizations. Some of the volumes of this series are remarkable, in that they illustrate the *total absence of everyday life* in a given community at a given time. With the Incas, the Aztecs, in Greece or in Rome, every detail (gestures, words, tools, utensils, costumes, etc.) bears the imprint of a *style;* nothing had as yet become prosaic, not even the quotidian; the prose and the poetry of life were still identical. Our own everyday life is typical for its yearning and quest for a style that obstinately eludes it; today there is no style, notwithstanding the attempts to achieve one by resurrecting former styles or by settling among their ruins and memories – so much so that *style* and *culture* can now be distinguished and opposed. The series consecrated to the study of everyday life gives only a muddled and confused idea of it, and does not succeed in isolating what was specifically quotidian after trade and monetary economy had become generalized with the establishment of capitalism in the nineteenth century. From then on the prose of the world spread, until now it invades everything – literature, art and objects – and all the poetry of existence has been evicted.

Thus the difference between our inquiry and others on material life and culture stands out from the start. For the historian who is not content with dating events it is essential to know how people were clothed and in what sort of dwellings they lived in various communities, classes, countries and periods. Histories of furniture and of costumes are of the greatest interest,* but we are concerned with the fact that peasant cupboards had a certain style (where peasants had cupboards) or with the fact that household utensils – pots, pans, bowls – varied from one place or one class to another; in other words our inquiry bears upon an understanding of the interdependence and simultaneous distinctness of the forms, functions and structures of such things. Though they were subject to a possibly endless number of variations, which it may be extremely rewarding to catalogue, they maintained a certain unity of form, function and structure which constituted their style. If we want to understand former societies – or our own – we should neither dissociate dwellings, furniture, costumes or food by filing them into systems of differing significance, nor consider them as a single general concept – such as culture, for instance. Furthermore, when markets became common between the capital and the provinces everything (objects, people, relations) changed under the influence of this predominant feature that turned the world to prose.

Written shortly after the Liberation in 1946 the *Introduction à la critique de la vie quotidienne*† bears the mark of the prevailing circumstances. In France at that time economic and social existence were in the process of reconstruction and many people believed that they were building a new society, when all they were really doing was to re-establish the old social order in a slightly modified form. The book contains an interpretation of Marxist thought which is relevant to the present inquiry; it challenges both philosophism and economism, refusing to admit that Marx's legacy can be reduced to a philosophical system (dialectical materialism) or to a theory of political economy. The term *production* acquires a more forceful and a wider significance, when interpreted according to Marx's early works (though still bearing *Das Kapital* in mind); production is not merely the making of products: the term signifies on the one hand 'spiritual' production, that is to

---

* Cf. F. Braudel: *La Civilisation matérielle*, Paris, 1967.
† Vol. I, first edition, Paris, 1946; second edition, Paris, 1959.

say creations (including social time and space), and on the other material production or the making of things; it also signifies the self-production of a 'human being' in the process of historical self-development, which involves the production of social relations. Finally, taken in its fullest sense, the term embraces *re-production*, not only biological (which is the province of demography), but the material reproduction of the tools of production, of technical instruments and of social relations into the bargain; until they are shattered by de-structuralism, a society's social relations remain constant, their reproduction being the outcome of a complex impulse rather than that of inertia or passivity; this impulse, this many-faceted phenomenon that affects objects and beings, which controls nature and adapts it to humanity by humanity, this *praxis* and *poiesis* does not take place in the higher spheres of a society (state, scholarship, 'culture') but in everyday life. Such is the basic assertion or theoretical postulate of the *Introduction*. In other words a society, according to Marxist theories, is 1) an economical *basis*: labour, producing material objects and wealth, and the division and organization of labour; 2) a *structure*: social relations, both structured and structural, determined by the basis and determining relations of ownership; 3) a *superstructure*: jurisdiction (acts and laws), institutions (amongst others the state) and ideologies. Such is the main outline; however popular interpretation reduced the superstructures to a mere shadow of the basis; the operation was then given the philosophical name of materialism, used dogmatically (and very un-dialectically). This outline became inapplicable as a consequence of its drastic simplification; it only produced an endless series of controversies on the utility of superstructures.

The *Introduction à la critique de la vie quotidienne* took part in these controversies. Scholarship pertains to the superstructures in connection with ideologies, and it is effective since science plays an essential part in material production. Ideologies are made of understanding and interpretations (religious or philosophical) of the world and knowledge plus a certain amount of illusion, and might bear the name of 'culture'. A culture is also a *praxis* or a means of distributing supplies in a society and thus directing the flow of production; it is in the widest sense a means of production, a source of ideologically motivated actions and activities. This active role of ideologies had to be reinstated in the Marxist plan in order to prevent its degenerating into philosophism and economism; the notion of production then acquires its full significance as production by a human being of his own existence. Furthermore, consumption thus re-enters the plan as dependent upon production and with the specific mediation of ideology, culture, institutions and organizations. In this revised form there is a feedback (temporary balance) within determined production relations (capitalism) between production and consumption, structures and superstructures, scholarship and ideology. This implies first that culture is not useless, a mere exuberance, but a specific activity inherent in a mode of existence; and second that class interests (structurally connected to production and property relations) cannot ensure the totality of a society's operative existence unaided. Everyday life emerges as the sociological point of feed-back; this crucial yet much disparaged point has a dual character; it is the *residuum* (of all the possible specific and specialized activities outside social experience) and the *product* of society in general; it is the point of delicate balance and that where imbalance threatens. A revolution takes place when and only when, in such a society, people can no longer lead their everyday lives; so long as they can live their ordinary lives relations are constantly re-established.

Such a 'revisionist' or 'rightist' conception of dogmatic theories gave rise, in fact, to an extremist (leftist) political attitude. Rather than rebuild French society during the crisis and try to secure the leadership in this reconstruction, would it not be better to make the crisis an occasion for a 'change of life'?

Notwithstanding its lofty though short-lived aims the *Introduction à la critique de la vie quotidienne* is dated. At that moment of history (1946), in France at any rate, there was still a general belief in the possibility of man's self-realization through productive and creative activities. Different forms of activity might, it is true, be stressed according to different class ideologies; some, owing to their upper-class prejudices, had a rather condescending attitude to work of any kind and manual labour in particular; others, imbued with religious fervour, preached the spiritual value of work considered as effort and mortification; certain social groups praised all intellectual activities (in 1946 the term 'cultural' was not yet in use). But notwithstanding such controversies on the nature and essence of 'creativity', one fact emerged: work was endowed with an ethical as well as a practical value; people still hoped to 'express' themselves through a profession or a trade; among workers and labourers, among 'labourites', not a few saw a true dignity in manual labour and found vindication for their class-consciousness in such views. These views coincided with a political plan, elaborated by competent organizers, whereby society would be reconstituted according to principles of labour and the labourer; in this ideal society production would play an important part and social rationality would assume the dual aspect of an extensive social promotion of the working classes and a general replanning of the economy. From a sociological point of view the French nation, just after the Liberation, still formed a socio-economico-politico-ideological whole, notwithstanding – or perhaps because of – desperate struggles, controversies and political clashes. This whole appeared (or re-appeared) virtually complete; the second Liberation – the social change that was to follow shortly in the footsteps of the political Liberation (victory over the oppressor) – would consolidate this unity; project and expectation would coincide in an historical moment. But this moment was not to be; it faded away and was soon almost completely forgotten. At this turning point of history, with such prospects ahead, alienation assumed a new and deeper significance; it deprived everyday life of its power, disregarding its productive and creative potentialities, completely devaluing it and smothering it under the spurious glamour of ideologies. A specific alienation turned material poverty into spiritual poverty, as it put an end to the fruitful relations arising from the direct contact of creative workers with their material or with nature. Social alienation turned creative awareness – and the basic 'reality' of art – into a passive awareness of disaster and gloom.

This was the time when writers and poets were also trying to discover or rediscover true values. Their quest led them towards nature and towards imagination, into the realm of make-believe or that of basic primordial reality. Surrealism, naturalism, existentialism, each in its way put the stress on social 'reality' endowing it with the inherent potentialities of reality. This critical exploration of a familiar, misunderstood reality – everyday life – was thus related to humanism, and its claim to rejuvenate the former liberal humanism or to replace it by a new revolutionary form owed something perhaps to the post-Liberation climate. The new humanism did not aspire to enlist rhetoric and ideology in the cause of a reform of superstructures (constitutions, State, government) but to 'alter existence'.

Certain observations made at the time have become, after twenty years, sociological and journalistic commonplaces. In 1946, as today, the discrepancies in everyday life from one social class to another resulted more from the type of income received (wages, salary, fees, unearned income) and the manner in which it was administered and distributed, than from its size. A high standard of rationality was attained by the middle classes where the head of the household, husband or father, held the purse strings; he gave the woman, wife or daughter, a household allowance and put aside the remainder in the form of savings; if he did not economize and save but chose to enjoy the present rather than invest in the future he went counter to his conscience, his family and society. A typical middle-class family saved and invested at the least possible risk for the best possible income; the good father founded the family fortune or increased it, and it was transmitted by legacy, even though experience had proved that middle-class fortunes were dispersed by the third generation and that the only way to avoid this was to raise one's financial standard. Consumption was the wife's province – and the importance of her function is still increasing – though in 1946 it was still relatively limited.

In those days the peasantry still practised a natural or closed economy; their means were extremely restricted; administration was divided equally between the woman, who was in charge of the house and out-houses (garden, chicken-run, etc.) and the man who took care of the cultivation of the land. Savings were in kind – seeds, preserved fruit, etc. – and were usually squandered at festivals. As for the working classes, they led a hand-to-mouth existence having neither the possibility nor the inclination to save; the husband's pay was handed over to the wife, usually untouched, and she allotted a small sum to her mate for his personal expenses, if he was a good husband and she a good housewife. Such women spent without bargaining, paying what was asked for reasons of pride as much as of humility. The labourers did not stint; they had inherited from their peasant ancestry a taste for good food, good wine and a certain degree of comfort; a taste that had been eradicated from the lower and middle classes.

Such is the sociological content of the *Introduction à la critique de la vie quotidienne;* but the book goes further, attempting to capture a panoramic view, rather than to dwell too much on minutiae and on purely practical distinctions between communities and classes.

The result is a sort of contrasting diptych, where the first panel represents the *misery of everyday life*, its tedious tasks, humiliations reflected in the lives of the working classes and especially of women, upon whom the conditions of everyday life bear heaviest – child-bearing and child-rearing, basic preoccupations with bare necessities, money, tradesmen, provisions, the realm of numbers, a sort of intimate knowledge of things outside the sphere of material reality: health, desire, spontaneity, vitality; recurrence, the survival of poverty and the endlessness of want, a climate of economy, abstinence, hardship, repressed desires, meanness and avarice. The second panel portrays the *power of everyday life*, its continuity, the permanence of life rooted in the soil, the *adaptation* of the body, time, space, desire; environment and the home; the unpredictable and unmeasurable tragedy forever lurking in everyday life; the power of woman, crushed and overwhelmed, 'object' of history and society but also the inevitable 'subject' and foundation; creation from recurrent gestures of a world of sensory experience; the coincidence of need with satisfaction and, more rarely, with pleasure; work and works of art; the ability to create in terms of everyday life from its solids and its spaces – to make something lasting for the individual, the community, the class; the re-production of essential relations, the feed-back already mentioned between culture and productivity, understanding and ideologies, which is at the bottom of all the contradictions among these terms, the battlefield where wars are waged between the sexes, generations, communities, ideologies; the struggle between the adapted and the non-adapted, the shapelessness of subjective experience and the chaos of nature; mediations between these terms and their aftermath of emptiness, where antagonisms are bred that break out in the 'higher' spheres (institutions, super-structures).

An important problem now emerges from this context: the problem of the Festival, of which play and games are only one aspect. The *Introduction à la critique de la vie quotidienne* stressed its peasant origin and the simultaneous decline of Style and the Festival in a society dominated by the quotidian. Style has degenerated into culture – subdivided into everyday culture for the masses and higher culture, a split that led to specialization and decay. Art can replace neither style nor the Festival, and is an increasingly specialized activity that parodies the Festival, an ornament adorning everyday life but failing to transform it. However, the Festival has not completely disappeared and, though it only survives in meetings, parties and funfairs that are a poor substitute and fall short of the required glamour, these are none the less pleasant enough imitations on a reduced scale. A project to resurrect the Festival would thus appear to be justified in a society whose characteristics are an absence of poverty and the growth of urbanism; and a revolution, whether violent or non-violent, consequently acquires the new significance of a liberation from the quotidian and the resurrection of the Festival. The revolutions of the past were, indeed, festivals – cruel, yes, but then is there not always something cruel, wild and violent in festivals? The revolution of the future will put an end to the quotidian, it will usher in prodigality and lavishness and break our fetters, violently or peaceably as the case may be. This revolution will not be restricted to the spheres of economy, politics and ideology; its specific objective will be to annihilate everyday life; and the period of transition will also take on a new meaning, oppose everyday life and re-organize it until it is as good as new, its spurious rationality and authority unmasked and the antithesis between the quotidian and the Festival – whether of labour or of leisure – will no longer be a basis of society.

After twenty years we may summarize and clarify the intentions of this book; but the time perspective that makes them clearer does little to disguise their artlessness. We should not, however, overlook the fact that when it was written we were just emerging from the two festivals so generously organized by the Popular Front and the Liberation and that the disruption of everyday life was then an integral part of revolutionary activity and of revolutionary romanticism in particular. But the revolution betrayed our hopes and became part of everyday life, an institution, a bureaucracy, an economic control and a rationalization of production in the narrowest sense of the term, so that, confronted with this state of affairs, we were left wondering if the word 'revolution' meant anything any more.

Only when considering the life of the working classes – and by redeeming and extolling their creative ability – did it become clear that there was a power concealed in everyday life's apparent banality, a depth beneath its triviality, *something extraordinary in its very ordinariness*. This was less clear and more questionable if we considered urban rather than country or village life, and more questionable still in relation to family life, notwithstanding the hardships women so bravely bore and which endowed them with a certain dignity. Where exactly did our artlessness lie? Perhaps the theory of everyday life had become contaminated by a form of populism, magnifying the life of the proletariat, of the man in the street – of people who knew how to enjoy themselves, how to get involved, take risks, talk about what they felt and did. It implied both an obsession with the working classes (values of trade and labour and the comradeships of labour) and a philosophical obsession with the genuineness concealed within the ambiguity of experience and within artificiality and spuriousness.

Are such assertions, petitions and projects irredeemably outdated, should we give them up for good and all, or can they be reformulated more artfully? This question will be answered later. None the less our critical analysis of everyday life involves, in retrospect, a particular view of history and the historicity of everyday life can only be compiled by exposing its emergence in the past. Undoubtedly people have always had to be fed, clothed, housed and have had to produce and then re-produce that which has been consumed; but until the nineteenth century, until the advent of competitive capitalism and the expansion of the world of trade the quotidian as such did not exist, and the point we are making here is crucial, it is indeed one of the major paradoxes of history. In the heart of poverty and (direct) oppression there was *style*; in former times *labours of skill* were produced, whereas today we have (commercialized) *products* and exploitation has replaced violent oppression. Style gave significance to the slightest object, to actions and activities, to gestures; it was a concrete significance, not an abstraction taken piecemeal from a system of symbols. There was a style of cruelty, a style of power, a style of wisdom; cruelty and power (the Aztecs, Rome) produced great styles and great civilizations, but so did the aristocratic wisdom of Egypt or of India. With the rise of the masses (who were none the less still exploited) and with democracy (the masses still being exploited) great styles, symbols and myths have disappeared together with collective works such as cathedrals, monuments and festivals. Modern man (the man who praises modernity) is the man of transition, standing between the death of style and its rebirth. That is why we must contrast style and culture, to show up the latter's fragmentary character, its lack of unity, and why we are justified in formulating a revolutionary plan to recreate a style, resurrect the Festival and gather together culture's scattered fragments for a transfiguration of everyday life.

Second stage

This summary of theories formulated in an earlier work is given here for a specific reason. The sequel to the *Introduction*, the *Critique de la vie quotidienne* itself, was to have developed and clarified these theories and elaborated the assertions; thus the main section of the work would have dealt with the historical evolution of everyday life showing:

a) the gradual dissociation of quotidian and non-quotidian (art, religion, philosophy) and the consequent dissociation of economics and direct returns, work and production, private and public affairs;

b) the decay of style that ceases to influence objects, actions and gestures and is replaced by culture, art and aestheticism or 'art for art's sake';

c) man's estrangement from nature, accompanied by a sense of loss (of nature and the past) and an absence of rhythm; the dwindling of tragedy and temporality;

d) the substitution of signs – and later *signals* – for symbols and symbolism;

e) the dispersal of communities and the rise of individualism (not to be confused with self-realization);

f) the profane displacing but not replacing the sacred and the accursed;

g) the division of labour stressed to the point of specialization and the subsequent loss of unity compensated by ideology;

h) anguish arising from a general sense of meaninglessness, the proliferation of signs and signifieds failing to make up for the general lack of significance.

The *Critique de la vie quotidienne* was to have related these facts to the bourgeoisie as a consequence of their ideologies (rationalism based on a narrow-minded interpretation of laws and contracts), of their disproportionate sense of private property and of the excessive importance attributed to economics. The projected work would also have shown that all attempts to save the situation were doomed to failure, since capitalism had to be preserved; that art could neither re-assemble the disjointed fragments, transform that which eludes 'culture', replace style nor infuse the quotidian with non-quotidianness; that ideologies (aesthetics, ethics, metaphysics, positivism or a more or less subtle form of rationalism) were equally inadequate for such a task and only serve to enhance the commonplace. Everyday life is the vital element in which the working classes thrive, and they could – or might – challenge and change it; but it is the bourgeoisie who control the quotidian, and they try, without much success, thanks to their higher incomes, to make it into one long holiday so as to avoid its drudgery. In the past this might still be done; the Dutch bourgeoisie in the seventeenth century did just this, when they wanted to enjoy the fruits of their labour: the leading citizens, comfortably established in their era and their homes, found it a stimulating experience to see their opulence reflected in the works of contemporary painters, where they were also able to admire their numerous conquests over the unruly ocean, over distant countries and over their oppressors; in those days art was a link between fidelity and freedom, adventure and stability, insignificance and significance, new perceptions and lively feelings, or, in a word, between style and culture; but such times cannot be restored. The modern bourgeoisie banks on the absurd illusion of replacing art by aestheticism.

This section of the projected work was to have been the first of a triptych, the other two panels of which were an analysis of ideologies and a theory of the individual (with a complementary theory of individualism) called respectively 'Mystified Conscience' and 'Frustrated Conscience'.

Though written in part, this work was never completed or published, because the author soon realized that the momentous changes taking place in society at the time had transformed his 'subject' to the point of making it unrecognizable or virtually nonexistent. However, the exposition of our present inquiry can only benefit from references to this 'history' of recent times that reveals a number of significant facts.

Between 1950 and 1960 the social conscience, and the ideology stemming from production, creation and the humanist notion of work, lost their clarity of outline – slowly, in terms of days and weeks, very fast in the perspective of history. Social liberation had miscarried; the working classes – who increased, as it were, both in quantity and in quality – were losing ground socially and politically; the workers were being dispossessed of their conscience, and attempts to build a new society based on this conscience had not succeeded. Furthermore the model for such a society, the USSR, had fallen into disrepute, as the failure of the Liberation in Western Europe was echoed by the failure (or near failure, which is in some respects worse) of Stalinist socialism; the notion of a revolution and the entire socialist ideology were depreciated and were losing their radicalism – their ambition to reach the very roots of humanity and of society.

After ten years it is hard to say what exactly happened; yet there is little doubt that the way to historical truth had been blazed and many a half-truth had been uncovered. Basically capitalism (somewhat modified but structurally identical) and the bourgeoisie (outside and above its many national and international components) had regained the initiative. But had they ever lost it? Possibly between the years 1917 and 1933; but from 1950 on the situation was reversed. Militarily over-run and reduced to impotence, fascism had served its purpose: as a strategic episode in the battle of the international bourgeoisie it had its after-effects, for the bourgeoisie as an international class had succeeded in absorbing or neutralizing Marxism and deflecting the practical implications of Marxist thought, by assimilating rational planning while perverting the society from which this philosophically superior rationality originated. The dialectic trend of history had been turned – momentarily – against itself and had been annihilated; dialectic thought had lost its roots. Thus an attitude of mind and conscience that had seemed to be deep and lasting was universally deprived of significance. The role and the ideologies of the working classes were losing their distinctness; and a new mystification was being launched: the middle classes would only retain a minimum of power and wealth; perhaps . . .; but none the less it was they who were still in the limelight and directing the play, because their 'principles' and their 'culture' were 'superior' to those of the working classes.

Clearly such a process is extremely complex. To begin with, it is a process. Here the questioner intervenes asking, 'What? How? Do you really mean to say that there was a vast conspiracy to expropriate the working classes, that an invisible conductor directed the operations from behind the scenes?' The question is allowable, but it concerns once again history and the historian. Evidently there was never a fully conscious 'cause', a theoretically defined 'situation' or a carefully planned 'class strategy'. And yet class strategy, situation and design existed. A class cannot be considered as a philosophical 'subject' any more than can a society;

but they possess unity, wholeness, totality, in a word 'system'. Let us reformulate the question thus: 'Who was responsible?' It is an important question, but its importance is secondary because the main point is to understand what the consequences were of the tremendous amount of personal initiative, social tragedy, ideological undertakings and of activities of all kinds during this crucial period.

The 'process' passed over the heads of most people like a tidal wave over bathers by the sea; those who managed to keep their heads above water had their share of ducking and buffeting, but they survived by swimming with the tide. This process assumed different aspects:

a) the introduction of neo-capitalism, which was an institutionally modified version of former capitalism (competitive, then monopolistic) with production relations unchanged;

b) the redirecting of creative activities with revolutionary tendencies, by blurring and, where possible, eradicating productive conscience in so far as it was creative;

c) the simultaneous liquidation of the past and of historical influences challenged by the temporarily successful strategy.

At the time of the Liberation, France was still suffering from the after-effects of the years immediately preceding the Second World War: stagnation, birth control and the money-mindedness of the ruling classes under the Third Republic. This was undeniably an old country and predominantly agrarian, its institutions based on a compromise between industry and agriculture and between the city and the country, and such characteristics naturally involved a certain amount of sterile illusions, nostalgias and increasingly outdated traditions. The Marxists had claimed that they alone were capable of injecting new energy into the nation, and had not succeeded in so doing. Now the renewal was taking place without and therefore against them. But was it a genuine renewal? A revolution that miscarries always bears the mark of failure; though it may appear to be successful and may be described by its well-wishers as a 'silent' or 'invisible' revolution, it is in fact no better than a parody.

What were these traditions that had survived from an age of

peasants and artisans and of competitive capitalism? What ideologies and 'values', what half-significant systems vanished unobtrusively at that time, decayed or discarded? It would be as
difficult as it would be tedious to relate; furthermore such questions are not our concern but that of the historian of ideologies
and institutions. To put it in a nutshell: this was the end of a form
of rationalism whereby reason is an individual attitude and rationalism an opinion (profane, lay, anti-religious or even anti-clerical).
Outside philosophical scholarship, rationalism had been associated for a long time with science and technology on the one hand,
and with the state on the other. During the period in question, the
positive or effective aspects of rationalism predominated; social
planning (a world-scale distortion and integration by the bourgeoisie of a Marxist notion) and organization (first at business level
only but later generalized) were its province. The concept of
rationalism underwent a change; now it was state-concerned and
political (though officially state-concerned organizations were
apolitical). The concept of *organization* (isolated from transitional
organicism) merged into that of *institution* in neo-capitalist social
practice (which may, up to a point, be thus defined, so long as the
relation between these concepts is made clear and the boundaries
of a now 'operative' rationality are specified).

Together with the decline of rational thought (and the liberal
theory of thought as the province and embodiment of freedom)
there was a tendency to ignore individual ethical notions of the
quality of execution and of labour and of self-realization in one's
craft. Such ethics – which were an ideological representation
mediating between product and labour or between trade value and
'value' in the philosophical sense – as well as the placing of a value
on creative activity, had once been universally acknowledged, but
were now restricted to the members of a few more or less 'liberal'
(or so-called) professions (medicine, law, architecture, engineering,
etc.), where they served as a cover for the fact that they were combining into organized bodies which formed the social and institutional backbone of the new France. Faith in the dignity of work
and the worker had been drained from the working classes and
was replaced by rhetoric and nihilism.

Where man still depended on nature, where he was still inspired by the monuments of the past, fear reigned invisible – fear of want, of disease, of the unknown, of woman, of the child, of sexuality, of death and the dead. This fear gave rise to defence and protection mechanisms, incantations and magic. One of the objectives of the *Critique de la vie quotidienne* was an analysis of superstitions involving words and gestures and their function in displacing and negating this deep-rooted fear. In the period we are studying the predominance of rationalism was incompatible with such fears, and indeed they seemed to recede; but they were merely displaced, not eradicated. Terror now replaced fear, terror of impending atomic warfare and the threat of an economic crisis; not any longer the terror of nature but, notwithstanding the change to ideological and practical rationality, the terror of society. Such terror did not do away with the former fears either, but was simply added to them. As a consequence the minor superstitions of everyday life, far from being expelled, became 'over-specialized' ideological constructs such as horoscopes and exotic beliefs that fostered, rather than overcame, the need for security, moralism and moral order, and were, in fact, the reverse of rationalism. Security was becoming institutionalized.

The former superstitions that used to pervade everyday life and give irrational value to objects (a crust of bread, a piece of string, an old candle-end) now receded before a greater and more deep-rooted irrationality that was an extension of official rationality; tragedy was dying out because it had merged with terror and was repressed by rationality; nature was receding too, for even the manual labourer had lost contact with his material in the concatenation of actions and gestures. Yet a sort of general *naturalization* of thoughts, reflections and social contacts still transpired that was like the verso of rationalism, the meeting-place of irrationalism and rationality. According to Marx, objects reflect abstract forms that seem to belong to them, to be part of their nature as trade value is reflected in wares: social and moral forms appear as given in a society, and so do forms of art, aesthetics and aestheticism, and the ritualized forms of social relations. The rational is considered normal according to the norms of a society sufficiently self-conscious and organized for the misunderstanding (or metonyme) to take root; and the normal becomes customary and the customary is taken for natural, which in turn is identified with the rational, thus establishing a circuit or blocking. The consequence of such apparent (and contrived) logic – naturalism understudying as rationalism – is that all contradictions are abolished, reality is rational, reality is ideality, knowledge is ideology.

It now becomes necessary to ask two questions, or two series of questions. First, this society was changing face; change and an ideology of change, particularly in France, had replaced the stagnation of an earlier period when the ideologies were those of a well-to-do bourgeoisie unconsciously accepting its self-annihilation through the widespread practice of birth control. To what extent had this society changed? Could such terms as capitalism, bourgeois society, liberal economy, etc., still apply to France or to any other country? If not, what could such a society be called? Should it have a name, or ought one to be content with an inconclusive study of change or simply with suggestions for a pattern of change?

Such questions are of a general interest and might be asked by the scientifically minded in general, though each specialized science will have its own specific methods of inquiry – and foremost among these will be sociology; but the second series of questions has a more restricted scope. Does the *quotidian* still have any significance in this society and, if this society's basic preoccupations are rationality, organization and planning, is it still possible to distinguish a level or dimension that can be called *everyday life*? *Either* the quotidian in such a society is taken to stand for what is organized and rational, and it is everything – *or* it is nothing. Surely this concept must disappear at the same time as the singularities, survivals and extensions from an age of peasants and craftsmen or from that of the bourgeoisie of competitive capitalism.

Let us consider to begin with the first series of questions.

What should the new society be called?

Until the first rather confused formulation of this question between 1950 and 1960 (gradually made more explicit thanks to sociology) it was customary to speak of 'society' without further qualification, thus making of social reality an entity, a 'social nature' opposed to the individual or superimposed on the community; or to speak with polemical intent of 'capitalist' or 'bourgeois' societies – designations that, without actually disappearing, have lost today much of their impact and authority.

Later, sociologists borrowing from Saint-Simon launched the term 'industrial society'. It was indeed clear that, for the great modern nations at any rate, industrial production, involving the increasingly important role of state and organized rationality, was acquiring an unprecedented magnitude. Industry was not a complement of agriculture; the two did not happily co-exist, but the first absorbed the latter so that agriculture, in fact, became industrialized. On the other hand the real distinctions between 'capitalism' and 'socialism' were not those exposed in their respective ideologies. There were, moreover, a number of common elements in these two political régimes which claimed to be radically and systematically contradictory; foremost among these was the rationality devolving from the industrial society's organization of productive labour and business concerns. Could it be that they were only two variants of one species?

The term 'industrial society', though supported by theories, provoked a great deal of controversy. Here, in brief, are the arguments of the opposition. Is there *one* industrial society or are there *many*, and does each nation find (or fail to find) its specific course in and by industrialization? Can socialism be defined simply as a method of rapidly industrializing underdeveloped countries, or does it lead by new methods to a specific form of society and civilization? Can it be asserted, even if the substitution of socialism for capitalism no longer appears inevitable, that the world-scale expansion of industry and the industrialization of the world are conducive to homogeneity, to identical (because rational) structures in all countries? Will the discrepancies increase, or will they gradually vanish? The suggested term would appear to imply a premature solution to such problems.

Furthermore to accept such a term we must ignore the fact that agricultural production has only been totally superseded in certain areas and that 'world agriculture' persists. However, an 'agricultural society' completely independent of industrialization is now inconceivable, and this fact gives rise to violent antagonisms. The suggested term with its attendant concepts and theories does not allow for the formulation of questions, and in addition stresses economic *expansion*. Sociology might, indeed, take different aspects of social reality into consideration, but if it tends to favour economics it must inevitably over-emphasize *development* at the expense of quality (the greater or lesser complexity of social relations, their fruitfulness or sterility) for economic rationality; and there is the further risk of its overlooking other determining factors. Is industrialization possible without urbanization? Would the main feature of a so-called 'industrial society' not be (apart from a quantitative increase in material production) the expansion of cities, or rather of an urban society? Would not the logical procedure for a 'social science' then be to start from this double – or double-faceted – proposition: *industrialization and urbanization*? For the operation cannot fail to be scientifically questionable if the two aspects are dissociated, the one being set above the other and taken to a scientific extreme.

In other words, the term 'industrial society' is exact in a different sense from that given to it by its promoters. Industry or the economic capacity for material production has not been rationally mastered; the theory is still incomplete, even where socialism is concerned; industrial expansion is only meaningful (acquires orientation and significance) when understood *as* this *double process* and *through* it. Industrial theory has given rise to techniques (organization and planning), but it was only with Marx that these were in any way significant; since Marx, and more especially since the working classes were dispossessed of the 'values' of production, we have fallen short of the meaning instead of elucidating and realizing it. Urban existence gives significance to industrialization, which in turn contains it as a second aspect of the process. From a certain critical angle (at which we may place ourselves) it is possible to see urbanization and its problems as dominating the industrial process. What scope has an 'industrial society' if it fails to produce a fruitful *urban life*? None, unless it be *to produce for the sake of producing.* A class can produce for profit, *vide* the bourgeoisie. But a society, even when the bourgeoisie or a portion of the bourgeoisie are in power, cannot readily produce for the sake of producing, and if it seems to do so it is really producing for power and domination, that is for war; otherwise every trace of ideology, culture, rationality and significance disappears. Does the one necessarily rule out the other?

In brief, only a portion of the facts to be set forth and explained are condensed in the suggested term; it comes up against a number of problems that cannot be elucidated – let alone formulated and solved – through its categories. This theory is an ideology, a form of modernized rationalism, and its extrapolations and additions are contrived by a skilful dissimulation of the tragic element; it tends towards a mythology of industrialization. Its theoretical exposition *reflects* (rather than signifies) a lack of meaning and the way such a society replaces absence by illusion; it *reflects* the mistaken identification of the rational with the real, the exact identification of absurdity and rationality (limited and ratifying its limitations).

Certain theoreticians, rightly impressed by the important role of *technicality* in the so-called industrial society, have suggested the name of *technological society*. They maintain that the image of a 'technological environment' is more specifically characteristic of such a society than that of a 'natural environment'.

This proposition includes a number of indisputable facts from which it draws a definition, a concept and a theory.

It is a fact that in our society technology has become a determining factor, not only by revolutionizing productive conditions and involving science directly in its technical achievements. Indeed theory and appreciation go much further, and it is, unfortunately, only too true that technology – unmediated by a controlling mind or a significant culture – gives rise to a particular form of social and industrial conscience. Technology is *reflected* in the social and individual conscience by means of images and objects and their related words. For instance a photograph obtained with a maximum of technological means and a minimum of 'subjective' intervention becomes part of remembrance and daydreaming in the family album, in the periodical or on the television screen. The technical object with its dual functional and structural character, perfectly analysable and 'transparent', is given no definite status; it completely invades social experience: a town may become a technical object; sound-packets obtained through highly perfected techniques provide musical components; a sequence of images technically noteworthy – by the quality of the photography, the continuity and the montage – becomes part of a film; a barely modified car or bicycle is offered to the public as a piece of sculpture; three or four pieces of technical objects are exhibited as 'plastic space'; with Op and Pop art aestheticism is added to the technicistic trend. The glance that is cast upon a technical object – passive, concerned only with the way it works, with its structure, how it can be taken apart and put together, fascinated by this backgroundless display all in transparent surface – this glance is the prototype of a social act; therein lies the effectiveness of television. The real message, says McLuhan, is the medium or machine; no; the message is pure reflection: the eye on the image infinitely reproduced in the form of social relations, a cold eye and, as such, possessing feed-back, balance, coherence and perpetuation; images change, the eye remains; noises, sounds, words are auxiliary and subsidiary, symbols of impermanence.

What has become of Hegel's theory of art as a partial system, a compendium of significances bestowed on selected objects serving as active *mediations* between the other systems and sub-systems that constitute a society (material requirements, ethics, law, politics, philosophy)? According to this theory the partial system is only a mediation, but one with a pregnant actuality that confers cohesion on society. Now the reflection of our relation to a technical object, the 'medium' (screen, set, etc.), reflection of a reflection, replaces art as 'mediation'. Culture is a decaying myth, an ideology superimposed on technology.

To the intensive consumption of technological tokens we may now add the highly consumable commodity: aestheticism, or words describing art and aesthetics. Technicality decked with aestheticism and lacking any specific artistic mediation or culture is one of the more obvious justifications for the term *technological society*.

We shall now give our reasons for rejecting this term. It may be asked if such a society is still a society precisely in so far as it is technological; it claims to be a technical object and sees itself as such; it tends to eliminate all the mediations that gave social experience its complexity and connected material production to ideologies, principles and the often contending groups of signs and significances that enlivened social existence. Furthermore the expression 'technological environment' is questionable, for it would be more apt and exact to say *urban environment* since technology only produces an 'environment' in the city and by the city; outside the city technology produces isolated objects: a rocket, a radar station.

In so far as the term 'technological society' is correct, we may assume a transformation of technicality – that was formerly limited and repressed by the effects of birth control – into an autonomous economically and socially determining factor. Such a factor is operative only by means of a social 'layer' tending to become a caste or class: the *technocracy*. Our definition undergoes a metamorphosis, and it now seems more befitting to say 'technocratic society'. However, technocratic influences are active only in organizational and institutional spheres, their rationality directed towards specific ends and means, so that we should really say 'technocratico-bureaucratic society' and thus deprive the term of its authority.

And not only its authority, for this proposition exposes its inaccuracy as well. Indeed, what strikes the critical observer in the present society is a *deficiency of technicality*. The first and foremost of the technocracy's shortcomings is that it does not exist, that it is a legend and an ideology and that the alleged reign of technology is, in fact, a cover for the obverse. All the vast achievements of technology, such as the conquest of space, rockets or missiles, have a strategic value; they spell power and political prestige, but they have no social purpose, no current utility that might influence everyday life and improve it; everyday experience benefits only from 'technical fall-outs'. As to gadgets, they only simulate technicity, and under our critical scrutiny technicality and technicity prove to be *substitutes*, the application of technology to everyday life a substitute for technocracy which is itself a substitute for the true leaders of economy and politics. While our society appears to be pacifically evolving towards a superior rationality, to be changing under our eyes into a scientific society where great scholarship is rationally applied to the understanding of matter and of human reality, this scientificness only serves to justify bureaucratic rationality and to prove (illusively) the competence of the technocracy; technicity and 'scientificness' metamorphosed into autonomous entities re-echo each other, justify each other, and act as substitutes for each other. A *system of substitutions* emerges, where every compendium of meanings – apparently independent and self-sufficient – re-echoes another in endless rotation. Is this what is hidden behind rationality and our society's rational behaviour?

Is this situation final? While dispensing with historicity and with the historical as method, might it be the outcome of history? It would seem on the contrary to be the product of a specific predicament, the challenge of political régimes and systems, a new form of world-scale competitiveness with all the consequences this implies. In this predicament – arms race, rapid depreciation of military and technical equipment, obsolescence of technological objectives – technicity becomes revolutionary; its role is that of an unfulfilled revolution (though it claims the status of an independent factor), weighing on the whole of social experience while breaking away from it – that is the paradox – to provoke stratospheric incidents in political as well as in cosmic space. Such a predicament threatens moreover to become structural. The future alone contains the answer to such problems.

In short the designation 'technological society' is also only partly appropriate, and that in other ways than those suggested by its promoters. If this relative truth is seen as absolute it becomes an error, an ideological illusion and a myth to justify a situation, to conceal the fact that it is unbearable and to promote its historical novelty at the cost of history and historicity.

What of the term *affluent society*? Our society's rapid promotion to affluence could well be seen as a characteristic feature by which to define it. Indeed, industrial production and 'technology' could lead to an unlimited productivity by way of the total automation of production. Unfortunately for the definition (borrowed from the American ideologists Galbraith, Rostow, etc.) automation is accompanied by a number of restraining effects that might well be more serious than most theoreticians believe; total automation and affluence could lead to a total depreciation of certain commodities produced in excess, and thus undermine the very foundations of trade value. Is it this prospect, rather than the threat of unemployment to the working classes, that restrains automation?

This is not the place to dwell on such problems. In the so-called affluent or even lavish societies, in the United States and the highly industrialized countries of Europe, nuclei of poverty and material want still subsist. Furthermore, a new form of want is being generated everywhere: though basic needs are now catered for (at what cost?), productive societies show no concern for the more refined or 'cultural' needs of the individual nor, on the other hand, for basic needs that might be termed 'social'; this new poverty takes root and spreads, *proletarianizing* new social strata (clerks, sales-assistants, certain technicians, members of the 'liberal' professions, etc.).

Furthermore, new shortages crop up in the so-called affluent society. In our countries we suffered formerly from shortages of bread but never from a lack of space; corn is now plentiful (bread remaining scarce in some parts of the world), but space is in short supply. The overcrowding of highly industrialized countries is especially pronounced in the larger towns and cities. Time is also becoming scarce, and desire. We saw how the distribution of commodities in short supply became a 'science' trying to prove its basic 'scientificness'. Last and not least of our objections is that affluence has no value and significance if it fails to recreate the Festival and if festivals are not its objective. Thus we can reject this definition like the previous ones on the grounds that it is only exact in part and extrapolates these half-truths to become absolute.

Society of leisure perhaps? Indeed, the most remarkable aspect of the transition we are living through is not so much the passage from want to affluence as the passage from labour to leisure. We are undergoing the uneasy mutation of our major 'values', the mutation of an epoch.

Who can deny that leisure is acquiring an ever increasing importance in France and in all so-called industrial societies? The stress of 'modern life' makes amusements, distractions and relaxation a necessity, as the theoreticians of leisure with their following of journalists and popularizers never tire of repeating. A new universal social phenomenon, the holiday, has displaced anxiety and is becoming its focal point.

This term, like those that preceded it, is based on facts; but other facts exist that make it unacceptable. Time-tables, when comparatively analysed, reveal new phenomena: if the hours of days, weeks, months and years are classed in three categories, *pledged time* (professional work), *free time* (leisure) and *compulsive time* (the various demands other than work such as transport, official formalities, etc.), it will become apparent that compulsive time increases at a greater rate than leisure time. Compulsive time is part of everyday life and tends to define it by the sum of its compulsions. Modernity is therefore not self-evidently included in the age of leisure. It is true that the 'values' that were formerly attached to work, trade and quality in creative activity are disintegrating and those attached to leisure are in the process of coming into being; but if people think of their holidays all the year round, this does not imply that the situation has created a 'style' giving a new significance to leisure; people may be looking for such a style in the atmosphere of holiday resorts, but there is little evidence of their having found it. . . . Leisure contains the future, it is the new horizon, but the transition promises to be long and dangerous. Only the total automation of production could make a society of leisure possible; but a couple of generations would have to be sacrificed in the venture, so great would be the investment of capital required for its realization. The prospect then is one of unremitting labour to bequeath to future generations a chance of founding a society of leisure that will overcome the demands and compulsions of productive labour so that time may be devoted to creative activities or simply to pleasure and happiness. In the meanwhile labour and its drastic division of productive operations continues to dominate social experience. In automated industry there is no longer any contact with the material or even with the machine itself, but this non-labour (control, supervision) is none the less daily work. Careers replace trades everywhere, without alleviating – indeed, more likely, aggravating – the worker's compulsion. Today leisure is first of all and for (nearly) all a temporary break with everyday life. We are undergoing a painful and premature revision of all our old 'values'; leisure is no longer a festival, the reward of labour, and it is not yet a freely chosen activity pursued for itself, it is a generalized display: television, cinema, tourism.

The term *consumer society* has increased in popularity since the period under consideration (1950–60). It has been proved by convincing statistics that in highly industrialized countries the consumption of material and cultural goods is on the increase and that so-called 'durable' goods (cars, television sets, etc.) are acquiring a new and ever greater significance. These observations are correct but trivial. The theoreticians of the 'consumer society' mean or imply something more by this term; they assert that once upon a time in the pre-history of modern society, when capitalist economy and industrial production were still in their infancy, production was not controlled by demand, and that contractors were ignorant of market and consumer alike and their haphazard production was launched to await the expected and desired consumer. Nowadays, we are told, the organizers of production are aware of the market, not only of solvent demands but of the desires and needs of the consumer; thus consumer activity would have made its momentous debut in organized rationality; everyday life, in so far as it exists, would be taken into consideration and (integrated as such with scientific rationality) embodied in the experience of a highly organized society; there would no longer be any reason to consider it as a level of reality.

Our answer is first that in France we have not noticed any serious attempts at social and cultural 'market research' but only at research into *specific* needs, and therefore into solvent demands. It would indeed be too easy to show how badly and belatedly the *social* needs peculiar to *urban* existence have been studied.

Moreover, even specific needs are not submitted to unbiased research; the manner of the inquiry reacts on the needs and becomes a part of social practice that freezes them. There exist, besides, other more powerful methods of directing needs than market and motivation research. What, for instance, is the role of advertising? Is the advertiser the magician of modern times working out spells to entrap and subjugate desire, or is he merely a modest, honest intermediary investigating public requirements and broadcasting the discovery of new, exciting products to be launched shortly on the market in answer to such requirements? No doubt the truth lies between these two extremes. Does advertising create the need, does it, in the pay of capitalist producers, shape desire? Be this as it may, advertising is unquestionably a powerful instrument; is it not the first of consumer goods and does it not provide consumption with all its paraphernalia of signs, images and patter? Is it not the rhetoric of our society, permeating social language, literature and imagination with its ceaseless intrusions upon our daily experience and our more intimate aspirations? Is it not on the way to becoming the main *ideology* of our time, and is not this fact confirmed by the importance and efficiency of propaganda modelled on advertising methods? Has not institutionalized advertising replaced former modes of communication, including art, and is it not in fact the sole and vital mediator between producer and consumer, theory and practice, social existence and political power? But what does this ideology disguise and shape, if not that specific level of social reality we call everyday life, with all its 'objects' – clothing, food, furnishing?

The term we have just examined is not entirely satisfactory. The transition from penury to affluence is a fact; in this society of a modified capitalism we have seen the transition from a state of inadequate production to one of boundless, sometimes even prodigal, consumption (waste, luxury, ostentation, etc.), from privation to possession, from the man of few and modest needs to the man whose needs are many and fertile (in potential energy and enjoyment); but like all transitions it is not easily accomplished, dominated as it is by inexplicable compulsions and trailing shreds of a past age in its wake. It is the transition from a culture based on the curbing of desires, thriftiness and the necessity of eking out goods in short supply to a new culture resulting from production and consumption at their highest ebb, but against a background of general crisis. Such is the predicament in which the ideology of production and the significance of creative activity have become an *ideology of consumption,* an ideology that has bereft the working classes of their former ideals and values while maintaining the status and the initiative of the bourgeoisie. It has substituted for the image of active man that of the consumer as the possessor of happiness and of perfect rationality, as the ideal become reality ('me', the individual, living, active subject become 'objective'). Not the consumer nor even that which is consumed is important in this image, but the vision of consumer and consuming as art of consumption. In this process of ideological substitutions and displacements man's awareness of his own alienation is repressed, or even suppressed, by the addition of a new alienation to the old.

We have already discussed the all-pervasive presence of an extraordinary phenomenon, the enormous amount of *signifiers* liberated or insufficiently connected to their corresponding signifieds (words, gestures, images and signs), and thus made available to advertising and propaganda: a smile as the symbol of everyday happiness, that of the informed consumer for instance, or 'purity' signified in the whiter-than-white of a detergent; as to the discarded signifieds (styles, the historical, etc.) they are left to get on as best they can, occasionally reinstated as advanced learning – the prerogative of the élite – or retrieved to be turned into consumer goods (furniture, houses, jewellery, inspired from works of art or antiques) and thus occupy a level of social reality.

Since the beginning of all these changes and the birth of modernity, sociologists, economists and politicians have frequently stressed the significant role of the state. As a reaction to Marx and often in open protest against him, they reject the most remarkable of his theories, that of the state's decay. In most cases they seem oblivious to the fact that they are reverting to Hegelian theories, opposing Hegel to Marx, and that today we are still experiencing such an opposition. Will this age witness the triumph of Hegelianism and of the totalitarian state rather than achieve the philosophy of a human totality? The state has certainly acquired in all countries more authority since the war than it ever possessed before, even in the countries of the 'Third World', in 'socialist' countries and in the Anglo-Saxon countries that had, until recently, avoided the demands of state control, economic programming and organized rationality; Yugoslavia alone perhaps is still free from its grip. The powers of decision are exerted from on high, strategies and strategical variables are elaborated and opposed above our heads. But on what are these powers exerted, what foundations support them and whom do they implicate? What, if not everyday life, bears the weight of institutions? They subdivide it and distribute it between themselves according to compulsions representing and realizing the requirements of the state and its strategies. Such questions may seem pointless, like all protests against state control, but it would be more pointless still to accept the situation without a murmur or to elaborate theories in support of the state and to whitewash it. Moreover the structure is already showing signs of decay in France and elsewhere and both 'public' and 'private' relations have their own problems to face.

Though technology has achieved a remarkable degree of perfection it is always at state level – space and nuclear research, arms and strategy – that results are obtained. We saw the discrepancy between these and the technical trivialities of everyday life, between the importance of real technical constructs and the petty gadgets with their ideological wrappings. Thus after an internal split culture too is decaying; secluded in their ivory towers we have subtle intellectuality, complex literary word-play and a certain amateurism in styles and history; down below sprawl the vulgarizations, puns in poor taste, rough and bawdy games, the culture of the masses.

Thus what commands our attention is a *difference of levels* and not the rational equality of demands, consumption and communication; a difference that is programmed and organized so that the pyramidal structure of modern society rests on the broad base of everyday life which is the lowest level.

In Western neo-capitalist countries there has been no overt programming of production, no total rationalization of industry; yet a kind of programming, a sort of total organization has sneaked in unobtrusively; offices, public organizations and subsidiary institutions operate on this basis, and though the structure lacks coherence, grates and jolts, none the less it works, its shortcomings hidden behind an obsessive coherence and its incapacity for creative integration disguised as participation and communality. And what do these organizations organize, if not everyday life?

Around 1960 the situation became clearer, everyday life was no longer the no-man's-land, the poor relation of specialized activities. In France and elsewhere neo-capitalist leaders had become aware of the fact that colonies were more trouble than they were worth and there was a change of strategy; new vistas opened out such as investments in national territories and the organization of home trade (which did not exclude the exploitation of 'underdeveloped countries' for manpower and raw material and as sites for investments – only they were no longer the main preoccupation). What did the leaders do? All areas outside the centres of political decision and economic concentration of capital were considered as semi-colonies and exploited as such; these included the suburbs of cities, the countryside, zones of agricultural production and all outlying districts inhabited, needless to say, by employees, technicians and manual labourers; thus the status of the proletarian became generalized, leading to a blurring of class distinctions and of ideological 'values'. This well-organized exploitation of society involved consumption and was no longer restricted to the productive classes only; capitalism, while requiring that people 'adapt' to modern circumstances, had adapted too. Formerly the leaders of industry produced haphazardly for a problematic market; limited family business concerns predominated adding their bourgeois treble to the chorus praising the wonders of trade, of quality, of dearly beloved labour. In Europe after the war a few gifted and intelligent men (who they were is not our concern) saw the possibility of exploiting consumption to organize everyday life. Everyday life was cut up and laid out on the site to be put together again like the pieces of a puzzle, each piece depending on a number of organizations and institutions, each one – working life, private life, leisure – rationally exploited (including the latest commercial and semi-programmed organization of leisure). The *new town* was the typical, significant phenomenon in which and on which this organization could be *read* because it was there that it was *written*. What, apart from such features as the negation of traditional towns, segregation and intense police supervision, was inscribed in this social text to be deciphered by those who knew the code, what was projected on this screen? Everyday life – organized, neatly subdivided and programmed to fit a controlled, exact time-table. Whatever the size of his income or the class to which he belonged (employee, clerk, minor technician), the inhabitant of the new town acquired the generalized status of proletarian; furthermore the new towns (Sarcelles, Moureux, etc.) were strangely reminiscent of colonial or semi-colonial towns, with their straight roads crisscrossing at right angles and their frequent police patrols*; but these were more forbidding and austere, perhaps on account of there being no cafés and pleasure-grounds: the colonizers of the metropolis do not encourage levity . . .

The following inferences may be drawn from what precedes:

a) In France as in other neo-capitalist countries the changes in social practice had not eliminated the notion of *everyday life*; we were not confronted with a choice between modernity and everyday life. But the concept of the quotidian had undergone a metamorphosis by which it acquired a greater not a lesser significance; it had lost some of its implications, the striking contrast between want and affluence, between the ordinary and the extraordinary, for instance, but otherwise it was unchanged, even consolidated.†
In the modern world everyday life had ceased to be a 'subject' rich in potential subjectivity; it had become an 'object' of social

---

* These were not the only significant features and should not be singled out from the others; thus we should not underestimate the role of semi-programming, National Accounts and preoccupations with consumer-research in France; mortgages and hire-purchase must also be considered among these features.

† The author admits that he hesitated for some years before reaching such conclusions. More than once between 1950 and 1960 he considered abandoning both concept and inquiry, and this explains the time-lapse between the first volume (*Introduction à la critique de la vie quotidienne*, 1946) and the second (1962).

organization. Far from disappearing as subject of reflection, however (which it could not have failed to do if the revolutionary movement had prevailed), it was more firmly entrenched than ever.

b) All the suggested definitions of our society have proved unacceptable. How can the distinctive features that have emerged during this inquiry be summarized and formulated? We propose the following term: *Bureaucratic Society of Controlled Consumption* whereby this society's rational character is defined as well as the limits set to its rationality (bureaucratic), the object of its organization (consumption instead of production) and the *level* at which it operates and upon which it is based: everyday life. This definition has the advantage of being *scientific* and more *precisely* formulated than any of the others*; moreover it owes nothing either to literature or to a 'social philosophy' extraneous to social reality.

What happened in France between 1950 and 1960?

We are now in a position to answer this question in greater detail though we wish to make it quite clear that our concern is neither with matters of State and administration, with strictly urban problems, nor with the (incomplete) control that trade has achieved by influencing the consumer; it is better to leave such matters to the economist, though we refute *economism* by a radical analysis.

a) There is a contrast, almost a contradiction, between cyclic and linear (rational) time and, more specifically, between cumulative (social) and non-cumulative processes. Marx's theory of accumulation must be brought up to date, for in *Das Kapital* and connected works it is based on the history of England and Western Europe alone, whereas in the past century new facts have come to light. Thus there are other things besides capital that are subject

---

* This definition is not incompatible with certain others such as 'monopolistic capitalism of State', for instance; but in our opinion it allows for a more thorough analysis of the society's functions and structure and it goes further into actualities and potentialities than the latter, which appears to stress the economic aspect and denotes a certain partiality for *economism*, ideology and 'values' in the society it defines.

to accumulation: for instance knowledge, techniques and even, to a certain extent, populations, though here opposing tendencies check or arrest the process; memory is a typical process of accumulation and therefore an essential component of mechanisms that materialize and technicalize such a process. But everyday life is not cumulative. In a society, physical habits alter from one generation to another, gestural conventions change, intentional physical expressions (serving as a means of communication) such as mimicry, gestures, grimaces, are modified, but the structure of bodies does not change. Physiological and biological needs and their corresponding achievements are shaped by styles, civilizations and cultures; means of satisfying and frustrating such needs evolve and, in so far as they are physiological and biological, these deficiencies and activities show a certain stability that might suggest the presence of a 'human nature' and a progressive continuity. Emotions and feelings change but they are not stored up; neither are aspirations. The number of calories required by an American millionaire and a Hong Kong coolie is identical, the coolie if anything requiring more than the millionaire. Physical performances, erotic achievements, the time required for growing up or growing old and natural fertility oscillate on a relatively limited scale. The number of objects that a person can actually use in a lifetime cannot increase indefinitely. In short the effects of accumulation on everyday life are superficial though they cannot be completely eliminated. Everyday life, when it changes, evolves according to a rhythm that does not coincide with the time of accumulation and in a space that cannot be identified with that of cumulative processes. Thus an illusion is created of the unbroken continuity of houses, buildings and cities from the oriental town of proto-history down to the present day . . .

However, a society loses all cohesion if it cannot re-establish its unity; that is why modern society tries to control the changes that take place in everyday life. The depreciation of goods and 'fashions' is accelerated by the process of accumulation; mental fatigue sets in at shorter and shorter intervals till it overtakes that of machines, technical appliances, etc.; our society seems to be heading for disaster and self-destruction while war maintains peace here and there by various methods.* Everyday life is preserved in mediocrity or it must perish (violently or otherwise, but always under compulsion).

Thus the conflict between accumulation and non-accumulation is resolved in the methodical subordination of the latter and its organized destruction by a rationality bordering on the absurd but excelling in the manipulation of people and things.

b) Remarkable changes have taken place in the *semantic field* considered as a whole (that is, the whole of society as the theatre where meaning is enacted in various specific contexts). *Symbols* had been prominent in this field for many centuries, symbols derived from nature but containing definite social implications. However, in the early stages of our civilization there was a perceptible shift from symbols to *signs* as the authority of the written word increased, and especially after the invention of the printing press. Today a further shift, from signs to *signals*, is taking place, if it has not already happened. Though the signal figures in the semantic field together with the symbol and the sign, it differs from these in that its only significance is conventional, assigned to it by mutual agreement; in this respect it can be compared to certain signs such as letters that compose articulated units (words and monomials) but that are otherwise meaningless. The signal commands, controls behaviour and consists of contrasts chosen precisely for their contradiction (such as, for instance, red and green); furthermore, signals can be grouped in codes (the highway code is a simple and familiar example), thus forming systems of compulsion.

This shift to signals in the semantic field involves the subjection of the senses to compulsions and a general conditioning of everyday life, reduced now to a single dimension (re-assembled fragments) by the elimination of all other dimensions of language and meaning such as symbols and significant contrasts. Signals and codes provide practical systems for the *manipulation* of people and things, though they do not exclude other more subtle means. If we try to figure out how the 'new man' uses his memory, we shall see that he must register once and for all each action, gesture and

* We shall come across the notion of obsolescence again further on.

word of 'another' as though these were *signals*. What a terrifying vision of future humanity this image conjures up!

c) The redirecting of creative energy from works of art to shows and displays of reality (the cinema, television) has notable implications. 'Displays of reality' have become a display trade and a display of trade offering a perfect example of a pleonasm, though such redundancy is seen as a satisfactory stability (feed-back) by the rationalists of organization. The result, however, is a fairly vivid awareness of creative impotence and of the deceptive nature of a form of consumption that takes no account of styles and of the achievements of the past. The natural outcome of this situation was an attempt to compensate ideologically for these short-comings; whence the theory of 'participation' followed by the theory of 'creativity'. Former certainties fail that were related to a content (real or apparent). Form without content is deceptive, though it is accepted as 'pure' form and thus assumes the role of structure; but none the less the sense of a *loss of substance* prevails, a tragic sense more pregnant than the 'disenchantment' with rationality that Max Weber (who still had faith in rationality) analysed. Where did the sense of substantiality of former ages come from? Was it from nature or from the apparent uniqueness of so many things and the consequent value attached to them? From tragedy and death, or from style and the ethics of art as the substantial mediator of form? We may well ask!

d) Before the Second World War there were still traces of an older society surviving in France and elsewhere in Europe. Industrial production had not yet swamped and absorbed the remains of peasant production and crafts; villages still thrived and the countryside surrounded the town even in industrial countries; the legacies of *pre-capitalism* had not yet been set aside as folk-lore (nor exhibited as such for tourist consumption); industrial products co-existed with the products of rural crafts. Such objects possessed a symbolic value that was already outdated, and contradictory into the bargain; some stood for what was rare and valuable (jewels, ornaments, etc.); others represented riches and profusion in the midst of penury: thus the massive cupboard or sideboard, the cumbersome double-bed, the long looking-glass or the grandfather clock reflected an almost mythological past and became status symbols for the aristocracy and the middle classes alike; and the same could be said of buildings. These superimposed strata of variously dated objects lost their sentimental value in the period we are discussing through the intervention of a form of capitalism that organized and controlled consumption and the distribution of so-called *durable* consumer goods. In other words trade economy, stimulated by neo-capitalism, invaded what is sometimes known as 'material culture', eliminating the residue of these strata. The apparent exceptions were works of art and styles of high or low periods; objects bearing the mark of creation were reserved for the 'élite', a special market and a specific branch of production (copies and imitations of original works) taking charge.*

Third stage: after 1960

To subdivide and organize everyday life was not enough; now it had to be *programmed*. The Bureaucratic Society of Controlled Consumption, assured of its ability and proud of its success, is attaining its goal and its half-conscious intentions are coming to light: to cybernetize society by the indirect agency of everyday life.†

Everyday life in France is organized according to a concerted programme; the so-called superior activities (applied sciences, etc.) are not only increasingly aware of the quotidian, it has become their special province. Daily life is the screen on which our

* The *Critique de la vie quotidienne* in its projected design was to have formed a triptych with 'Mystified Conscience' and 'Frustrated Conscience'. Conscience has not ceased to be frustrated, but today we can add to the theory of individualism (of contacts and communication) a new claim: the right to solitude, to privacy and to escape from contemporary terrorisms. As to the mystification, it has spread; furthermore the term has permeated even journalism; and lastly, ideologists, now over-selfconscious, present ideology as non-ideological and as a safeguard against mystifications ('pure' science, advanced culture, etc.); which accounts for our discarding the project.

† Cf. the next chapter and, in due course, vol. III of *Critique de la vie quotidienne* of which this section is a summary.

society projects its light and its shadow, its hollows and its planes, its power and its weakness; political and social activities converge to consolidate, structure and *functionalize* it. The other levels of society (with the exception of the state, which operates on a much more exalted plane) only exist in relation to everyday life and the utility and significance of constructs is estimated in direct proportion to their structural effect on it.

If tragedy still exists it is out of sight; the 'cool' prevails. Everything is ostensibly de-dramatized; instead of tragedy there are objects, certainties, 'values', roles, satisfactions, jobs, situations and functions. Yet there are powers, colossal and despicable, that swoop down on everyday life and pursue their prey in its evasions and departures, dreams and fantasies to crush it in their relentless grip.

The great event of the last few years is that the effects of industrialization on a superficially modified capitalist society of production and property have produced their results: a programmed *everyday life* in its appropriate *urban setting*. Such a process was favoured by the disintegration of the traditional town and the expansion of urbanism. Cybernetization threatens society through the allotment of land, the widescale institution of efficient apparatus and an urban expansion adapted to specific ends (directing offices, the control of circulation and of information).

Thus the dividing process that can still be seen in the new towns is finished and is being replaced by the practical reconstruction of a kind of unity, a tendency officially called 'urbanism'. The problem of synthesis returns to the fore; the 'man of synthesis' is very much in demand, and there are many candidates among philosophers, economists, sociologists, architects, town planners, demographers and other technicians; nearly all of them bank inconspicuously on a certain 'robotization' shaped on their own synthetic model which they would programme; the more intelligent among them hope to achieve this by a spontaneous, or democratic, rather than an autocratic, method.*

---

* It may not be amiss to repeat here that we have no regrets or nostalgias for former times; we do not incriminate the 'machine' whether electronic or otherwise; on the contrary. A programmed non-automation of the productive

Our theories are more or less in agreement with those of American critical sociology; but though this sociology has elucidated a number of important facts it has neglected the essential concepts of everyday life and modernity, urbanization and urbanism; lacking a general theory of society, of ideologies and of economics (theory of expansion) it has left the last word to the economists. Unlike Riesman, we do not contrast an 'outer-directed' with an 'inner-directed' man; moreover we would prove that though man is directed, even prefabricated, by outer circumstances (compulsions, stereotypes, functions, patterns, ideologies, etc.) he sees himself none the less as more than ever self-sufficient and dependent only on his own spontaneous conscience even under robotization. But we would *also* try to prove the failure of such tendencies through 'irreducibles', contradictions that resist repression and transposition. Can terrorist pressures and repression reinforce individual self-repression to the point of closing all the issues? Against Marcuse we continue to assert that they cannot.*

American critical sociology – notwithstanding the weight of orthodox industry-sponsored 'research' – has raised a number of important questions, amongst which is that of the *social function of business concerns.* We are now aware, through published works corroborating practical experience, that the big 'modern' business concern is not content with the status of economic unit (or group of units) nor with political influence, but tends to invade social experience and to set itself up as a model of organization and administration for society in general. It usurps the role of the city and takes over functions that are the city's by right and that should, in the future, be those of an urban society: housing, education, promotion, leisure, etc.; furthermore it constricts and

---

apparatus leads to a programmatizing of the consumer, whereas automation would (perhaps) free creative energies and make them available for works of art. The Bureaucratic Society of Controlled Consumption is heading for fresh contradictions, as only industrial production can be automated and the consumer is elusive and must be tracked down. By displacing basic problems such a society collapses; it is a failure where social life is concerned as the liquidation of humanism proves.

* Marcuse, *One Dimensional Man*, London, 1968.

alienates privacy by housing its dependants in hierarchized dwellings. Its control is sometimes overpowering and, in its own way, the business concern tends to level out society, subordinating social existence to its totalitarian demands and leading to 'synthesis'.

Cybernetization appeared to operate through the police (Orwell) or through bureaucracy; however conditioning, seeping through the channels of a highly organized everyday life, succeeds mainly on the level of woman or 'femininity'. Yet femininity also suggests feminism, rebellion and assertiveness. The robot and the computer are, we repeat, production apparatus; to by-pass this appropriation involving a rational world-scale programming, consumption is organized on the pattern of production; only *desires happen to figure among the irreducibles,* and the consumer, especially the female of the species, does not submit to cybernetic processes; while the robot – for the time being – has neither desires nor appetites; his memory alone is unimpeachable. As a result, not the consumer, but consumer-information is treated to conditioning – which may perhaps restrict cybernetic rationality and the programming of everyday life . . .

We have just added a ticklish problem to our theory, a poisonous flower to a pretty posy: could the organization of everyday life (with its 'brilliance', scintillation and 'modernism') be the French high-road to americanization? We return to a question formulated earlier on: are we heading for a world-scale homogeneity that would foster or reveal a single absolute system, or, on the contrary, for a state where discrepancies and resistances must inevitably bring about the disruption of the whole structure? Do economically developed nations provide a model, both theoretical and practical, for the relatively underdeveloped, and does expansion feed on development to the point of integration? Will ideology and technology – or the expansion of productivist ideology – prevail in Europe and in France? Is the americanization of France heading straight for success, under cover of an anti-American policy and using for its ends a social group, the technocrats, at first reactionary but finally submitting in the hope of satisfying a thirst for power? The answers to these questions will have to be deferred.

2   The Bureaucratic Society of Controlled Consumption

Coherence and contradiction

We shall now examine some of the features of this society that justify our definition of it, not in order to exhaust the subject but to prove our theory. If scholars take the trouble to attack this definition they will certainly direct their fire mainly against its lack of 'scientificness' and try to demonstrate that its value is purely subjective and its range polemical. In our opinion, however, polemics do not detract from 'scientificness'; on the contrary, knowledge thrives on irony and on opposition, and theoretical conflicts prevent it from stagnating; but such controversies are as old as philosophy and scientific research and are far from nearing extinction. We assert that for us a 'pure' science that holds action at arms' length is not a real science even when it is true. 'Pure' epistemology and a rigorous procedure provide a strategical withdrawal and cover against serious onslaughts, and a cover too for 'operations' whereby problems are distributed according to personal values and interests that are best left unaired if protests and disputes would be avoided. The fact of standing back to get things into perspective does not involve a withdrawal into formal learning; however, this last being a caricature of the first, we are prepared to add to certain assertive formulae our own: 'Scientism against science! Rationalism against reason! Rigorism against rigour! Structuralism against structure!' etc. As for critical objections, are they not perhaps the best way to positivity? Our definition can only be refuted by those who refuse to name this society as a whole and consider it as a compendium of phenomena, devoid of concept and theory.

A hundred years ago Marx published the first part of *Das Kapital*, a work that includes both a scientific exposition of social reality and suggestions for realizing the possibilities of this society. This involved:

a) a *whole* perceptible to reason (dialectic), possessing self-regulating devices that were spontaneous but restricted (competitive capitalism tending to produce a rate of average profit), and therefore incapable of becoming permanent, of eluding history and change;

b) a specific *cause:* society ruled and administered by a class, the bourgeoisie (united, notwithstanding conflicting ambitions), possessing the means of production;

c) a *form* perceptible to understanding: trade (exchange value) with an unlimited capacity for expansion, constituting a 'world' with its logic and its language and inseparable from a *content*: social labour (defined dialectically: qualitative and quantitative, individual and social, specialized and general, simple and complex, particularized, or rather divided and standardized according to social averages). In this way it was possible to see how social labour might eventually control the 'world' of trade and set a limit to its senseless expansion;

d) a *social structure*, mediating between the base (organization and division of labour) and the *superstructures* (institutions, ideologies, public offices and moral, artistic and intellectual 'values') by means of the structured–structuring relations of production and property; the main ideology then being *individualism* (disguising and vindicating the society's basic character);

e) a coherent *language* answering at one and the same time the needs of practical experience, of science and of the Revolution (or of the world of trade, of the scientific understanding of this world and of the action that would control and transform it); a language that emerged and took shape in *Das Kapital* in relation to specific referentials (dialectic reason, historical time, social space, common sense, etc.); this attitude implies the collaboration of scholar and revolutionary, of learning and action, of theory and practice;

f) *specific contradictions* within the given whole (particularly between the social character of productive labour and the profits of 'private' property);

g) this society's possibilities of quantitative *expansion* and qualitative *development*.

After a century, what remains of Marx's masterly plan is a question of 'capital' significance that has not yet received an answer. It is not enough to say that the works of Marx are necessary for an understanding of the second half of the twentieth century yet not sufficient for such an understanding; but here we can do little more than make this assertion and give a brief outline of the insufficiencies to be supplemented. The creative cause (collective, productive) has grown vague; is the organizing cause political leadership, the army, the state, bureaucracy? It disintegrates on all sides and can no longer be seen as the cement that holds the structure together. But is there even a structure, a unity? If the structure is decaying, it is not solely, as the followers of Lukács maintain, in and for the individual conscience; the general character of social relations and foundations is not all that is going to pieces; the whole structure defined by Marx a hundred years ago is collapsing for want of a revolution that would have sustained and furthered 'human totality'. The world is fragmented and so are individual nations; we have fragments of culture, of specialized sciences and of systems and 'sub-systems'. And all the possibilities are now strategical prospections. Though the working class and its function seem to be disappearing, it is our last hope. Institutions and public offices with the ends and values that sustain and justify them can only be described as the 'cause' if one ignores the meaning of the word, and it is not easy to overcome the feeling that the state works for its own objectives rather than for the rational functioning of a society served by responsible and self-effacing statesmen. Specialized systems of values are conducive to systems of communication, but what have they to communicate apart from their own rules of conduct, their empty shell? 'Values' that preserve an apparent substantiality are intended to forbid what they conceal; thus the ideal of every state bureaucracy is moral rectitude, and the more corrupt and corrupting it is, the more it will stress this ideal. The very notion of 'values' is suspect, as Nietzsche was well aware, precisely because he was a theoretician of values; they are not so much ideologies as organized substitutes; the 'hidden structure' is composed of a series of *substitutes* corresponding in number to the institutions and public offices; technology is the substitute for the technocracy and rationality for public offices, each circling round the other (social pleonasm); the 'system' in so far as it exists is concealed by the 'sub-systems' and is a system of mutual and multiple substitutes; nature provides a substitute for those who wish to avoid contradictions or conceal them; the culture of the élite is a substitute for the culture of the masses, and so on and so forth.

Is it possible to analyse such a society *according to its own categories*? But of course; it suffices to analyse *functions* (institutions), *structures* (groups and strategies) and *forms* (systems and channels, media of information, censorship, etc.); all one has to do is take it to pieces like a mechanical object, a car: engine, body, equipment and appliances. ... We strongly oppose such a procedure, for a society cannot be reduced to separate parts without something being lost in the process, namely its unity – or what is left of its unity that enables it to go on functioning as a unit without completely disintegrating. According to its own categories this society is no longer a society; which assertion allows for the diagnosis of a *malaise* that can, however, only be ascertained after resorting to a further analysis. The difficulty, as much for the society as for such significant social constituents as the city, is to avoid organicist metaphors without losing sight of the whole, and (especially) without forgetting distortions, lacunae, cracks and crevices.

What we want to demonstrate is the fallacy of judging a society according to its own standards, because its categories are part of its publicity – pawns in a game of strategy and neither unbiased nor disinterested; they serve a dual practical and ideological purpose. A century ago individualism provided philosophers and scholars (historians, economists, etc.) with categories and images, and it was necessary to raise this veil in order to catch a glimpse of reality and thence of possibility; today ideologies have changed and they bear names such as functionalism, formalism, structuralism, operationalism or scientism; they parade as 'non-ideologies' in order to merge more readily with the imagination; they disguise the basic fact – or factual basis – that everything stems from everyday life which in turn reveals everything, or, in other words, that the critical analysis of everyday life reveals 'everything' because it takes 'everything' into account.

To sum up:

a) Is the quotidian definable? Can it serve as the starting point for a definition of contemporary society (modernity), so that the inquiry avoids the ironic slant, the identification of a fragmentary or partial sphere, and encompasses its essence and its unity?

b) Does this method lead to a coherent non-contradictory theory of the contradictions and conflicts in social 'reality', to a conception of the real and the possible?

To these questions, formulated in the most scientific way possible, our reply is a condensation of the previous assertions. Everyday life is not a discarded space–time complex nor a clear field left to individual freedom, reason and resourcefulness; it is no longer the place where human suffering and heroism are enacted, the site of the human condition. It has ceased to be a rationally exploited colonial province of society, because it is not a province and rational exploitation has availed itself of more refined methods than heretofore. Everyday life has become an object of consideration and is the province of organization; the space–time of voluntary programmed self-regulation, because when properly organized it provides a closed circuit (production–consumption–production), where demands are foreseen because they are induced and desires are run to earth; this method replaces the spontaneous self-regulation of the competitive era. Thus everyday life must shortly become the one perfect system obscured by the other systems that aim at systematizing thought and structuralizing action, and as such it would be the main product of the so-called 'organized' society of controlled consumption and of its setting, modernity. If the circuit is not completely closed it is not for want of purpose or strategical intent but only because 'something' irreducible intervenes, 'something' that is perhaps Desire, or Reason (dialectics) or even the City. . . . The only way to stop the circuit from closing is to conquer the quotidian, attack it and transform it by making use of another form of strategy. Time alone will reveal whether it will be possible for those who are willing to recapture in this way the lost harmony of language and reality, of significant actions and learning.

This coherent logical theory is also conducive to practical action, but it presupposes a preliminary action or thought-action; certain conditions are required for a conception of the quotidian and a theory of quotidianness, the first being that one must live or have lived in it; it is also essential not to take it for granted but to see it in critical perspective. Short of these two conditions understanding becomes impossible and our words will fall on deaf ears – and none are so deaf as those who refuse to hear.

Everyday life weighs heaviest on women. It is highly probable that they also get something out of it by reversing the situation, but the weight is none the less on their shoulders. Some are bogged down by its peculiar cloying substance, others escape into make-believe, close their eyes to their surroundings, to the bog into which they are sinking and simply ignore it; they have their substitutes and they are substitutes; they complain – about men, the human condition, life, God and the gods – but they are always beside the point; they are the subject of everyday life and its victims or objects and substitutes (beauty, femininity, fashion, etc.) and it is at their cost that substitutes thrive. Likewise they are both buyers and consumers of commodities and symbols for commodities (in advertisements, as nudes and smiles). Because of their ambiguous position in everyday life – which is specifically part of everyday life and modernity – they are incapable of understanding it. Robotization probably succeeds so well with women because of the things that matter to them (fashions, the house and the home, etc.), notwithstanding – or on account of – their 'spontaneity'. For adolescents and students the situation is reversed, since they have never known everyday life; they would like to take part in it but are afraid of being caught up in it, and all they know about it is through their parents, a vague potentiality in black and white. There exists an ideology or mythology of maturity for their personal use that belongs to parents, connects paternity and maternity, culture and submission.

What of the intellectual? He is in it all right! Intellectuals have careers, wives, children, time-tables, private lives, working lives, leisure, dwellings in one place or another, etc.; they are in it, but in a slightly marginal position so that they think of themselves as being outside and elsewhere. They have a number of successful means of evasion, and all the substitutes are at their disposal – dreams, make-believe, art, culture, education, history and many more besides. They frequently even accept the system of methods by which social experience and everyday life are submitted to compulsion, conditioning, 'structuring' and programming, calling it 'social science', 'urban science' or 'organizational science'; intellectual honesty in such 'operationalism' is not imperative. The more serious specimens of this breed of theoreticians elaborate sub-systems and specific codes to organize a society, that in turn organizes everyday life in approximate categories such as environment, dwellings, furnishings, horoscopes, tourism, cookery, fashions – all the specialized activities that provide subject-matter for pamphlets, theses, catalogues, guide books. These honest theoreticians impose their own limits to their endeavours and refuse to question invisible patterns, ignore the significant absence of a general code. Scientism and positivism provide excellent subjects for discussion and perfect substitutes which oppose and imply each other: pragmatism, functionalism, operationalism on the one hand, and on the other problems tactfully left to the experts. Criticism, protests, objections or any attempt to seek an opening 'elsewhere' are dismissed as utopia by these ideologists; and how right they are! They are supported by a special brand of reason and restricted rationality (their own). ... Such was in fact the objection raised against Marx, Fournier and Saint-Simon in the nineteenth century, for reflection necessarily involves a form of utopia if it is not content to reflect and ratify compulsions, blindly accept authority and acknowledge circumstances; it implies an attempt to interfere with existing conditions and an awareness of other policies than those in force.

Utopia? Yes indeed; *we are all utopians*, so soon as we wish for something different and stop playing the part of the faithful performer or watch-dog. 'Dogmatism!' cries our objector. 'You give a definition to which you stick and from which you draw exorbitant conclusions.' By no means; we selected our definition – namely the Bureaucratic Society of Controlled Consumption – from a choice of suggested definitions after examining their assertions and their foundations and discarding the others as unsound; moreover we concede the *relativity* of our definition; were it dogmatic and absolute, all hope would be lost, all issues closed; whereas we have undertaken to prove the existence of *irreducibles*, contradictions and objections that intervene and hinder the closing of the circuit, that split the structure. 'This is no more than literature, poetry, lyricism!' So now we have incurred the final insults; yet they can be worded more subtly as: subjectivism, the fight for the lost cause of individualism, romanticism. To be sure, we do not acknowledge the segregation of learning and poetry, any more than that of science and action, abstract and concrete, the immediate and mediations, positive and negative, assertions and criticism, facts and opinions, object and subject; not without stressing in each case the inadequacy of such philosophical categories – at the same time as their utility and necessity. In other words we refute *segregation* in favour of an unbiased constructive attitude of mind based on practical and theoretical understanding. Those who see only assumptions in our assertions and who uphold segregation in the name of epistemological precision may find some difficulty in maintaining their position to the very end without compromising with their painfully torn consciences or giving in to the suffering of that unity which is the postulate of philosophy and also of that which is beyond philosophy.

Once upon a time there was a sad, restricted, oppressed existence. The land, divided into a thousand and one domains, was ruled by King God and Queen Death. Yet derelict and oppressed as it was, this existence never lacked style; basically religious or metaphysical (does the basic ideology matter?), style reigned and permeated its every aspect. . . . Were we to continue this story we would see that these people lived in extreme poverty but were nevertheless snug and warm. There has been incalculable progress since those good old days – and who does not prefer everyday triviality to famine if the choice were to be made, and wish the populations of India an ordinary everyday life? 'Social security' even when it is unquestionably bureaucratic may be better than neglect and abandonment to a world of misery; indeed, it is, and we have no intention of denying 'progress', but only of understanding its obverse, the price that has to be paid for it. There is little cause to show open-mouthed admiration as the reign of death recedes from our planet; it recedes before the nuclear threat – which has the advantage of being something we can place and name. We do not wish to cry over spilt milk but to explain such tears and how they inspire 'rightist' censures of our society, a clear and a guilty conscience for ever misunderstanding potentialities.

At this point we must formulate a few simple (but practical) questions, though we cannot give them our full attention here. How is it that the more or less derelict and decaying centres of large cities are restored and occupied by well-to-do, educated middle-class citizens, and that those from the film and the theatre world move there from 'smart' neighbourhoods and 'residential districts'? Because of this attitude the city is being turned into the most precious and valued possession of the privileged classes and the greatest asset of consumption, to which it confers a specific significance. Why do the wealthy ruling classes snap up and monopolize antiques? Why do people flock to all the ancient towns and cities of Italy, Belgium, Spain, Greece? Those systems for the consumption and exploitation of leisure and curiosity, the tourist organizations, cannot alone account for this phenomenon; there must be something else: nostalgia, the breaking up of everyday life, modernity's immodesty and ostentation in the display it gives of itself to itself, or simply the appeal of the past? It is precisely to avoid such nostalgias and fixations that it is necessary to *understand;* for understanding, or the desire to understand, leads to comparative studies and to the *history of everyday life*. But such a history, though possible and essential, would be no better than a catalogue of details (objects) or a series of misunderstandings, were it not to stress the unity of each society and each period, that is social relations, methods of production and ideologies.

The history of everyday life must therefore include at least three sections: a) styles; b) the death of styles and the birth of culture (nineteenth century); c) the establishment and the consolidation of everyday life, which would show how in the past hundred years or so it has become more crystallized with each successive failed revolution. Everyday life is both the cause and the result of these failures; the cause, because it serves as obstacle and barrier, and after each tremor social existence is reorganized around the quotidian; the result, because pressures and compulsions tighten their grip after every successive failure – that of the Liberation being the most significant.

Science should not shun these theories and problems on the pretext that they lack seriousness. Indeed, we consider that games and play would be the most apt subject for scientific inquiry, that the ludic aspect of social life should not be left to philosophers while scholars are already studying strategies and formalized games. Inversely, we suggest that science should not be entitled to provide intellectuals, technicians and high officials with a clear conscience – not a cumbersome commodity and highly quoted on the market– for there is nothing worse than a clear conscience that has been rationalized, institutionalized and bureaucratized by science; we have no qualms in asserting that it is the rotten fruit on the tree of science. The ruling classes have always used science as their justification; we oppose our science to theirs.

An unbelievable amount of contradiction comes to light in this society of structure and structuring, functionalism, applied rationalism, integration and coherence. First there is the conflict between demands for seriousness (why shy from resounding words and not say straight out: the demand for truth and truthfulness?) and the absence of any absolute criteria or general code by which to understand and judge. Then there is loneliness, set to music and silence, and contrasting with the multiplication of messages, information, news. 'Security' assumes an importance that is out of all proportion in a world of cosmic ventures and nuclear threats.

There is a striking contrast between the incredible performances – at social and technical cost – to save a sick child, a wounded man, prolong the agony of the dying; and the genocides, the conditions in our hospitals and of medicine in general, the difficulties encountered in obtaining remedies. Satisfaction and dissatisfaction go hand in hand or oppose each other according to the place or the people. Contradiction is not always on the surface, not always outspoken; sometimes people avoid mentioning or even noticing it, but it is there none the less, latent, implicit. Are we discovering the unconscious, the significant 'desires' concealed beneath the signified? No need to go so far, for we are discussing everyday life.

Many sociologists have suggested that the working classes of the world prefer the *security* of a job, a status and assured leisure to revolutionary ventures, that they have 'chosen', 'opted' and rejected their historical mission. Assertions such as these are highly suspect, particularly the last; in so far as these facts are true they must be imputed to the establishment of everyday life rather than to the 'choice' of security and the rejection of creative insecurity; moreover the proletariat cannot abandon its historical mission without renouncing its status, for if it 'chooses' to be integrated in a society governed by the bourgeoisie and organized in view of capitalist production and profit it must cease to exist as a class. For the proletariat, integration equals disintegration, and the suicide of a class is, to say the least, hard to imagine – and harder still to enact. What we see is in fact a society tending tactically and strategically towards the integration of the working classes and partially succeeding – by the repressive organizations of everyday life through compulsions and by a persuasive ideology of consumption more than by consumption itself – at the cost of sacrificing the integration of its other elements, adolescents, communities, women, intellectuals, sciences, cultures. The result of compelling the proletariat to renounce its status – of handing it a knife, as it were, to commit *hara-kiri* – will be the suicide of capitalism as a society, for it cannot fail to be dragged with the proletariat in its downfall.

Among the contradictions that come to light let us select at random that between the death of the ludic spirit, the dreariness of everyday programming in its rational organization, and the scientific discovery of chance, risk, play and strategy at the heart of natural processes and social activities.

Thus by studying the basic stratum – everyday life – new contradictions emerge, varying in significance but of a general nature; among the more important is the opposition between technical ideologies or technocratic myths and everyday reality; but worse still is the contradiction that consists in considering compulsion as the basis of social order and a social programme, and simultaneously using the ideology of Liberty as a face-saver, notwithstanding the repressions and oppressions that reflect a very different attitude and objective.

The roots of unrest

Our society contains its own self-criticism, for the requisite critical perspectives and concepts obtrude without being formulated or expressed as such; they are apparent in the lacunae of social experience so long as these are not stopped up with the ever-present verbal mists that can so easily be taken for substantial 'reality'.

Satisfaction is the aim and objective of this society and its official justification; every known and imagined need is – or will be – satisfied. Such satisfaction consists in saturation obtained, as far as solvent needs are concerned, with all possible alacrity. Needs are seen as clearly defined gaps, neatly outlined hollows to be stopped up and filled in by consumption and the consumer until satiety is achieved, when the need is promptly solicited by devices identical to those that led to satiety; needs are thus incessantly re-stimulated by well-tried methods until they begin to become rentable once again, oscillating between satisfaction and dissatisfaction, both states being produced by similar manipulations. Thus controlled consumption does not only plan objects for consumption but even the satisfaction obtained through these objects; play on motivations denies and destroys motivations precisely to the extent of its hold over them and without, moreover, ever stipulating the rules of the game.

It is impossible to ignore the fact that a sense of unrest really prevails. 'Values' usually undergo a general crisis where satiety is generalized; there is a slump of ideas, philosophy, art and culture, significance vanishes to re-emerge in disguise; a void makes itself felt – a terrible lack of significance filled by nothing but rhetoric; though the situation has a certain significance or significances – of which the first is perhaps that 'satiety' (of needs, 'environment', space and time) cannot provide an end, is devoid of finality and of meaning. For a distinction must be made between satisfaction, pleasure and happiness. Pleasure was once the prerogative of the aristocracy who knew how to give it a meaningful place in their lives; but the bourgeoisie can, at best, only achieve satisfaction; and who will discover happiness?

This sense of unrest that pervades everyday life is one of the main themes of contemporary literature. All the works of the past few decades that have left their mark are those which, directly or indirectly, portray it; in the more or less permanent crisis of the theatre, the cinema, literature and philosophy these are the works that are remembered, however successful others may have been for a time. Some depict everyday life in sadistic or masochistic detail, or they represent it as more degrading even than it is; others, whose authors evidently deplore the death of tragedy through satiety, try to restore tragedy by exposing the devices that provoke and ratify satiety. Through this residue of culture (not to be confused with what is officially known as 'cultural'), our society's inherent unrest becomes a social and intellectual phenomenon.

We have seen that this society is undergoing a remarkable *expansion* (economic, quantitative, measured in tons and kilometres) and a limited *development*. There is little change in basic class relations (structured – structuring) – or the relations between production and property by which society is subjected to one class (the bourgeoisie) possessing full administrative power – except in terms of class strategy (the consolidation of everyday life); and class strategy does not tend towards development but towards the 'balance' and 'harmony' of expansion as such. The development, complexification and enrichment of social relations including those of city life are left to 'culture' and institutionalized on that score. In consequence the *technical mastery* of material experience is not counterbalanced by the adaptation of man to his own personal experience, his body, his needs, time and space. The discrepancy between expansion and development echoes a further and more basic discrepancy between (technical) *mastery* and *adaptation*. These familiar propositions acquire significance only if we specify their terms: *expansion* refers to the process of industrialization, *development* to urbanization. According to our theory (which has already been formulated and will be further developed) urbanization gives significance to industrialization; an aspect of the general process that is basic today after many decades in which the former was subordinated to the latter; but if the situation is now reversed class strategy still maintains this subordination, thus provoking an intolerable situation where a *city crisis* is added to all the other permanent crises.

Its limitations are an integral part of this society, being the limitations imposed by capitalist production as such. But at no level and on no terms can we accept and ratify *economism;* it is wrong because it ignores the basic elements of society. However, this is no excuse for supplementing it with philosophical and sociological theories that are equally short-sighted.

Our society has no idea where it is going, with its ceaseless superficial modifications so totally opposed to that perpetual change which is the basic aspiration of the 'modern mind'. It gropes, blindfold, in a dark tunnel, seeking an exit, a way of escape . . . or marks time. . . . Perhaps, rather than marking time, it is in fact committing suicide while standing still . . .

There is little point in dwelling on the destruction of the past by the massive consumption of works of art, styles and cultures, but we shall consider, instead, the devices inherent to this consumption. *Obsolescence*, before becoming a technique, was the subject of careful study; experts are well acquainted with the life-expectancy of objects: three years for a bathroom; five for a living-room; eight for a bedroom; three for a business, a car, etc.; such statistics are part of the demography of objects and are correlated to the cost of production and profit; production-organizing offices know how to exploit them to reduce life-expectancy and accelerate the turnover of products and of capital. Indeed, the scandal has reached world-scale proportions in the case of the car industry.

To this now familiar theory we add two observations; first, the *obsolescence of needs* should be taken into consideration, for those who manipulate objects to make them less durable likewise manipulate motivations, and it may well be these social expressions of desire that they are really attacking and destroying; for if 'intellectual' fatigue and the obsolescence of objects are to have a rapid effect, needs must also become outdated and new needs take their place; this is the strategy of desire. Secondly, productive power is such that it would now already be possible to achieve an extreme *fluidity* of existence, of objects, dwellings, towns and of 'living', so that 'real life' need not still stagnate in everyday life; but both in theory and in practice obsolescence uses transitoriness as a means of exploiting everyday life. In this light a contrast or contradiction appears between institutionalized *durability* objectively structured (according to a logic of procedures, those concerned with state and administration, among others, including the administration of towns, environment and dwellings that are regarded as lasting), and the manipulated transitoriness of rapidly deteriorating objects. When transitoriness is not suffered but desired, willed, qualitative and appealing, it is the *monopoly of a class*, the class that dictates fashions and tastes and has the world for its playground; on the other hand the deterioration of objects (quantitative, measurable in terms of time, suffered, unwilled and unwanted) is part of a *class strategy* directed towards a rationalized (though irrational as procedure) exploitation of everyday life. The cult of the transitory reflects the essence of modernity – but reflects it as a class strategy* and is in total contradiction to the cult of, and the demand for, stability and permanence.

This is a society with rational aims and pretensions, with principles of finality as its major preoccupation, with a whole-scale, full-time organization, structured, planned and programmed; scientificness supplies its mechanisms (how and on what are mere details so long as there are computers, electronic brains, IBM calculators and programming); mystifications are passed off as scientific discoveries and a fool, if he introduces himself as an

* Cf. *Utopie* (Paris), I, pp. 96–107, the article by J. Aubert, with notes by J. Baudrillard.

expert, is acclaimed and respected. Here, moreover, irrationality thrives and prospers; if we probe into the private lives of the members of this society we find that they are, in many cases, fortune-tellers, witches, quacks, star-gazers ... indeed, one has only to read the papers; it is as though people had nothing in their daily lives to give them a meaning, a direction, apart from publicity, so they fall back on magic and witchcraft. Perhaps they hope in this roundabout way to *adapt* their desires, discover and orientate them. Thus the rationality of economism and technicity produces its opposite as their 'structural' complement and reveals its limitations as restricted rationalism and irrationalism pervade everyday life, confront and reflect one another.

Everyday life and its sources of information (the press, the cinema) are infested with *psychologism* and psychological tests such as: 'Discover who you are', 'Learn to know yourself.' Today psychology and psychoanalysis are not only clinical and therapeutic sciences but ideologies, particularly in the United States. Such an ideology requires compensations which are provided by occultism. Horoscopes might form the subject of a methodical inquiry, their themes classified, their texts considered as a *corpus* or coherent and clearly defined body, and a *system* could be drawn from horoscopes in general (and thence a sub-system for our society); but we shall not attempt such an undertaking as it would not advance our particular problem, though horoscopes do affect it in a certain way. What, indeed, do people expect from horoscopes, why do they consult them, how do they interpret the signs and how are they influenced by the interpretations? A zone of *ambiguity* is established half way between belief and make-believe, yet directed towards action by justifying individual tactics so that those concerned believe and do not believe what they say, and behave as if they believed, while following their own inclinations, feelings or interests – their vaticinations.

We should not, however, overlook the fact that horoscopes involve the fragments of a universal vision, the zodiac, the constellations, destiny inscribed in the stars, the heavens as divine writing that only the initiate can decipher. This is the symbolic heritage that inspired architecture, was sealed into great monuments of past cultures and summarizes a topology – the division and orientation of space and the projection of time on to cosmic and social space for the use of shepherds and peasants and later of the inhabitants of towns.

It seems that the influence of this cosmogony is not quite spent. For instance the particular significance of cycles, and numbers governing cycles (twelve and its multiples), survives to this day. Life is trapped in an intermediary zone between cyclic and rationalized linear time. And everything points to the fact that now a new cult of the Cosmos is emerging from our poor, down-trodden everyday life; it is emotionally – or irrationally – situated between two opposite poles: horoscopes on one side, and on the other cosmonauts, their myths and mythologies, the exploitation of their achievements for purposes of propaganda, space exploration with its quota of *sacrifice*. Countering this re-emerging cult of the World – or the Cosmos – complementing and compensating it, is another more 'human' cult, that of Eros. Eroticism is obsessive nowadays, though this obsession only superficially reflects an intensification of virility (or femininity) and a greater aptitude for sexual pleasure. We see it rather as a symptom of the obverse, a lack of virility and femininity, frigidity, not overcome but self-conscious, and a demand for compensations. The cult of Eros denotes a desire to restore former *interdictions* so that *transgressions* – investing erotic acts with a lost significance – become possible; whence the impressive number of collective rapes and sadistic or masochistic rituals. Interdictions are extended to everyday life even when their ideological justification is absent: *vide* the obstacles – psychological, physiological (real or fictitious), ideological and political – set up against the use of contraceptives. Man's *adaptation to his desire* is arrested mid way between the real and the possible, between experience and make-believe; his adaptation is also blocked by basic repressions, the foremost – an heirloom of religion – is the ideological relation of fecundation to the sexual act that sanctions and consecrates physiological phenomena and blind determinism. It is because such religious traditions survive that sexuality, debarred by society from *adaptation*, seeks an outlet in new forms of religiosity.

Satiety and a stubborn quest for satisfaction, dissatisfaction and unrest contradict, confront and reflect each other as they merge; show-consuming turns into a show of consuming, and the past – works of art, styles, historic cities – is avidly consumed till boredom and satiety set in. In such circumstances it is impossible to avoid escapism (the desire to get away from everyday life), and as a result escapism and flight are promptly and easily salvaged by tourist organizations, institutionalism, programming, codified mirages and the setting in motion of vast controlled migrations. Whence the desecration of the quest and its objects by the questers themselves, as historic towns and regions, museums and galleries are submerged under the flood of consumers who thus consume nothing but the all-pervading, increased and multiplied presence of their fellows.

A summary analysis suffices to show that there are two distinct types of leisure 'structurally' opposed: a) leisure integrated with everyday life (the perusal of daily papers, television, etc.) and conducive to profound discontent as it creates situations like that of the Kierkegaardian character who, before his horrified wife and terrified children, tore his newspaper to shreds screaming: 'Everything, everything has now become possible!'; b) the prospect of departure, the demand for evasion, the will to escape through worldliness, holidays, LSD, debauchery or madness.

A stroll through the land of make-believe

The experimental and conceptual gropings of contemporary philosophy and sociology have discovered one thing at least, and that is social make-believe – not to be confused with individual imagination or with the vast symbolic heritage of the past.*

The best examples of social make-believe are to be found neither in films nor in science fiction, but in women's magazines, where experience and make-believe merge in a manner conducive to the

---

* Among the experts of social make-believe we mention at random: G. Bachelard, J.-P. Sartre, E. and V. Morin, R. Barthes, Jean Duvignaud, H. Raymond, and of course the authors of plays, science fiction, films, etc., whom it would be too lengthy to name.

reader's utter bewilderment. Indeed, a single issue may include practical instructions on the way to cut out and sew up a dress or precise information such as where and at what price to buy another, alongside a form of rhetoric that invests clothes and other objects with an aura of unreality: all possible and impossible dresses, every kind of dish from the simplest to those whose realization requires the skill of a professional, garden chairs and occasional tables, furniture worthy of a castle or a palace, all the houses and all the flats are presented to the reader with the codes that ritualize such 'messages' and make them available by programming everyday life. The reader, according to his personal taste, invests this subject-matter with a concrete or an abstract interpretation, sees it as pragmatic or imaginary, imagines what he sees and sees what he imagines. Here too literature and publicity are distinguished only by the different way in which each is laid out on the page to attract the eye of the reader, the rhetoric of advertisements being often more literary (and better written) than the reading matter, which adopts the methods of publicity and fills the same metaphorical function of making insignificance 'fascinating' and translating everyday life into make-believe so that the face of the consumer lights up with a smile of satisfaction. Such publications insinuate into each reader's daily life all possible daily lives, including the unrestricted (or presumed such) everyday lives of the demi-gods, happiness made possible.... It is a fact that women do read these practical texts on make-believe fashions and these make-believe sections (including publicity) on practical fashions, thus proving our theory of a level of reality where superficial analysis only perceives juxtaposed sectors (living, food, clothing and fashions, furnishing, tourism, towns and urbanism, etc.), each sector governed by a system and forming a kind of social entity, but where we discover sub-systems that make possible the functional organization of everyday life and its subjection to compulsions that are anything but unselfish. Let it be remembered that our aim is to prove that a system of everyday life does not exist, notwithstanding all the endeavours to establish and settle it for good and all, and that there are only sub-systems separated by irreducible gaps, yet situated on one plane and related to it.

LEVELS OF SOCIAL REALITY

Strategies of power and opposition
Perspectives and prospectives
Conceptual and theoretical knowledge
(gradually descending towards experience)

Ideologies of property, rationality and the state

Images and ideologies ('culture' fragmented and specialized)

Principles (ethics, aesthetics, aestheticism, patterns and models, ideologies seen as non-ideologies such as scientism, positivism, structuralism, functionalism, etc.)
Organizing *sub-systems* that are justified by principles
The ideology of consumption
Publicity as ideology

Illusions and myths related to ideology and to current rhetoric

MAKE-BELIEVE (social) (involving individual make-believe and collective symbolisms)

Language
vocabulary
oppositions — *metaphysical* function (of writing)
links — *metonymical* function (of speech)

Rhetoric
words
images
things

Emotional projections consolidating make-believe or actualized as adaptation

POESIS and PRAXIS

Adaptation (of a human being to his natural being)
bodies
time
space
desire
'Values' nascent or vanishing: festivals, leisure, sport, the city, urbanism, nature, etc.

Everyday life

Compulsions (determinisms noted by science, mastered by technology)
biological
geographical
economic
etc.
multiple but united in the social mastery of nature and in *praxis*

This theory, which we shall not develop here, is summed up in the diagram on page 87, and our commentary of this diagram will serve as defence and justification.

The diagram is more or less consistent with the tri-dimensional code (cf. *Le Langage et la société*, chapter VII), that is, with the theory distinguishing three dimensions of reality expressed in speech: symbols, paradigms and links. Indeed, the two theories define the same phenomena, one in terms of levels, the other in terms of dimensions. Compulsions might, for instance, be graded from 0 to 100; for the inhabitants of a 'large community', that is for conditions in an urban settlement and a particularly significant standard of everyday life, the total of compulsions would approach the highest grade, while it would decrease in the case of a suburban district dweller and decrease further if we consider the well-to-do citizen living in a residential area in a big town. Adaptation and compulsion have conflicting and complex relations; he who *adapts* to circumstances has overcome compulsion, but the technical mastery of 'natural' determinisms is not sufficient; one could say, roughly, that more compulsion (controlled and codified) equals less adaptation, but the relation is not one of logical inversion but of dialectical conflict; adaptation absorbs compulsions, transforms them and turns them into products.

Such conflicts and problems of everyday life involve *fictitious* solutions, superimposed on the *real* solutions when these are, or seem to be, *impossible*. Thus problems and the search for solutions overstep the frontier of make-believe, 'projections' unobtrusively fill the gap between experience and make-believe and people project their desires on to one group of objects or another, one form of activity or another: the home, the flat, furnishing, cooking, going away on holiday, 'nature', etc. Such projections invest the object with a double existence, real and imaginary.

We have seen that language is a medium of make-believe, and the contradictions that arise at this level; and we shall have more to say on the subject later. There is a displacement, a decay of symbols and a general shift towards signals and towards syntagmatic links at the expense of symbolism and opposition. So long as make-believe exists, the displacement is not total, and, moreover, metalanguage (or words about words) acts as compensation.

Art formerly represented a form of *adaptation* (of time, space, desire); the work of art gave a perceptible shape to time and to space, frequently even on a social scale as for instance in cities, architecture and monuments. Aesthetics tends to operate more on the level of make-believe, in the form of discussions on, and interpretations of, art, or rhetoric; as to aestheticism, with its discussions on art-discussions and on aesthetics, its illusory adaptation, fictitious metamorphosis of everyday life and verbal consumption, it occupies an intermediary position between make-believe and ideology; all depends on the 'quality' of the discussions.

Style also implied *adaptation* when objects, instead of being considered only as such and put to a definite restricted use *qua* objects, were the common property of social experience; that consumption can exist without such an adaptation and, simply through a prescribed and exact correspondence of needs and goods, is a postulate of the society of consumption; indeed, its ideology (and publicity as ideology) is founded on this postulate that is assumed to be the basis of satisfaction.

It is of some significance to note that the diagram on page 87 also illustrates the theory of objects and activities as 'sectors': clothing, food, furnishing, 'living' and environment and possibly sex and sexuality; and can also be applied to towns and urbanism, and to the motor-car. Not that it applies literally to each specific sub-group or sub-system, but it can be theoretically adapted to a specific sector while still, apparently, maintaining its essential outline; each theory would require a modulation of the initial diagram so as to fit and define the sector in question; thus the amount of compulsion and the success of adaptations vary according to the theory; certain objects refuse to be restricted to the level of experience or of make-believe and become emotionally or imaginatively charged because they are both perceived (socially) and expressed, while others attain a 'superior' status and become ideologically overcharged; thus the 'detached' house is experienced by the inhabitant as something to which he has a chance of adapting, but also as dream and ideology; the same applies to clothes (ready-made, ready-to-wear, *haute-couture*) or to food (ordinary meals, good cooking, dinner parties and banquets), each level having its specific context of images and verbal commentaries. Make-believe as such is part of everyday life, everybody expects his daily (or weekly) ration; yet make-believe has a specific role in relation to everyday experience (compulsions and adaptation): it must disguise the predominance of compulsion and our limited capacity to adapt, the bitterness of conflicts and the weight of 'real' problems, and sometimes it can further adaptation or circumscribe experience.

Publicity does not only provide an ideology of consumption, and it does more than create an image of the 'I' consumer, fulfilled as such, realizing himself in actions and coinciding with his own ideal. It is based on the imaginary existence of things; it evokes them and involves a rhetoric and a poetry superimposed on the art of consuming and inherent in its image; a rhetoric that is not restricted to language but invades experience; a display window in the Faubourg Saint-Honoré or a fashion show are rhetorical happenings, a language of things. But, although we shall return to the subject of publicity later, for the time being we must concentrate on trying to define the outline of our unrest and our discontent.

The sense of disappointment that pervades consumption has a number of causes, and we are far from understanding them all; but we have succeeded, none the less, in locating one of them in the absence of a determined split or division between the consumption of things and that of signs and images deriving from these things. The act of consuming is as much an act of the imagination (fictitious) as a real act ('reality' itself being divided into compulsions and adaptations), and therefore metaphorical (joy in every mouthful, in every perusal of the object) and metonymical (all of consumption and all the joy of consuming in every object and every action). This in itself would not matter if consumption were not accepted as something reliable, sound and devoid of deception and mirage, but there are no natural frontiers separating imaginary consumption or the consumption of make-believe (the subject of publicity) and real consumption; or one might say that there exists a fluid frontier that is always being overstepped and that can only be fixed in theory. Consumer-goods are not only glorified by signs and 'good' in so far as they are signified; consumption is primarily related to these signs and not to the goods themselves. How then can frustration and disappointment be avoided if people have nothing more substantial than signs to get their teeth into? Adolescents today want to consume now, at once, and such a market has been duly and effectively exploited. Thus young people tend to lead a marginal everyday life, their own yet unchanged, opposed to that of their elders yet in all ways identical to it; their presence overshadows adult values, possessions and trades, and yet as 'adolescents' they are marginal; they are incapable of formulating, still less of imposing, their values, so that what they consume, both negatively and massively, are the adult objects that surround them with their material existence and their signs. This situation fosters deep and multiple frustrations that are inadequately compensated by a brutal assertiveness.

The case is still more distressing for the working classes, who live in the midst of signs of consumption and consume an inordinate amount of signs, as everyday life is, for them, mainly dominated by compulsions with a minimum of adaptation. Consciousness, in such circumstances, craves for make-believe and is inevitably disappointed by it, because the methods of enslavement and exploitation to which the working classes have to submit disguise their true condition, and they are not aware of being exploited and enslaved in their daily lives and daily consumption to the same degree as they are in the sphere of production. In the 'good old days' the working classes were unaware of the structure of production and therefore of their being exploited; the ideology of exchange, 'work for wages', served as a cover for the real conditions of production, the structured–structuring relation (sale of working energy, ownership and administration of the means of production by one class). This relation has become vaguer still since then, and the ideology of consumption only increases its vagueness. Consumption is a substitute for production and, as exploitation is intensified, it grows proportionately less obtrusive The working classes cannot help being discontented for they are the first of the social strata to be acquainted with such frustration;

their class consciousness is not easily restored and yet does not entirely disappear but becomes a class 'misunderstanding', and as such is involved in all claims and protests that spread unobtrusively from questions of pay (that are never adequately solved) to the organization of their daily lives.

We have already noted the ambiguity of women's status today. Everyday life, to which they are consigned, is also their stronghold from which they try, nevertheless, to escape by the roundabout method of eluding the responsibilities of consciousness; whence their incessant protests and clumsily formulated, directionless claims.

For the intellectual, make-believe, flowing with the waters of rhetoric, language and metalanguage, is the permanent substitute for experience that allows him to ignore the mediocrity of his condition, his lack of power, of money and the humiliating fact of having to submit to compulsions and myths in order to climb a few rungs of the social ladder and become a popular writer, a famous journalist, an eminent technician or government advisor, etc.

In consequence, protests, objections and claims do not cease and cannot be eradicated as each particular group in turn objects and protests trying to make the most of the situation. The rejection of this society by ever-renewed groups of adolescents is the most significant; it is a total rejection, all-encompassing, hopeless, fruitless, absolute and endlessly recurring. Such groups fall into two categories, the violent and the non-violent, for their refusal implies an attempt to evade everyday life and establish a new existence of creation and adaptation that has various aspects: vagrancy, drugs, passwords, complicities, etc.

The middle classes have, of course, been had once again! By whom, it is difficult to say, for if class strategy possesses an active 'subject' it can never be caught red-handed, because it is 'made up' after the event by experience; but the middle classes, who serve as pivot in the manoeuvre, are also its victims, and their particular relation to objects and property is becoming a general relation. This intermediary stratum of society has always craved satisfaction ever since it first came into existence: itemized satisfactions and items of satisfaction; authority and power have never been its lot (neither has creativity, but for different reasons), and it is impossible to speak of 'style' in relation to it – an absence of style would be more to the point; thus the circumstances that characterized it have spread to the whole of society, with the exception of the ruling classes or contemporary equivalent of the aristocracy who have no everyday life. (The image, however, by which they are made popular presents them in the setting of a superior brand of this commodity; in extreme cases they have not even a fixed abode; these demigods reproduce in their opulence and power a revised version of vagrancy and the tramp, wandering from yacht to Grand Hotel to Château; but they are not on the same plane as the ordinary citizen; like fairy-tale heroes they provide common mortals with a tangible image – sold at a high price – of make-believe; that which was possible and all that was possible have taken shape. Here is another everyday life, unrecognizable yet recognized with its swimming-pools, white lacquered telephones, antique furniture ... yet there remains one insuperable superiority: the demi-gods do not live in the quotidian, whereas the common mortal, his feet glued to the ground, is overwhelmed by it, submerged and engulfed.) The middle classes wallow in satisfactions and are yet half-aware of being swindled; they carry very little weight, have only a smattering of wealth, no power and no authority, but their way of life seems to have conquered the whole of society including the working classes, so that they must live henceforth like the proletariat or only a fraction better. Thus, as it has been said and repeated, social strata take the place of classes; and moreover the middle classes, by denying the status of 'class' to the workers, have acquired in relation to these proletariat a sort of dignity and eminence, a superior standing – in short, a class consciousness, so that they are, unwittingly, furthering the cause of the bourgeoisie. At present, this intermediary stratum of the society of controlled consumption is slowly merging with the proletariat and though white-collar workers, small technicians and clerks put up a stubborn resistence to this state of affairs it spreads none the less, not because of ideological pressures but simply through the obvious similarity of their everyday lives and the identical evasions from such lives in packaged tours and trips.

Resist it as he may, the middle-class citizen is uneasily aware that in the society of consumption the consumer is consumed – not himself in flesh and blood, who is still as free as the labourer; not himself, but his life-time. The theory of alienation is reputed to be out of date; indeed, certain forms of alienation may perhaps have vanished, such as, for instance, sexual alienation, though even this is not certain and the basis of sexual repression (the 'natural' relation, practically and culturally enforced, of the sexual act to fecundation) is very far from extinct. New types of alienation have joined ranks with the old, enriching the typology of alienation: political, ideological, technological, bureaucratic, urban, etc. We would suggest that alienation is spreading and becoming so powerful that it obliterates all trace or consciousness of alienation. We commit for trial, here and elsewhere, ideologists who would class this theory among antiquated philosophies; notwithstanding their would-be sardonic insinuations concerning ideological 'conspiracies' and their 'instigators', they further the cause of class strategy; with a clear conscience, neither better nor worse than the others: those who know and those who understand nothing about anything. What is new is that the theory of alienation is left with a diminishing philosophical referential and has become a *social practice*, a class strategy whereby philosophy and history are set aside so as to confuse the issue and successfully inhibit any consciousness of the actual state of total alienation. Such a strategy has a number of moves at its disposal; the pawns are the middle classes who are totally unaware of their alienation, although they have served as models for most chroniclers of this phenomenon. One fine morning the middle-class citizen passes out like a Victorian lady, or like the Kierkegaardian character he starts shouting 'Everything is now possible!'; he is no longer content with exchanging reality for make-believe and vice versa, with jumbling the levels, he wants something else; consuming satisfies him and yet leaves him dissatisfied; consuming is not happiness, comfort and ease are not all, joy does not depend on them; he is bored.

This society wishes to *integrate* its members, communities, individuals, atoms and molecules, to integrate them with itself though it is no longer considered a 'subject'; this is its problem and one of its major contradictions. Not that it lacks integrating powers, though these are mainly prevalent in the spheres of trade and consumer-goods, but still active on the cultural level too; while everyday life integrates those who accept it and even those whom it does not satisfy; these last who would like something more fulfilling are rapidly and totally engulfed none the less, and to them the most convincing incitements to revolt only sound like so much noise. Has not this society, glutted with aestheticism, already integrated former romanticisms, surrealism, existentialism and even Marxism to a point? It has indeed, through trade, in the form of commodities! That which yesterday was reviled today becomes cultural consumer-goods; consumption thus engulfs what was intended to *give meaning and direction*. It is all very well to dismiss meaning and to consider the quest for meaning absurd, to assimilate the absurd to the real and the rational; but a great gap widens, a gap that the philosophers can face unflinchingly, but one whereby our society – which has no other ideological props – is deprived of its integrating powers. For culture – that abstract translation of economic and technological demands – is of no avail; whence the paradox, frequently discussed but only superficially analysed, of a society whose function is integration and participation and that cannot succeed in integrating any one of its groups – neither adolescents, intellectuals, districts, towns, business concerns nor women. Typical of such an imposing and impotent society is the United States of America. When the French and European bourgeoisie possessed an ideology (the universality of Reason) and a social practice (the creation of nationality) they had integrating powers, but the channelling of such universalizing ideologies into the restricted rationalities of technology and the state has reduced their former strategical power to nothing, with the result that impotence prevails in cultural and especially in integrative spheres.

In these circumstances new ideologies are required and feverishly sought after. It was evidently impossible to live on the American funds of 1950 to 1960: de-ideologization, an increasingly harmonious release of tensions, the abolition of classes. 'End ideologies!' was the rallying cry of the American attack, and such a battering ram and such artillery made short work of Europe's ancient fortresses; massive landings of specialists (sociologists, psychologists and others) followed in the wake of this onslaught. With what result? Now Europe is little more than a battlefield of broken philosophies and theories, with here and there a lone and much beleaguered citadel or fort still resisting (Marxism, historicity). The American attack coincided with the downfall of Stalinist dogmatism; and now the demand for more subtle ideologies is intense both in America and in Europe, so that it is necessary to refine the concept itself of ideology. We believe that today this concept includes, on the one hand, theories purporting to be non-ideological and 'rigorous' and, on the other, a large proportion of social make-believe, fostered by publicity (that tends to become both ideology and experience); today an ideology must not be seen as such, it must make no appeal to emotivity, involve no allegiance to specific leaderships, but don a scientific disguise, short of imitating a certain psychoanalysis or a certain occultism and foolhardily staking on the irrational.

At an inferior level of the build-up, as a sop to the lower classes, we have *economism*. Vulgar and vulgarized, it has no easy life because it works as an ideology of expansion, as productivism, as organizing rationality or as the prospect of imminent affluence. Such concepts, though already discarded in the United States, have still a rosy future before them in underdeveloped France and may well be included officially, one of these days, in a university curriculum or that of some other state-sponsored institution. Economism has the considerable advantage of uniting a decayed Marxism and a degenerate bourgeois rationalism; furthermore, it conveniently clothes the organization and the rationalized exploitation of everyday life.

But there are other more subtle undertakings. The ideology of *femininity*, or of happiness by and in femininity, is only another form of the ideology of consumption (happiness through consuming) and the ideology of technicality (women possessing the technique of happiness!), but with something more appealing.

The ideology of culture or culturalism supports the unsteady theory of the coherence and singleness of culture, which is the official theory; but, in fact, culture is atomized and sub-cultures of various denominations are no novelty: country life, city life, aristocracy, proletariat, bourgeoisie, 'underdeveloped countries', culture of the masses, etc.; but so many 'sub-cultures' – even when disguised in the Harlequin cape made for the purpose by one of them (namely 'classicism') – do not make a culture; the fragmentation of specialized knowledge and labour is not conducive to unity. Culture is not a myth, it is worse: it is a state ideology. Unity of culture can only be found at the highest level, that of cultural institutions; whence 'mass culture' and consumption are supplied with 'best quality products' and works that are said to be 'unadulterated'.

Functionalism, formalism and structuralism have this in common with scientism and positivism: they all parade as non-ideological. Yet the ideologizing process is clear enough, and consists in extrapolation-reduction whereby the ideology makes absolute truths of relative, specific concepts. The importance of the ideology of *language* entitles it to a chapter to itself; it is related on the one hand to the remarkable discoveries of the budding science of *linguistics* and on the other to 'language phenomena' that pertain to everyday life. Let it suffice to note for the time being that this ideology is based on a simultaneous representation of language as the *key to social reality* (which becomes perceptible by means of its specific forms of speech) and as a *system* (including and involving the unity of reality and intelligibility); whereas the theory we shall be introducing in the following chapter stresses the fact that we are surrounded by *metalanguage*, words about words, or the decoding of former messages without the faintest claim either to novelty or to the decoding of 'reality'.

Publicity is a 'language phenomenon' that requires our particular attention; not the least of the problems that it raises is its efficiency, the character and scope of its influence. We hope to show how, by a process of substitution – one among its many processes – publicity assumes in part the role formerly held by ideologies: to clothe, dissimulate and transform reality, that is to say production relations.

Ideology in its former capacity (possessing the power to grip, liberate and integrate, that once characterized rationalism) could only subsist if everyday life could be seen as an actively coherent system; and this view is impossible. Such a system should first be proved by experience, for if everyday life is to be seen as a system this system must be structured and closed. Unfortunately for this theory, as soon as the quotidian is presented as a system (a compendium of meanings) it collapses and is seen to be meaningless, a compendium of non-meanings, to which we try to append a meaning; indeed, everyday insignificance can only become meaningful when transformed into something other than everyday life; in other words, it is not possible to construct a theoretical and practical system such that the details of everyday life will become meaningful in and by this system. Furthermore there is no system because there are so many sub-systems situated, as we have seen, not *within a single system* but at *different levels of reality*, the lacunae and gaps between them filled with floating mists . . .; and the only system sufficiently comprehensive to be worthy of the name is the system of *substitutes* – so comprehensive, in fact, that all 'theories', 'analyses' and 'inquiries' risk turning into substitutes to save trouble and uphold a 'system' that only exists in words!

A few sub-systems

Theoreticians of structuralism frequently use the word 'system'; but their vocabulary is sadly lacking in precision. For the word has gradually become vague and indeterminate, and though exactness may be included in its connotations and its rhetoric it has certainly no part in its denotation, which signifies about as much as 'what's-its-name' or 'thingummybob'. Yet the fact remains that a system is a unity or it is nothing,* for if there are more than one the existence and effect of each will be only relative and none can stand alone. In such circumstances it would be more correct to speak of sub-systems, though of course, this puts an end to the authority and dignity of the structure, prerogatives of the one

* As Michel Foucault has demonstrated in the last pages of his book *Les Mots et les choses*, Paris, 1966. which is as sybilline as could be wished.

absolute system surrounded by prophetic mistiness. ... Sub-systems were already implicit in Hegelianism with the theory of an all-encompassing philosophico-political system, a circle surrounding circles, a sphere containing spheres.

The conditions required for the existence of sub-systems are:

a) a distinct, specific and specialized (social) activity; objectives corresponding to this activity, specific, classifiable and that can be labelled; situations determined by the relation between activity (social agent or subject; groups and individuals) and objectives, so as to constitute an indissoluble whole;

b) organizations and institutions justifying one another at state level or at the level of another state-sponsored institution; the institutions make use of the organizations as 'implements' with which to manipulate social activity while a competent devoted bureaucracy promptly ransacks the common weal, so that a hierarchy – or hierarchies – is rapidly constituted;

c) texts (forming a *corpus*) that ensure the communication of activity, the participation of its organizing actions, the sway and authority of the corresponding institutions; these texts are sometimes already organized into codes, or they consist of documents, treatises, manuals, guides, or the illustrations and literature of publicity, from which the explicit corpus and code may be analytically deduced; such analyses, when successful, reveal and define what some linguists (Hjemslev, A. J. Griemas) call *connotational language*.

According to this definition, fashion is a sub-system;* so is cookery when it renounces the status of a regional, household craft consisting of orally transmitted recipes, to become a formalized, specialized activity, the object of manuals and gastronomical guides with a hierarchy of place-names and dishes, and serving as pretext for social rituals; however it is, for the most part,

---

* Cf. R. Barthes, *Le Système de la mode*, Paris, 1966. It is hardly necessary to say that in his work the methodical analysis of the language of fashion is first rate. However, the 'experience' of fashion (sociological: women, materials, prices – in brief, the system's impact or importance) is lacking. Such was the author's intention. Our concern (with the insertion of fashion into everyday life) precedes or follows his.

successful in eluding systematization and retains its household and regional character. Sub-systems are the result of a sort of nucleus of significances favouring a certain sphere of social space so that it acquires powers of attraction and repulsion; this is an *isotope* (A. J. Griemas). The nucleus of language attracts activity, depriving it of its spontaneity, and transforming actions and skills into signs and significations at the expense of adaptation. Such a process takes place in the sphere of make-believe.

Tourism might also be called a sub-system in the so-called consumer society; 'culture', too, that appears as an entity in this light; sexuality and eroticism could also be classed under this heading; but, from the viewpoint of programmed everyday life, nothing can beat the motor-car.

Practical and explicit inquiries into the role and function of the motor-car are remarkably inconclusive to date; there are a number of essays and studies on the subject that might serve as introductions to our analysis, but most of them are more symptomatic than informative. We shall, however, leave to others the task of compiling a methodical treatise, since our aim is to prove the existence of a 'sub-system', a specific semantic field invading and influencing everyday life, and to this end we shall show that:

a) The motor-car is the epitome of 'objects', the Leading-Object, and this fact should be kept in mind. It directs behaviour in various spheres from economics to speech. Traffic circulation is one of the main functions of a society and, as such, involves the priority of parking spaces, adequate streets and roadways. The town only puts up a feeble resistance to this 'system' and wherever such resistance occurs it is duly quashed. Certain experts use the general term 'urbanism', with its philosophical and rational implications, to designate the effects of traffic circulation carried to their extreme limits. Space is conceived in terms of motoring needs and traffic problems take precedence over accommodation in self-termed technical rationality; it is a fact that for many people the car is perhaps the most substantial part of their 'living conditions'. It might be interesting to point out some curious phenomena: motorized traffic enables people and objects to congregate and mix without meeting, thus constituting a striking example of simultaneity without exchange, each element remaining enclosed in its own compartment, tucked away in its shell; such conditions contribute to the disintegration of city life and foster a 'psychology' or, better, a 'psychosis' that is peculiar to the motorist; on the other hand the real but limited and pre-established dangers do not prevent most people from 'taking risks', for the motor-car with its retinue of wounded and dead, its trail of blood, is all that remains of adventure in everyday life, its paltry ration of excitement and hazard. What is also significant is the place of the car in the only global system we have identified, the system of substitutes; as a substitute for eroticism, for adventure, for living conditions and for human contact in large towns the car is a pawn in the 'system' that crumbles away as soon as it has been identified. It is an unimposing technical object, depending on relatively simple functional requirements (it must move, therefore work – using and wasting a considerable amount of energy – light up the way before it, change direction and speed) and structural requirements (engine, chassis and body, equipment), and figures also in a simple, unimposing functional and structural social complex where it plays an increasingly important part; it gives rise to an attitude (economic, psychic, sociological, etc.), assumes the dimension of a complete object and has an (absurd) significance; in fact the motor-car has not conquered society so much as *everyday life* on which it imposes its laws and whose establishment it ensures by fixing it on a *level* (levelling it). Today the greater part of everyday life is accompanied by the noise of engines, and is taken up with their 'rational' exploitation and the demands of the motor industry and motor repairs.

b) This is not the end; a car is not merely a material object with certain technical advantages, a socio-economic means and medium involving demands and compulsions. It fosters *hierarchies:* an obvious hierarchy determined by size, power, cost, and a more complex and subtle hierarchy depending on *performance.*

There is a certain amount of lee-way between the two hierarchies, so that they do not exactly coincide; a margin or interval separates them in which there is room for talk, discussion and controversy, in a word for speech. A definite point in the material scale does not correspond precisely to a point on the performance scale; thus I might climb a rung or two by becoming a champion (for a minute or a day?) within a specific restricted circle; there are limits, of course; but what are they? When I overtake a more powerful car than that which I am driving, I change my place in the first hierarchy by climbing a rung in the second, that concerned with performance and requiring foolhardiness, ability and cunning, therefore freedom; my achievement becomes a topic of conversation with my passengers, later with my acquaintances and friends to whom, especially if I have taken some risk, I am sure to boast of my feat; in these circumstances the hierarchy is no longer oppressive and compulsive, but integrative.

We note that this characteristic of automotive objects is similar to that of the human body in its relation to sport; there is a physical hierarchy (weight, strength, height, etc.) and a hierarchy of performance, but also a telescoping of the two.

Moreover this dual hierarchy corresponds (*approximately* therefore fluidly – and therein lies its general significance and its specific significance for the theoretician) to the social hierarchy: there is analogy (not homology) between social standing and the grading of cars. As the two scales do not coincide there is an incessant shift from one to the other with no definite cause for interruption, and this undefined, indefinite, reversible and ever-recurring – yet imperative – character of the rating allows for an infinite variety of combinations, contradictions and computations.

c) As a result the practical significance of the motor-car, as an instrument of road communication and transport, is only part of its social significance. This highly privileged object has a second, intenser significance, more ambiguous than the first, real and symbolic, practical and make-believe and its hierarchization is both expressed and implied, sustained and enhanced by its symbolism. The car is a status symbol, it stands for comfort, power, authority and speed, it is *consumed as a sign* in addition to its practical use, it is something magic, a denizen from the land of make-believe. Speech becomes rhetorical and unrealistic when referring to the motor-car; this significant object has a significant retinue (language, speech, rhetoric), its various significances involving, intensifying and neutralizing each other as it stands for consumption and consumes symbols, symbolizes happiness and procures happiness by symbols. The motor-car's roles are legion: it is the sum of everyday compulsions, the prime example of the social favours bestowed on mediator and medium and it is a condensation of all the attempts to evade everyday life because it has restored to everyday life hazard, risk and significance.

d) This object has its own code, the Highway Code, a fact that speaks for itself. Volumes are filled with semantic, semiologic and semiotic interpretations of the Highway Code that is the epitome of compulsive sub-codes disguising by their self-importance our society's lack of directive and of a general code. It demonstrates the role of signals; but the scholar who wishes to complete a thorough semiologic (or sociologic) interpretation of the motor-car must include in the basic corpus – in addition to this code – further documents such as legal, journalistic or literary tracts, advertisements, etc. The Leading-Object has not only produced a system of communication but also organisms and institutions that use it and that it uses.

At this point the situation becomes comical, or rather *absurd*. Such sub-systems, we are convinced, can only lead to pleonasm, to destruction through tautology as the object destroys everything and then itself. The tourist trade, whose aim is to attract crowds to a particular site – historic city, beautiful view, museum, etc. – ruins the site in so far as it achieves its aim: the city, the view, the exhibits are invisible behind the tourists, who can only see one another (which they could have done just as well elsewhere, anywhere). Fashion? How many women are really fashionable? A handful of models, cover-girls and demi-goddesses, who quake in their shoes lest they should cease to be fashionable because fashion, which they make, eludes them no sooner launched, and they must keep up with it or rather ahead of it in a perpetual giddy-making overtaking. Formal cookery is on the way out; the unenlightened customer has come to appreciate rites, appearances and settings more than the actual dishes, so that hotel and restaurant owners, on the look-out for easy profit, substitute form for quality; the enlightened customer will have to discover the little café, the simple, unpretentious restaurant run by an ambitious chef. As to the motor-car – notwithstanding its specific attraction as desecrator of town and countryside – saturation point will soon be reached here too and is indeed, to the horror of traffic experts, already in sight in the form of final freezing and inextricable fixity. In the expectancy of this ever-receding, fascinating culmination, motorists in America and Germany spend long hours in roadside motels contemplating the flow of traffic on the motorways* and evidently finding the pastime extremely (if not totally) rewarding.

We are sufficiently familiar with obsolescence in theory and in practice to realize that the wear of motor-cars is foreseen, conditioned and programmed; we might even suggest (with a rather doubtful pun) that the automotive vehicle is the arch-symbol of autodestruction, and as such, though termed 'durable consumer goods' and involving permanent structures (thoroughfares, motorways, etc.) it takes place of honour in the system of substitutes.

One could say that publicity is a sub-system; yet such a hypothesis appears to be unacceptable. Rather, it is the language of trade at its most elaborate, complete with symbols, rhetoric and metalanguage, the means by which the traded object and its ambiguous (abstract–concrete, formal–practical) trade value subsist. The following theory taken from Marx's *Das Kapital* seems apt and conclusive: trade is a form, distinct from its content (social labour), and its contingent retinue (negotiations, palavers, words and sentences, gestures and rituals). This dialectical theory *reduces* the act of trading to its simple form just as, later, we shall see the semantic theory discarding words to redeem the essence of the act of communication, or language. Such a form, furthermore, is only isolated from its content and contingencies at a first operation; consequent stages of the inquiry restore both content and historical and sociological conditions of trade, which, when 'pure' form is under analytical observation, are set aside for further consideration – the content placed between brackets, the contingencies dis-

* See the caricatures by Sempé (though his humour, tinged with absurdity, is harmless enough and easily retrievable, that is, merging into acceptance).

carded. This allows the linking of form to a social experience, its gradual emergence and the creation of its own social experience so that it becomes, in fact, the experience. It would indeed be simple-minded to see trade value as a pre-established *system* concealed in the words and gestures of those concerned in trade (buyers, sellers, tradesmen, the capitalists of commerce, etc.). Trade as form contains a *logic;* as the product of labour it produces sequences, intelligibly linked actions; it is both a social and an intellectual phenomenon. This form even governs the language that preceded it, adapting it to its own ends; and the result is more than a simple connotational language – though certain groups such as tradesmen, for instance, do possess just such a semantic sub-system. Notwithstanding resistances – which may be unsurmountable – from former traditions and fixations as well as from revolutionary potentialities, trade tends (without ever entirely succeeding) to constitute a 'world' (or should we say that 'system' familiar under the name of capitalism?). And publicity, of course, describes objects intended for a specific use and possessing a trade value (quoted on the market), in a manner such as to induce the consumer to buy. That is how it started, that was its function in the nineteenth century: to inform, to describe and to provoke desire; and indeed, that is still one of its functions, now overshadowed, however, by others; in the second half of the twentieth century in Europe, or at any rate in France, there is *nothing* – whether object, individual or social group – that is *valued* apart from its double, the image that advertises and sanctifies it. This image *duplicates* not only an object's material, perceptible existence but desire and pleasure that it makes into fictions situating them in the land of make-believe, promising 'happiness' – the happiness of being a consumer. Thus publicity that was intended to promote consumption is the first of consumer goods; it creates myths – or, since it can create nothing, it borrows existing myths, canalizing signifiers to a dual purpose: to offer them as such for general consumption and to stimulate the consumption of a specific object. Thus it salvages and reconditions myths, the Smile Myth (the joy of consuming identified with the imaginary joy of the man or woman depicted consuming the object), the Display Myth (the social activity consisting in putting things on display and, in turn, producing such objects as the 'display unit', for instance).

Here we have a picture, the photograph of an athletic half-naked youth clinging for all he is worth, arm and thigh muscles tensed, to the rigging of a yacht that cleaves the water at full speed; tremendous speed is evoked by the flying foam and the tension of the ropes; the beautiful adolescent scans the horizon: what does he see that eludes the eye of the periodical-reader? Danger or Vision, or nothing at all? . . . Moreover he is doing nothing, neither landing nor turning; he is magnificent, that's all. The caption to this picture reads: 'A real man's life is marvellous, yes, marvellous! It's truly marvellous to find every morning the tonic freshness of your After-Shave . . .'

We append a few observations:

a) Here is a picture accompanied by a caption. Deprived of its caption the picture would have no meaning, or it might have any number of meanings; this is a commonplace. The caption without the picture would be absurd; this goes without saying. We note however the availability of signifiers (a naked man in the sun, the sea, the boat, etc.) and of signified (real life, plenitude, humanity). After-Shave X publicity hooks these vagrancies one to the other by means of a specific brand of consumer goods and with the object of promoting sales.

b) Former myths are thus restored: nature, virility, virility in natural surroundings, the naturalness of virility. With such themes myths as such are discarded – unless we concede to the term a very vague and general sense that would also include ideology. *Publicity acts as ideology*, imparting an ideological theme to an object (After-Shave) and endowing it with a dual real and make-believe existence. It appropriates ideological terms and links the salvaged signifiers to the re-conditioned signified without further reference to mythology.

c) A photographer working for some advertising agency happens to catch the 'spontaneous' attitude of this superb youth on the deck of a yacht and gives it a specific meaning – the pleasure of using a given after-shave – by the subterfuge of pictorial rhetoric and caption; or by the twofold *terrorism*: 'Be a well-groomed man.

Every morning become a tremendous guy who appeals to himself and to women. Use this After-Shave, or you will be nobody and know it . . .'

Thus publicity is the poetry of Modernity, the reason and pretext for all successful displays. It takes possession of art, literature, all available signifiers and vacant signifieds; it is art and literature, it gleans the leavings of the Festival to recondition them for its own ends; as with trade, which it takes to its logical limits, it confers on all things and on all beings the plenitude of duality and duplicity, the dual value of object (utility value) and of consumer goods (trade value), by a carefully organized confusion of these 'values' to the advantage of the latter.

Publicity acquires the significance of an ideology, the ideology of trade, and it replaces what was once philosophy, ethics, religion and aesthetics. The time is past when advertising tried to condition the consumer by the repetition of slogans; today the more subtle forms of publicity represent a whole attitude to life: if you know how to choose you will choose this brand and no other; this labour-saving device will give freedom to women; this fuel is your fuel. The extremely vast 'content' these appropriated ideologies constitute does nothing to diminish the apparent sincerity of publicity's concern with the public's well-being; the injunctions that interrupt films and news items on American television prove the depth of this concern: you are at home, in your living-room, in the company of the diminutive screen (rather than of the message it transmits, asserts McLuhan) and you are being looked after, cared for, told how to live better, how to dress fashionably, how to decorate your house, in short how to exist; you are totally and thoroughly programmed, except that you still have to choose between so many good things, since the act of consuming remains a permanent structure. The Smile Myth is out-ranked; consuming is no joke; well-wishing and helpful, the whole of society is with you, and considerate into the bargain, for it thinks of you, personally, it prepares for you personally specially personalized items; or better still, these items are delivered to your personalizing free will to be used at your leisure: this armchair, these assembled elements, this bed-linen, this underwear; this and not that. We had misjudged society; all of us; it is maternal and fraternal; our visible family is duplicated by this invisible one, better and especially more efficient, the society of consumption that showers consideration and protective charms on everybody. Who can be ungrateful enough to be uneasy?

The swivels turn at ground level. Consuming of displays, displays of consuming, consuming of displays of consuming, consuming of signs and signs of consuming; each sub-system, as it tries to close the circuit, gives another self-destructive twist, at the level of everyday life.

Sign-consuming deserves our particular attention. It has clearly defined properties; striptease, for instance, is the ritualized consumption of erotic symbols. But sometimes it is hard to tell it from madness; thus we have seen the craze for the 'Scoubidou', a symbol of uselessness, contrivance and absurd rationality, obsessive and joyless; and the craze for key-rings, symbols of property. In the space of a few weeks or a few months the craze is born, increases like a whirlwind, sweeping thousands of people off their feet, and then subsides without leaving a trace.

'Culture' is also an item of consumption in this society; not entirely similar to the others, however, for this particular, so-called free consumer activity (that is indeed a little less passive than most ways of absorbing ready-made goods) has an air of festivity that endows it with a sort of unity, socially real though fictitious, a part of make-believe. Works of art and styles are distributed for prompt consumption and towns are devoured with such a remarkable show of pleasure that it seems to denote outstandingly imperative needs and frustrations: foreigners, suburbanites, tourists of all descriptions hungrily devour its heart (where it still exists). Thus every object and product acquires a dual existence, perceptible and make-believe; all that can be consumed becomes a symbol of consumption and the consumer is fed on symbols, symbols of dexterity and wealth, of happiness and of love; sign and significance replace reality, there is a vast substitution, a massive transfer, that is nothing but an illusion created by the swivel's giddy twists.

Would this ironic image (illustration of a structural analysis) be a correct representation of the society in which we are living? Everyday life, as the ground on which people and things stand surrounded by eddies and whirlpools that gradually carry away people, things and the ground itself and merge in the vast maelstrom of trade? It may be a fraction over-dramatic. By stressing instability and change it overlooks our taste for solidity, durability and effort and the ascetic implications of such tastes. It might be truer to say that everyday life is a crust of earth over the tunnels and caves of the unconscious and against a skyline of uncertainty and illusion that we call Modernity, while overhead stretch the Heavens of Permanence; among the greater planets are Scientificness, clear, cold and somewhat shadowy, and the twin planets Virility and Femininity; there are stars, constellations and nebulae; high over the polar horizon we have Technology and elsewhere Youthfulness; there are *novae* such as Reliability, frozen, extinct stars like Beauty and the strange signs of Eroticism; among the fixed stars of the first magnitude we might place Urbanism and Urbanization (so long as we do not omit Naturalness, Rationality and a few others); and then the sub-lunar planets, Fashion (or 'fashionability') locatable in the vicinity of Femininity, and Sportiveness, etc.

What philosophy does it boast, this society devoted to the transitory, all-consuming, self-termed productivist, inconstant and dynamic, worshipping balance, honouring stability and venerating coherence and structure, this incoherent society for ever at breaking point? Is it neo-Hegelianism, neo-Platonism? Does it produce its own philosophy or challenge philosophical references that help to give meaning and value to reality? To put the question differently, how can a society function that considers creative ability unimportant and has built its foundations on an all-consuming activity (consuming, destructive and self-destructive), that is obsessed with coherence, makes precision an ideology and where the act of consuming is an endlessly recurrent diagram?

The answers to these questions must be postponed, for by referring to the *consumption of signs* we have prepared the way for our inquiry into linguistic phenomena.

3   Linguistic Phenomena

The decline of referentials

Scholars of contemporary linguistics can be divided into two
groups. There are those who consider language as a social experience and examine the morphological, syntactic and lexical
characteristics of the languages (or tongues) in current use, including sub-systems and connotational speech (pertaining to
sexual and erotic experience, work and working life, city life,
without omitting written and literary language) in their inquiry.
The other method consists in seeing linguistics not as a specialized
but as a general science and, indeed, an exemplary one; and on
this basis scholars focus their attention on general problems or
information and communication, their inquiry thus constituting
a sociological (historico-sociological) and cultural phenomenon.
But this leads us to question the significance of such inquiries, of
even if they have any significance, if the fact of seeking or rejecting
a significance has a significance.

   The following theoretical point should be considered: words
and groups of words (specific significant units, monomials) indicate
this or that, they *denote*. There is an intimate relation between
denotation and *signified*, yet the first concept covers more than
the second. The word 'chair' signifies a concept, the concept of
'chair'; it does not matter whether the object 'chair' exists or not;
the signified 'chair', completely independent, is a kind of formal

absolute. Now, 'I bought this chair in the Faubourg Saint-Antoine' is a statement involving a *context* that is not only linguistic but practical and social; we cannot situate or define a thing, the object 'chair', the reality 'road', the French language, without French society and without specifications of space and of time. It is the context that endows a denotation with transmissible specification; the *denotative function* involves a contextual or *referential function*, presupposes a reference that specifies the signified's isotopism (or heterotopism), its isochronism (or heterochronism): the referential determines whether the signified are or are not situated in the same place at the same time. Is it possible to connect signs and ensure their concatenation without such a referential? Can the *context be reduced* to the words and phrases (groups of signs) preceding and following a given message, and has such a reduction a validity other than that of an arbitrary decision on the part of the speaker? An answer in the affirmative (with reservations) seems apt enough in the case of a written text; but where speech is concerned it is inadequate. If we accept the negative, we are justified in discarding linguistic methods, since the problem is no longer restricted to language – not that it is translinguistic, but the referentials are social phenomena (depending on sociology). We shall now reconsider and elaborate a theory discussed in a previous work,* stressing, to begin with, the significant *decline of referentials* at the beginning of the twentieth century.

A hundred years ago words and sentences in a social context were based on reliable referentials that were linked together, being cohesive if not logically coherent, without however constituting a single system formulated as such. These referentials had a logical or commonsensical unity derived from material perception (euclidean three-dimensional space, clock time), from the concept of nature, historical memory, the city and the environment or from generally accepted ethics and aesthetics. This phenomenon stressed the general character of a society as 'subject', and moreover the society possessed (or believed it possessed, which comes to the same) a general basic code of honour, honesty and self-respect.

* *Le Langage et la société*, Paris, 1966.

We have already noted society's innate tendency to relate productive activity to creative 'values', and although this attitude had different and often contradictory interpretations according to the various social classes and ideologies, it was none the less full of meaning. It was in this context that *Das Kapital* (1867) linked theoretical language to a philosophical 'consensus' that had previously been almost entirely unconscious or misunderstood. 'Man' and 'Humanity' were no longer seen as entities, abstract essences, any more than was the 'subject'; 'pure' philosophy was already outstripped and Man and Humanity were defined as actions and activities, specific concrete 'subjects' or 'agents' affecting 'objects' and aiming at 'objectives', both of which were equally specific and concrete, situated in an historical context. Notwithstanding (or because of) contradictions this society's *praxis* had unity.

However, around the years 1905–10 the referentials broke down one after another under the influence of various pressures (science, technology, and social changes). Common sense and reason lost their unity and finally disintegrated; the 'common-sense' concept of absolute reality disappeared and a new perceptible 'real' world was substituted or added to the reality of 'well-informed' perception, while functional, technical objects took the place of traditional objects. In 1910, in fact, the reign of electricity began with electric lights, electric signals and objects operated by electricity and this important innovation affected not only industrial production, it invaded everyday life, altering the relation of night and day and the perception of outlines. But this was not by any means the only innovation; there were others that were perhaps more significant and if we have singled out electricity it is mainly for its symbolic value.

We might say that from this date the sense of sight caught up with that of hearing that was formerly in the lead, making the grasp of perceptible reality more rewarding through the simultaneous progression of both senses; for it would indeed be a sign of prejudice to stress nothing but our losses. But is this really an acquisition? Yes, with reservations. It is not only that the complexity of our senses and of the information they impart has increased; the sense of hearing has acquired a greater aptitude for interpreting visual perceptions and the sense of sight for interpreting auditive ones, so that they signify each other reciprocally. The senses are more highly educated and their theoretical ability has increased; they are becoming 'theoreticians'; by discarding immediacy they introduce mediation, and abstraction combines with immediacy to become 'concrete'. Thus objects, in practice, become signs, and signs objects; and a 'second nature' takes the place of the first, the initial layer of perceptible reality. The paintings and the music of about 1910 seem to corroborate this theory. There was then a schism among painters, one school (in Central Europe) giving first place to the signified, the viewer contributing the signifier (if he could); another (in Paris) stressing the signifier and allowing the viewer to fill in the signified; this was cubism (Picasso, Braque, etc.). In both cases the massive intervention of symbols and the shift from the expressive to the significant split the unity of signifier and signified and the referential of perceptible reality vanished.

At about the same time the theoretical and practical possibilities of unprecedented speed changed the perception of motion. Static and mobile, like light and dark and like outlines, lost their status of independent, juxtaposed absolutes and became relative. Though the theory of relativity has no immediate connection with these social phenomena in the sphere of perception, the parallel is too striking not to be mentioned. With the loss of absolute time and space – the space of Euclid and Newton – perceptible reality lost its stable referentials – a fact that was promptly translated into the sphere of aesthetics; perspective changed, the vanishing point, a token of geometric space, vanished; it was the same with the tonal system in music, where the key-note is a token of a fixity granted to the section of sound continuum thus limited. The tonal system, like the system of perspective, was both learned and popular; both corresponded to perceptions that had been collectively elaborated over centuries, they were identified with common sense. Erudite music (harmony) and popular songs, complex pictorial compositions and art-school studies were dependent on identical principles, on rules considered permanent, universal and absolute;

rationalized systems, such as perspective and tonality, warranted a formal agreement between the artist – in search of *signifiers* for his emotions and imaginings – and the viewer or listener contributing his signified to the signifiers perceived. Moreover the work of art might also refer to more subtle signifiers, to the artist's more intimate subjectivity, anguish, regret, desire. Though related to a certain seemingly permanent rationality, all this collapsed around 1910 in Europe, where it was becoming theoretically apparent that 'our space' was just one among many possible spaces, and perhaps only existed in relation to us (at our level), while elsewhere, at different levels, there might be other spaces, other times. The discovery of relativity emphasized the presence of a new perceptible reality: the 'second nature' added to the first, the sign-object or object-sign. These were unavoidable practical changes in the criteria of evaluation as well as conceptual changes; but feelings and emotions were also disintegrating; psychology and psychoanalysis were to make suspect the innocence of the babe, a myth that compensated for original sin in the Christian faith, and they made spontaneity, purity and chastity equally suspect.

All the other referentials were to disappear in the wake of common-sense perception: Nature, Religion and the City; not to mention the philosophical Absolute, religious dogma and moral imperatives, which would involve a theory of ideologies as well as a theory of referentials. A more detailed account of these earthquakes would show that after each tremor a new and seemingly sounder faith sprang up, causing massive emotional *investments* and odd infatuations. Whenever the 'values' of work decline, leisure naturally prospers, and vice versa. This synchronic diagram of the upheavals gives only part of the picture; moreover these explosions–implosions have been going on for over half a century. History, as a well-established temporal process both comprehensible and identifiable, has ceased to be a referential since the historic phenomenon of the Liberation; ideology has sanctioned an aspect of social experience and 'culture', the accomplished fact, and historicity has disappeared; the historic city too only survives as a vague regret, as something quaint and picturesque or as commercialized, organized trade value for sightseers.

Then it was the turn of production relations – though these did not vanish entirely from the sphere of knowledge, or how could we know what we were talking about and who was talking? Consuming creates nothing, not even a relation between consumers, it only consumes; the act of consuming, although significant enough in this so-called society of consumption, is a solitary act, transmitted by a mirror effect, a play with mirrors on/by the other consumer.

Together with the reality of productions, the image and the concept of active, creative and productive 'man' tended to disappear, and consequently the image and concept of society as a body (a unity).

To avoid misunderstandings we stress the fact that we are not deploring the disappearance of ethical and religious criteria nor that of metaphysical and theological absolutes. The words of Nietzsche and of Dostoyevsky, 'God is dead', are perhaps less resounding than those heard two thousand years ago by a Greek sailor; 'The great god Pan is dead', but they still re-echo; though we may wonder if God was really dead for Marx and Marxist materialism, seeing that Marx accepted without sufficient proof the finality of evolution, the rationality of action and labour, the significance of life and the universe. We have no intention of judging modernity or trying to detect symptoms of decay, decline and decadence; if we take as our model the Grand Style, such symptoms cannot fail to transpire; and is there any reason why we should not fix our aim on such ideals as the greatest work of art – Venice – or the perfect style – Athens, Florence – in fact the City, so long as it subsists? If the verdict is severe when judgement is based on such criteria why should we not uphold it against those who find it unendurable? But this is not the problem, and we must discard Nietzschean theories, for our subject is more limited and precise. While avoiding sociologism (advantages of comprehensiveness grafted on to a specialized science) and finding fault with sociology up to a point, our subject is none the less sociological. For instance, the City was formerly conceived in opposition to the countryside, but with the countryside mediating between the City and Nature; in the last century, however, the situation has been reversed and the country is now seen and conceived in relation to the City, retreating before the invading City; the specific weight of each term has altered. This is the time of the City's explosion (which does not imply that urban experience and society are disintegrating as the former opposition is transcended and that nothing will be left). At the very moment when the City becomes a referential it ceases to be a material certainty; and what is there to fall back on for the citizen and the peasant alike? This complex of sociological phenomena cannot be without serious consequences. Logic, when isolated, cannot be used as a referential – except by philosophers and a few experts – for it prescribes coherence and rules for the transmission of a message that does not cancel itself out, and that apply to all messages. Science, or rather scientificness, tries to assume the role of referential nowadays, even that of universal code, an assumption that inverts the terms; science is by definition the knowledge of reality, but reality is not the reality of knowledge – and still less of scientificness, except where a metaphysic of knowledge is concerned.

Of all the referentials only two are still left standing; one, philosophy in the highest spheres of culture; the other, in the most trivial and commonplace sphere, everyday life. That is why philosophy has acquired so much significance; not just any philosophy, but Philosophy, the Message, that Philosophy which has fashioned throughout history an image of the Universe and of Man. . . . Its inconsistencies (unevenness, use and abuse of terms, metaphors, philosophical rhetoric) are overlooked and only the essence subsists as a reference for meditation and reflection. Philosophy may be necessary, but it is not enough, and, notwithstanding the efforts of many philosophers, this has always been the case. At the other end of the scale there is everyday life; but try to use it as a referential and it becomes unendurable. So, in fact, we are left with one referential and that the prerogative of higher culture! One might just as well say that all referentials have vanished and that what remains is the memory and the demand for a system of reference.

In these circumstances it seems that the only basis for social relations is speech, deprived of criteria, veracity and authenticity and even of objectivity. In other words such relations have no foundations, and speech, the form of communication, is now instrument and content as well; through a fog of verbosity the content sometimes makes a brief appearance and before it vanishes we are able to identify it as everyday life, but no one wants to see it or even know that it is there, no one can accept it; it is the subject of all conversations and no one mentions it. It is not desire, just everyday life. 'Here I must intervene!' cries our friend the objector. 'You speak of everyday life in almost psychoanalytical terms. Where, according to you, is everyday life situated? Everywhere and nowhere, obvious and invisible, we refuse to see it and we repress it; there is a consciousness of everyday life in everyday speech. If there is a connection between everyday life and the unconscious, between everyday life and desire, will you be so kind as to explain it.'

With pleasure. The first thing that distinguishes them is the historicity of everyday life, that it is born and simultaneously decays and prospers, that it is not something static underlying action and relations in a sphere outside history; it is a phenomenon and a concatenation of phenomena of a social or sociological order. If a hidden structure – that of substitutes – exists, it is an integral (though not an integrating) part of everyday life. Attempts to apprehend everyday life intellectually fail not because it vanishes into the unconscious, but because it collapses. And yet it is signified everywhere: in publicity, in techniques of happiness (or rather satisfaction), organisms and organizations. Moreover, what right have we to suggest that the unconscious is hidden behind consciousness like the wings in a theatre? The unconscious is only consciousness ignoring its own laws (or structures) and in this respect everyday life is indeed modernity's unconscious. What is desire? Psychologists, psychoanalysts and all those who formulate the question thus lack philosophical erudition, for desire is not; true philosophers know this and have known it for a long time. Desire 'desires', and in so far as this term that denotes a state of 'being' means anything, desire desires itself, desires its end, its disappearance in a flash of satisfaction. Only the signified is involved in the act of desiring one thing or another, being satisfied by it and finding satisfaction in it; the signifier, as psychoanalysts know, disappears. Moreover, everyday life figures in nearly every newspaper and magazine article – especially in women's magazines – yet it cannot be *systematized* as such, only taken to the limit where it (its unendurability) must explode; and that is what likens it to desire. But desire can be neither extinguished nor grasped, its very essence is unknown (or even if it *has* an essence); for it is elusive and when defined as instinctive or sexual it emerges in another form, as all-pervasive, but when redefined as a whole, as will for power, hidden reason, it breaks out in the form of cruelty, madness, violence, the unpredictable. We might say that everyday life is the place of desire, so long as we specify that it is also – indeed primarily – the non-place of desire, the place where desire dies of satisfaction and re-emerges from its ashes. A crafty question deserves an evasive answer, so we shall say that, yes, there is a connection between everyday life and the unconscious, between everyday life and desire; and yet, no, there is a distinction; mainly in that the power of material objects is part of everyday life, that everyday life tends to merge with material objects, whereas desire does not – which is the secret of its power.

The absence of referentials has consequences that are all the more serious since speech merges with image to create an illusion of structure, the image appearing as referential, although it has not (and cannot have) any such function. Image and speech re-echo each other, the image introducing a vast, undefined and variegated range of significances (of *signifiers*) that can only be *expressed* in speech (become *signified*). Speech hangs in space and appears to be supported by the image when it is the image that requires a support; but speech has nothing to lean on or to cling to either.

A close examination shows that the *uncoupling* of signifiers and signified is not a specific local and localized phenomenon but occurs when, for instance, an image – a photograph – is described in words as having different meanings which are expressed in these words; the commentator may, in fact, be mistaken, he can say too much or too little, miss the 'real' meaning. The decline of referentials has generalized the uncoupling; in the absence of a referential and a code providing *common places* (*topoi* and *koina*, social topics) the link between the two signs is insecure; we are already familiar with the floating stock of *meaningless signifiers* (stray images either conscious or unconscious). Once upon a time, works of art were significant constructs presented to the senses (sight, hearing, touch) but not disconnected; 'viewers' and 'listeners', who, as such, were not entirely passive, contributed the signified to the signifier, coupling the one to the other; the separation between the two aspects of sign and significance was not a divorce, it had nothing final about it and attraction was still actively connecting them so that they were not independent one of the other; thus spectator and listener could find what was signified in the signifier (meant in the meaning) and vice versa; the message was 'freely' re-assembled, yet its interpretation was based on a familiar code depending on a given referential; monuments, cathedrals, Greek temples and eighteenth-century palaces – all stylized works, in fact – were perceived in this way. The margin of uncertainty is not easily filled in when referentials are lacking; signifiers are massively and indiscriminately consumed in sign consumption, the coupling made anyhow, anywhere; thus a specific 'system' may hook itself on to disconnected signifiers. Fashion is just such a system: you can 'say it' with clothes as you can 'say it' with flowers; Nature, Spring, Winter, evening, morning, mourning, parties, desire, freedom – the 'system' makes use of everything including adaptation that becomes fictitious and make-believe; anything can be said – or nearly anything. Successful coupling is a matter of authority that can impose whatever it chooses – or almost; in some cases, it is true, 'almost' prevails.

And it is in everyday life that the coupling of signifier and signified takes place; more or less successfully, and rather less than more. Living is done there and signifieds are allotted to signifiers in the best possible way, everybody being convinced that his way is the best – which might account for the fascination of signs: floating in swarms and clouds they are free for all, ever available and, taking the place of action, they appropriate the interest formerly invested in activity.

Among the many complex processes of substitution, displacement and replacement, the most peculiar is that by which linguistic relations – or the relations established by forms of speech and language – replace those based on activity (work and division of work, co-operation in and for a 'work' or an 'output', emotions, etc.). Active groups with their active relations communicating through reference to habits, objects and objectives are replaced by groups whose relations are based on formal communication, means thus becoming ends and form content. Social groups based on productive activity (businesses, corporations) are now specific, isolated phenomena, and if they do aim at a general status it is through ideologies (the rationality of business, for instance). Large 'unofficial' groups based on speech and linguistic relations have taken over the role of the discarded groups almost entirely; they are, for the most part, more biological than social, consisting of groups of women, adolescents, old people, who produce nothing but talk; these people talk for the pleasure of talking, for a feeling of togetherness, to be 'in', to communicate without object or objective because that is the group's sole life and justification; it is the reign of talk, verbosity and gossip that goes into writing at the slightest provocation. This linguistic proliferation has socio-economic parallels in the proliferation of offices and office staffs, in the 'serious' hair-splitting that passes for rational efficiency and in the tactlessness of bureaucracies to whom 'private lives' are always suspect – because they are suspected not of 'privation' but of evading regulations. Language gives a value to things and things, furthermore, only acquire a social existence when they are named, denoted and systematized. (This assertion cuts both ways, for a 'thing' naturally only exists socially when it is named, yet if this statement is turned into a law it can be extremely dangerous, for it involves the justification of absolute power, the power of the one who 'names', that was formerly the prerogative of God and his representatives, then that of the Prince and his court; and so from triviality and tautology there is but one step to total authoritarianism!)

Language endows a thing with value, but in the process it devalues itself. Simultaneously it makes everyday life, is everyday life, eludes it, disguises and conceals it, hiding it behind the ornaments of rhetoric and make-believe, so that, in the course of everyday life, language and linguistic relations become *denials* of everyday life. Speech is duplicated, on the one hand continuing to serve as a tool for the practical analysis of reality (perceptible and social), fulfilling its function, which is to denote and describe situations; but it wastes away in the process. There are few things more curious and significant than a 'live' interview (as 'uninhibited' and spontaneous as possible), tape-recorded and submitted to a semantic analysis.* A couple of adjectives recur with an amazing frequency ('rotten', 'super'); two or three adverbs and adverbial phrases suffice to indicate the whole range of compulsions ('had to', 'automatically', 'it is', 'it isn't', 'that's how it is'); the same words are used – very inadequately – to denote the effects of compulsion, unpleasantnesses and disappointments; some terms serve to describe a thing emphatically or cynically, but without distinguishing it from things in general: object, gadget or simply 'that'; 'one' is used to modestly designate the speaker, having the advantage of designating others as well and thus dissolving personalities; 'we' is supposed to have undertones of daring, it asserts and rashly asserts itself; the other is usually 'they', they did this or that, they came; 'they' are interference, authority, administration, bureaucracy and power in general (before which words are defenceless and cringing); adaptation is even less adequately qualified and has to make do with an odd connotation or two: 'Aren't we snug in our little nest?...', 'What about it?' Such is the inadequate expression of true inadequacy, the inadequacy of experience. But let this suburban householder expatiate on his make-believe existence, the extraordinary advantages of suburban householding, let him forget compulsions and worries, and he becomes inexhaustable, he passes from 'cool' to 'hot', launches into artless rhetoric: compared to the city and its cramped living conditions his house stands for Nature, sunshine, greenery, health and above all for liberty (deludedly, since the suburb is only an offshoot of the city and still part of it, the 'householder' is still a city-dweller and even if he sees himself as outside the city and thinks he is opposed to it, he is not outside urban society), whereas the city and city life are artificial, morbid and enslaving.

* Cf. Institut de sociologie urbaine: *Les Pavillonnaires*, Paris, 1966, vol. II (N. Haumont).

Thus, according to 'habitat', the conditions and standards of everyday life – its sub-systems – obtrude in the very heart of language (notwithstanding, or rather because of, its inadequacies); speech both conceals and reveals, it says what it doesn't say. Everyday life is always hiding behind folds and circumvolutions, for it cannot exist if it is not self-elusive. Evasion is precisely the function of make-believe, and it fulfils it; ensnared as they are in everyday life, people tend to contrast it with the non-quotidian, home life with work, or work with leisure, and thus everyday life is duplicated and one of its halves is in the land of make-believe. That which is most everyday discards its quotidianness in the imagination, thus for many people – among them our suburban householder – *privacy* is the non-quotidian (a make-believe privacy, embellished and sheltered from the outside world, from view, from the sun, from the eyes of neighbours and even those of the family, by partitions, curtains, draperies; containing many objects; in the peace and silence of some quiet corner where nothing ever happens; and with a balance of space and time at one's disposal). For the inhabitant of a large building in a new town things will be very different, for his time-table is fixed, formulated, functionalized, inscribed on the walls, in what is left of roads, in shopping centres, parking spaces, bus stops and stations. The suburban householder talks in monologues, the new-town dweller talks in dialogues, with the authorities and with the absent but ever-present state; he speaks the language of wisdom, an organized wisdom claiming ever more organization. The rational neurosis of the suburban householder is echoed by the neurotic rationality of the other for whom make-believe is the rationality of commitments that fix his time-table and consume his life; the quotidianness of 'privacy' snuggling in the heart of everyday life is identified with a brief period of recuperation between days, weeks, months of commitments, after exhaustion. For each one the meaning of life is life without meaning; self-realization is a life without a history, total quotidianness, but unseen and evaded as soon as possible.

The following points should be stressed: if we immobilize reality and fix the mind on static categories we are confronted with a chart of opposites where each term echoes the other in an unambiguous relationship, work against leisure (and vice versa), everyday life against holidays (and vice versa); but when we cease to think in categories we see that, in fact, experience makes of each of these contrary terms a *substitute* for the other, so that leisure is a substitute for work, and work for leisure, going away on holiday and interrupting everyday life is a substitute for everyday life and vice versa. The difference between these two points of view is the difference between static reflection and thought, between structuralist ideology and dialectic logic.

But we cannot overlook the case of the city dweller living in the heart of the city (where such a thing subsists), who, even when he is impecunious, is a privileged person nowadays; in a few years the heart of every city (Paris, London, New York) will be owned entirely (apart from the odd exception) by the magnates of power and finance; but be that as it may, the city dweller today has a different relation to everyday life than that suffered unwillingly by the suburban householder or the new-town dweller, for in his case adaptation counterbalances compulsion. As we have said, even when he is not wealthy the city dweller reaps the benefits of past glories and enjoys a considerable latitude of initiative, the make-believe existence of his environment is less fictitious and unsatisfactory than that of his suburban or new-town counterpart; it is enlivened by monuments, chance encounters and the various occupations and distractions forming part of his everyday experience; city make-believe favours the adaptation of time and space and the city dweller appropriates its 'centrality' that provides a quantity of signifiers as yet incompletely isolated from the signified. In certain streets of central Paris it is still possible to hear a language that has preserved the freshness of a popular idiom, its liveliness and exuberance – for a little while . . .

Is it an extension of former times that survives with the styles of a past grandeur in some of the socially favoured neighbourhoods at the heart of older cities? We call to mind for instance the Gare Saint-Lazare, the Boulevard Saint-Michel, Saint-Germain-des-Prés or the Champs-Élysées in Paris; the Galleria of the Piazza del Duomo in Milan and that part of New York that stretches from Times Square to Central Park. Is there here a passive resistance –

stemming from a yearning for bygone days – against the onslaught
of everyday life, its full accomplishment so drably illustrated by
the suburbs of morphologically exploded cities, estates, new towns
and new neighbourhoods? Could this be seen as a promise, a sign?

Indeed it could. Though regrets do not fulfil promises they do
not forbid them either. In these favoured spots, the city, embryo
of the future urban society, doggedly resists and may finally
triumph; the 'hot' style is preserved and has a chance of survival
while the city's traditional values still override the mercenary ones
(tourists, coaches, etc.); encounters, chance or otherwise, proliferate in this setting and they dramatize everyday life, giving it
resonance and extension; conversations become meaningful, one
knows what one is talking about and why (to a certain extent) one
is talking; violence, endemic but repressed, at last explodes; news
succeeds news, piles up and all at once something new is about to
happen; the sense of play finds an outlet in old games restored or
improvised new ones. Yet there is surely something paradoxical
about this yearning for ancient customs and their reinstatement
and renewal, and it is certainly due to snobbishness more than anything else that a shabby flat furnished with bits of old furniture, a
dilapidated farm house or a tumbledown labourer's cottage lacking all comfort are seen as 'real finds' by wealthy eccentrics who
buy them for vast sums that have no relation with their intrinsic
value.

The city might be seen as an effective resistance to everyday life
and as its virtual conqueror; we could say that it is neither a realm
of make-believe high above daily compulsions nor a system of
signs for contemplation and consumption, but 'something else',
successfully overcoming a discarded, decayed, functionalized,
structuralized and 'specialized' everyday life. Could the city stand
for a potential referential – not the morphological town mapped
out on the ground and embodied in symbols and signs, but city
life and society? The notion is not unreasonable, but it involves a
risk; for what do urbanism and the city stipulate, what are their
practical basis and theoretical foundations? As yet we do not –
and we are not supposed to – know. For the time being we had
better avoid proclaiming a new entity, a new Platonic Idea, an

essence and proceed with caution so long as the *tendency* – towards an urban society – has not been elucidated and theoretically elaborated.

A cry of loneliness rises from the depths and the caves where, at the heart of everyday life, the most limited and specialized quotidianness lies coiled, the intolerable loneliness of unceasing communication and information. Efficient communication is now a possible–impossibility, an obsession and a torment; possible every minute of the day yet impossible because one of its conditions is lacking; can people (groups and individuals) communicate without referentials? Don't they communicate through a referential? If no irrefutable referential is at hand for them, around them, won't they look elsewhere (but where?) for a fictive referential, any referential? Now that semiological fields (not only common sense but also music and song, gestures, ritual behaviour, facial expressions), once unanimously accepted, have been discarded as referentials, what will take their place, for they must be replaced? Not only for individuals (large or small groups) when they are in each other's presence but for society as a body. The loftiest intellect (do not imagine, dear reader, that we are speaking with ironic intent, for we are indeed referring to the most penetrating mind, capable of unremitting inquiry into social and intellectual matters in general) asserts that if linguistic referentials have disappeared it is because language is now its own referential. The loftiest intellect ignores, or pretends to ignore, a) that in this way it withdraws into itself, sets out to use and abuse its own language; b) that it paves the way for (or follows the road of) popular conscience, or everyday life.

Such a tendency is obvious in literature from as early as the mid nineteenth century (failure of the Revolution, consolidation of capitalism, spread of trade and industry and of monetary power, etc.) and can be divided into three periods:

a) *the alchemy of speech:* the poet's words and sentences, freed from impediments sufficing to transform everyday life, transgress and transfigure reality (from Baudelaire to Joyce);

b) *language as second reality:* poetry being a second nature superimposed on the perceptible, social nature ('hot' lyricism, realism and surrealism, also expressionism, futurism, cubism, etc.);

c) *form as reality:* pure literature, the prose of life in all its coldness and starkness as, for example, in the 'new novel', but also in neo-formalism in general, in self-termed structuralist literature, etc.

This tendency is equally apparent in philosophy in three distinct movements:

a) *reflections on the philosophical Logos:* language seen as expression of absolute Reason, supreme subject, connected to a content, and form of this content – objective or metaphysical (Hegel and his followers);

b) *reflections on philosophical language* or on the vocabulary of philosophy taken to be the essence of philosophy, the heirloom and legacy of the philosopher: vocabulary, semantics, philosophical terms take first place;

c) *language as philosophy* seen from two different angles: fundamental ontology (Heidegger) and logical positivism.

The tendency is also perceptible in the scientific world, which is separate from philosophy yet connected with it:

a) *elaboration of specialized scientific idioms* since the mid nineteenth century;

b) *reflections on these idioms* and quest for a general linguistic metascience (positivist scientism), a metalanguage of specialized science;

c) *linguistics set up as a model for science and scholarship in general,* epistemology raised to the status of an exemplary systematic (exact) study, a model of intelligibility, reality and experience (both theoretical and practical, the science of information and communication parading as the science of sciences, sociological reality 'personified').

This triple development is indeed remarkable; through it emerge *intellectual structures* that are also *social structures* (and *superstructures* of society); it is both ideological and institutional. This society is functionalistic, formalistic and structuralistic, it draws its images (ideologies) from concepts of function, form and structure isolated and interpreted and supplemented by a philosophy; the images it projects (provided by its ideologies and launched on the market of ideas), derived from its own operational concepts, end in a cul-de-sac. In fact a society cannot properly consist of nothing but forms, functions and structures any more than it can consist of the sum of individuals, as Marx discovered when he diagnosed individualism as the main ideology of the bourgeois society; to *understand* it the three concepts should be used simultaneously without preference or prejudice; a study of this society based on these three key concepts leads to a further analysis based on the twin concepts of the quotidian and the modern, and thus we can appreciate the practical and ideological impact of these last as we discover how our society advertises and visualizes itself in relation to what it really is – how it recreates the astonishingly tenuous and amazingly tough links that hold it together and on which it is based, the unchanging quotidian, ever-changing modernity. The solution to this contradiction is to be found, as we now see, in the sphere of linguistic relations where stability and change are no longer opposed. Our society holds together and operates through speech, whence the emergence of the triple aspects of speech, reflection (philosophy), science and rhetoric whether literary or otherwise.

However our present purpose does not involve unfolding the motives and justifications for this triple tendency, nor its causes and the similarities between the three aspects. A chapter on the history of ideologies and ideas in the modern world has its place elsewhere,* but here we shall restrict rather than extend our scope, concentrating on what the preceding analysis has revealed, which is mainly the theory of levels and dimensions in language.

Metalanguage

The theory of metalanguage is based on logical, philosophical and linguistic research (and the critique of this research). It is defined as: a message (group of signs) controlling the code of the same or another message. When a person confides to another part of his code, by defining a word or by recapitulating to elucidate a meaning,

---

* Cf. *Introduction à la modernité*, Paris; but also vol. III of *Critique de la vie quotidienne*, Paris, in progress.

he is using metalanguage. Thus metalinguistic operations are
the normal, current, essential operations of speech (R. Jakobson).
Metalanguage, words about words, speech at one remove, is
present in ordinary speech, so much so that speech is unthinkable
without this preliminary transmission of a code, or without metalanguage which is part of the experience of speech. To borrow a
metaphysical metaphor, language is enclosed in a casing of metalanguage. The function of linguistics is to decipher, decode and organize the above operation; linguistics is metalanguage assuming
an epistemological status by setting itself above language. Metalanguage both precedes and follows the use of language – that is
of speech; it encloses speech, of which it is a condition and a
reflection.

By a justifiable abstraction of words, content and social context
from language, linguists are able to *penetrate* the form of language
(its inherent principle). Sociological analysis, on the other hand,
restores the context and shows in a different light linguistic forms,
functions and structures, the levels and dimensions of language,
and the secondary systems or sub-systems (connotational) included in conventional or denotative systems. Linguists may well
call such an analysis 'trans-linguistic' – implying that it is 'trans-
scientific'; for instance, if I show how Marx considered trade and
trade values as a form (identified by specific abstraction), then as
a logic, a language, a double chain of things and meanings, therefore as a 'world', and if I then assert that Marx was right and that
the first part of *Das Kapital*, where this theory is formulated, is
quite remarkable and too often misunderstood, according to some
people I will be committing a non-scientific action, launching into
ideology and subjective philosophy. Is it not presumption on the
part of a specialized science to set itself up as a rule of conduct and
to challenge the scientificness of methods that do not conform to
such rules? However, if some linguists do not see eye to eye with
sociological methods, it is their loss.

By restoring social context, the dialectical movement is thus
restored. If I consider trade with its values and wares as a simple
form I abstract the logic, the extensions, the language and the
world that are part of it; such an apparently exact method in-

volves errors and a deceptive portrayal, for only a dialectical
theory that keeps track both of social labour and of the context in
which the form evolves can grasp the reality of the problem –
namely the tendencies and contradictions enveloped and developed
within the form. For instance, should I consider the world of trade
in isolation, seeing it as wealth and its expansion as growth, I
would be unaware of the limitations imposed on it by the existence
of other 'worlds' such as ancient cities and potential cities, the
world that precedes and the world that follows the all-powerful
reign of industry and trade. By proceeding thus in all good faith
(ignoring or discarding Marx's theories), I compose a metalanguage of trade; I believe that I am politico-economically
minded, I gloss over the more violent tragedies of modernity and
everyday life; but the consequences of such an attitude, of such
'scientific' silence, are indirectly related to strategies that obstruct
the integration of so-called underdeveloped regions and countries
(as well as of so-called socialist countries) with the 'free' world,
the world where trade unfurls freely! In these circumstances a
would-be *science* can teach us nothing about *reality* – *metalanguage* cannot be seen as either harmless or innocent!

By restoring the dialectical movement – after the linguist's justified abstraction and formalization – contradictions that the linguist
had overlooked will be revealed. We repeat: the linguist is entitled
to his methods, but not to proscribe the exposition of such contradictions. There is *contradiction between referential and metalinguistic functions,* the latter eroding the former and supplanting
them; the vaguer the referential the more distinct and significant
grows metalanguage. Thus language and speech serve as referentials where metalanguage thrives; metalanguage discards and dissolves referentials and works on speech at one remove (or even
two); conversely, the disappearance of each successive referential
heralds a new extension to metalanguage (or a new specific sector
of metalanguage), so that metalanguage becomes a substitute for
language by assuming the attributes of referential-endowed language; the disappearance of each referential liberates a signifier
and makes it available, whereupon metalanguage promptly appropriates it, employing it for jobs 'at one remove', which contributes

to the decline of referentials, while metalanguage reigns, detached and 'cool'.

The theory elaborated here and elsewhere maintains that examination – with a strong lens and under a powerful light – of language and speech in social life, culture and science discloses a strange ambiguity: it is metalanguage that is always in evidence. The concept of the *message* (formally exact in the abstract theory of communication) must be submitted to a more thorough analysis. There exist pseudo-messages just as there are pseudo-events, pseudo-news and pseudo-novelty; and pseudo-production and spurious creations too – for only rationalist fanaticism can uphold the theory that works (of philosophy, art, literature), like mathematics and capital, conform to the law of accumulation that is restrained only by negligible factors. Accumulations of messages are illusory messages; they decipher former messages, they are talk about talk, proceed by recurrence and are acceptible as exegesis, as historical 'reflections', but not in so far as they deny their reference and relegate it to the shadows, and in so far as they request a refutation of their own historicity. A more or less innocent example of this type of message is that fairly popular contrivance, the book made entirely of unacknowledged quotations.

This may serve as introduction to a radical analysis of modernity, an analysis, needless to say, that shatters favourable preconceptions, biased enthusiasms and the apologist's rosy portrayals. There is no happy medium between the self-satisfied self-congratulations that every reader finds in the papers every day of every week, and this radical analysis. Our critical attitude to the second half of the twentieth century is similar to that which Marx adopted in his theory of the predominant ideology of the mid nineteenth century, the individual and individualism. If linguistic preoccupations dominate the scene today it is because we have passed unawares from language to metalanguage. Here complacent conscience whispers: 'All the better, things are as they should be, our problems are both practical and eternal.' To which radical criticism replies: 'Your castle is built on air, you believe you can step, with the help of language, out of illusion into a truth that you imagine is all around and ready at any minute to emerge; but you are wrong! We are now reaping the fruits of all the failed revolutions of the last hundred years or so in Europe, of the frustrated creative possibilities inherent in industrial production, and of the setting up of idols that only consume and devour. These preoccupations of which you boast reflect no great cultural wealth but are symptoms, rather, of a canker gnawing at the very roots of civilization. . . .' Here we list a few of these symptoms:

a) *Works of art.* How many of these – apparently conforming, in the same way as memory and learning, to the law of accumulation – do not owe their 'message' to metalanguage? The greater part; and among those that do not a large proportion reflect, be it only on the surface, identical tendencies. We are not alluding here to minor works, copies or imitations of great masters, but to the output of these masters themselves – influential works, highly original, expressive and significant (of novelty and modernity).

We do not have far to look for an example. Picasso will do; and we are not afraid of addressing him in person, apostrophizing him with the insolence his eminence demands: 'Pablo Picasso! You are the greatest living artist, and, as such, you are famous and famed, acknowledged all the world over. That your fame causes you some discomfort is self-evident, but how do you interpret this fame? Do you sincerely believe that all those crowds bow down before your genius? Where is the fault, the feint (your own), the fallacy? Do you know how Marx lived, how he died, how to this day his thought lives on? If it is true that you yearned for Revolution as a thirsty man yearns for water why has your work been accepted, assimilated, integrated? Does it bear witness to the Revolution or rather to its failure? Who are you, Pablo Picasso? Where are you? Are they yours, all those ghosts that peer through your canvasses, Velazquez, the Spanish School, Negro Art, Greek Civilization, the Mediterranean, the Minotaur and much else besides? Is only the Ocean lacking? You are the museum of make-believe. . . . You are a world's conclusion, the sum of an operation. The whole past lies there reduced to its elements, dismantled, dismembered, by a superb and spurious trick. The highest point of your life was reached at its end when you understood that your subject was the Painter and his Model; when with melancholy pleasure, untroubled humour and self-inflicted cruelty you said at last what you had to say, and you exposed the language of painting as a complex of signs, a writing. You said all there was to say: how the painter in relation to what he paints *is* enthusiasm and disparagement, tenderness and cruelty, admiration and disenchantment, respect and mocking desecration in succession. The Model is not simply a woman but the world and art. Thank you for those twenty or so canvasses, for this crowning self-destruction . . .'

And to whom, indeed, might not such a speech be addressed? To all those who contrived and adopted the metalanguage of Revolution, of love? It is even simpler for the philosopher; the theories, problems and categories of those who are faithful to the philosophical tradition get so inextricably mixed up with philosophical history that no one can unravel the skein, and in the best of cases the philosopher only reveals what Plato, Spinoza or Fichte 'really' thought. The philosopher philosophizes in/on philosophy as the poet writes in/on poetry, the novelist on novels (and novelists), the playwright on plays, the scriptwriter on the cinema, novels, plays and philosophy. Everywhere talk about talk at one remove, the 'cool', metalanguage and its shadows seen as original – and that are occasionally original when they are conscious of being shadows, cold and inconsistent, destructive and self-destroying.

Our questioner grows (understandably) impatient – and indignant. 'You've done a nice running-down job, I will say that for you! Have you no respect for anything, does nothing find favour in your eyes?' That is not the question – and furthermore it is badly put. The only question is whether or not our argument is valid, whether it counts and *accounts* for anything, if it has a hold and if it restores *something* – to object and objectives, to subject and subjects, that is to say, to operative strategies. Moreover the accusation is unfounded, for our radical analysis has not swept everything away and there are works of art still standing in the sites it has cleared, works that are generally considered, or have been considered, minor and that deal (directly or indirectly) with everyday life, mostly circuitously without naming it, but depicting it in such a way that it is better not to name it or describe it openly. If you want me to name these works here they are: *Ubu, Voyage au bout de la nuit, Demain les chiens, Under the Volcano, Naïves Hirondelles, L'Extricable, Les Choses*. If the questioner wants to know who we are talking about, our reply is: 'People I like, and all the worse for you if you don't know them. Moreover nothing compels you to see this list as final. Complete it if you feel like it.' 'All you are doing is trying to save your face. We were talking about everyday life – then you went off on a long diatribe against modern literature and art – after which you want to come back to everyday life again and pretend you never left it. Do you want me to believe that *Ubu* is everyday life?' 'That is just what it is. And furthermore I suspect you of hypocrisy, for you must know as well as anybody that Ubu stands for the Father, the Head, the Boss, the Master, in fact for the father-figure of everyday life. Ubu links everyday life and modernity; how otherwise can we explain why this barely outlined, spontaneous joke still obsesses us all to the extent that this era might be called the era of Ubu? Jarry succeeded in naming the unnameable, in making a statue of mud and a memorial to vileness. Moreover his work is not immune from radical criticism, for it provokes laughter by exposing the gory muddle and it invests with fictitious interest those things which destroy interest; it performs a *metaphorical function* and is indebted to *metalanguage*. Allusions to everyday life that make it a subject of irony and humour can only help to make it bearable* by hiding it under draperies of words and metaphors.

b) The vast *cultural consumption*, purporting to consume works of art and styles but in reality only consuming symbols (symbols of works of art, symbols of 'culture'). The consumer consumes metalanguage, thus lessening the wear of experience values; the sightseer in Venice does not absorb Venice but words about Venice, the written words of guide-books and the spoken words of lectures, loudspeakers and records; he listens and looks, and the commodity he receives in exchange for his money, the consumer goods,

---

* Like the books of Christiane Rochefort, for instance.

the trade value, is a verbal commentary on the Piazza San Marco, the Palazzo dei Dogi, or Tintoretto; but the experience value, the thing itself (the work of art) eludes his avid consumption which is restricted only to talk.

This is not a misuse of the term 'metalanguage', for it is really talk at one remove, talk about talk. The city (Venice, Florence), or the museum, the work of art, this painter, that group of painters, that particular painting, exist in the sphere of thought; it is impossible to perceive them other than through the work of historians, so that didactic speech is necessarily interposed between works of art and their understanding; such speech clears a narrow opening to a steep stairway that leads to the perception of styles and works of art and it bears the name of 'advanced culture'; but mass culture and the tourist trade have to make do with the consumption of words about words, or metalanguage.

Moreover metalanguage is far from modest and unassuming; on the contrary, it has high ambitions and it aims at 'furthering participation', at 'introducing to . . .' The City, Beauty, Nature, or Naturalness are served out to the tourist, the spectator, the bulk consumer. This metonymic function of speech is anything but artless; it bandies essences, entities and forms, creating in the hearer an illusion of participation. Speech passes with ease from the part to the whole – from a few aesthetic terms and the formulae of aestheticism to Art, from a few stones to the City, from a fashion-picture to Fashion; and from the relative to the Absolute. Metalanguage and its use by/for the consumer corresponds to the neo-Platonic vision – one more substitute! Let us not indulge in jokes about the harassed crowds sprinting through the Uffizi and the Palazzo dei Dogi, or stagnating like huge puddles under the downpour of descriptive words (the guides' enlightening information), yet seeing nothing, quite incapable of seeing anything, of doing anything but consume the commodities offered to them at a high price.

c) Whether concerted strategy, or the global effect of a mixture of contingent activities, the result is the same; we are confronted with a dual process: industrialization and urbanization. Marx perceived the first aspect of the process and understood how it should be dealt with, how to give it a significance by rational planning; his solution was 'social man' as potential of work and production. The working classes were to have taken upon themselves this historic mission, but instead they have been partially dispossessed of this mission (more or less, depending on the country and the region) and reduced to an economic pressure group, their place taken by political and technical bodies. Thus production has been organized to a certain (unequal) extent, but deprived of its significance; nature has been technically mastered, but without enabling man to adapt to his own vital and social nature. However, the second aspect of the process, urbanization, eluded Marx for historical reasons; when *Das Kapital* was published a hundred years ago urbanization was in its infancy. The process has never been understood; scientific inquiries have purely and simply *reduced* it to the organization and to the compulsions of industrial production, when it is precisely not reducible to industrialization but gives it meaning and direction, and it is at this level that *adaptation* (theoretical and practical) takes first place. The productive potential expressed and realized in industrial production might have been diverted towards that most essential of productions, the City, urban society. In such a city, creation of creations, everyday life would become a creation of which each citizen and each community would be capable.

Industrialization can only find its fulfilment in urbanization – carried out according to the *idea* of the City and of urban society, as a creation and not as an ideology. Industry in itself is only a means, and when means are taken for ends rationality becomes absurdity.

We have thus been unable to give to language – that is, to thought and active conscience – that which our practical and theoretical inquiry expected and required; metalanguage – words about acts and about the words that accompany actions – has taken the place of language; in other words, we are surrounded by emptiness, but it is an emptiness filled with signs! Metalanguage replaces the missing City that is missing because it has mis-fired. Everyday life stagnates like a great swamp hidden by mists and swarms of buzzing insects. Metalanguage is a grand substitute for the historical

missions that have been left undone, for responsibilities unfulfilled, but it exudes a feeling of latent guilt, a vague sense of
frustration and *malaise*.

The absurd

Flaubert invented the absurd in that ambiguous and misunderstood work *Bouvard and Pécuchet*.* In the preface to the Pléïade
edition it is described as a caricature of scientism and of the self-
taught scholar and at the same time as the development of the
character of M. Homais; but this does not tally with the author's
opinion of his book that he saw as deeply significant.

In the very centre of the city by the Bastille ('because of the
excessive heat the Boulevard Bourdon was deserted'), in a vividly
sketched urban landscape ('the inky waters of the Saint-Michel
canal, limited by its two sluices, were stretched straight as a plumb-
line. There was a barge loaded with logs in the middle and two
rows of barrels on the banks') – a commercial setting laid waste
by the week-end – something is going to happen, a chance yet significant encounter. 'Two men appeared, one from the direction of
the Bastille, the other from that of the Jardin des Plantes. . . . They
sat down at exactly the same time on the same bench.' They are
two transcribers, two men whose work consists in writing; one of
them had been engaged as copy clerk by a Head of Department
impressed by his talent; the other had been inspired to make the
most of his beautiful handwriting. But each of them had undoubtedly contributed – independently and unwittingly (having
probably, in his long-forgotten schooldays, left a written exercise
on his desk) – to a series that has added to the fame and fortunes
of a well known publisher (Larousse) and which bears the title
'Progressive Selection of Fifty Types of Handwriting. For Practice
in the Deciphering of Manuscripts. Including 1) Precepts of Be-

* It also figures in an earlier work: 'But the daring of their costumes was
counterbalanced by the respectability of their faces; . . . This assemblage of
half-naked women made him think of the inside of a harem; indeed an even
coarser comparison came into his mind. Every type of beauty was, in fact,
present . . .' *Sentimental Education*, London, 1956, pp. 150–51.

haviour for Children and Improving Anecdotes; 2) Examples of Invoices, Industrial Notices; 3) Examples of Epistolary Styles.' This long-forgotten booklet opens: 'The spectacle of the universe, the brightness of the sun, the extraordinary variety of plants and animals, all these wonders are proof of God's existence.' – in a beautiful round copperplate hand! But let us return to our two heroes. One is a widower, the other a bachelor, one more or less rakish, the other chaste, but they have in common an uneventful and very 'everyday' life and they are both equally reserved. Simultaneously they observe: 'How pleasant it would be to live in the country!', communicating because they were starved of communication. 'They thought more, so they suffered more.' So our two friends go to Chavignolles, in the hope of forgetting everyday life, of transcending it. After each abortive attempt they are back in the quotidian: cooking, the home, the neighbours, women. Their time is spent consuming; they consume things they have not produced and that are not even produce, not bread or furniture (though ancient, rustic furniture might be included) or tasty dishes or wine (though a drop from time to time is not unpleasant) or even objects; they consume works of art, culture, the whole of culture, all the books. Thus we follow Bouvard and Pécuchet through a nightmare of self-imposed cultural consumption, the consumption of books, of all written matter; this nightmare is our daily bread too. They are at work, and their endurance (our own) is tremendous; they dive head first into signifiers, they swim, swallow mouthfalls of the inebriating tide that carries them and though they are breathless they stick to it. Unrelenting and methodical they go through everything: first agriculture (since they had longed for the countryside, nature, freedom), next chemistry, physiology, astronomy, physics, geology, archeology, history, literature, linguistics, aesthetics, philosophy and education. The circuit is now closed since students of education learn about nature, agriculture, chemistry, philosophy, etc.; clumsily closed it opens again. Wending their way, circling around, Bouvard and Pécuchet chance upon systems, innumerable systems: spiritualism, materialism, Hegelianism; all that is rational is real; the absolute is both subject and object; when God assumed a material form he demonstrated a consubstantial union with nature: his death bore witness to essential death, death was part of him; but there is also the logical system according to which errors stem mainly from one cause and are the consequence of an erroneous use of words. Then there are the contrived systems like those of Allery, Pâris or Fenaigle. (For Allery each number is represented by a symbol, 1 a tower, 2 a bird, 3 a camel, and so on; Fenaigle divides the universe into houses containing rooms each of which has four walls with nine panels and a symbol in every panel.) Bouvard and Pécuchet also happen to be the casual and detached eye-witnesses of historical events such as the 1848 Revolution, the Coup d'État . . .

But what have they gained in the end, at the close of their circuit of the world of culture? Words, words and wind. They have not even consumed very many works of art but mostly secondary works, commentaries, exegeses, treatises, manuals and guides: metalanguage! Thus they are able to get their bearings (more or less) and find their way – to a certain extent – in the labyrinth of specialization. As to the signified, what, after all, was its status for the encyclopedists whom our heroes would emulate? Superfluity and pleasure. . . . They said as much; indeed, they said very little else. Thus our heroes saw nothing, acquired nothing, understood nothing but words and wind, and our friend Flaubert was well aware of it; that is what is signified, what he signified! . . . Yet Bouvard and Pécuchet are no fools, no more so than Flaubert, who identified with them; far from being stupid they wanted to educate themselves, acquire experience, raise themselves above the norm; had they lived today in 1968, as liberal left-wing intellectuals, they would have added to their collection of achievements existentialism, Marxism, technology, the social sciences, and they would have methodically perused *L'Éxpress*, *Le Nouvel Observateur*, *La Quinzaine littéraire*, supplemented, needless to say, by *Le Jardin des Modes*, *Elle*, and *Marie-Claire*.

When the circuit is closed nothing is left but to start again at the beginning. As transcribers, they have entered the realm they never left, the realm of written matter. So the only hope is that of receiving another legacy that will enable them to start all over again.

Who are Bouvard and Pécuchet, apart from being a pair of

famous characters among those who are condemned to immortality? Our own reflection? By a strange twist of irony they were *written* before their creator took any interest in them: 'There were once two clerks . . .'; yet thanks to intellectual courage this tale of two clerks, this sad little story of two poor devils nourished on handwriting and metalanguage, became a work of art; a new kind of laughter was born, bitter and silent. So they were no fools, trapped by words, stumbling over props and backdrops; they managed to acquire some experience: 'Bouvard was amazed at the contrast between the things around him and that which was said, because it always seems that words should be in harmony with the setting and that high ceilings are made for lofty minds . . .'

Here then is the absurd. The Death of God is grandiose and tragic; but his 'demise'? One vaguely imagines (context, referential, or simply connotation?) the stricken family, the widow's tears, the orphans' sobs, the burial rites, the solicitor's arrival, the unsealing of the will and the family misunderstandings over the division of the estate. And that is the end of speculative or theological Good Friday, notwithstanding the priest ('the priest rose; his presence was required elsewhere'). Such are the words of Pécuchet (the crafty devil).

This then is how in his pseudo-novel Flaubert, that crafty devil of a pseudo-bourgeois, informs the world of what awaits it when revolutions misfire; he makes it an occasion for revealing how, in his opinion and according to what, as an eye-witness, he has observed, revolutions misfire: half of man (and of men), the worse half, wants to change something and asserts whenever it gets a chance that everything must be changed; the better half, the jolly good fellow, finds life all right as it is.

The absurd is laughter and comedy with a difference, it is not irony and it is not humour; here neither the situation nor the action are funny; indeed, there is no clearly defined situation or action; they are not required. The story does not have to be 'credible'; credibility has vanished with the referentials, and this contributes to a sense of ease and linguistic freedom. If there is a common place it is everyday life, from which we soar on the wings of language. The laughter derives from words and nothing but

words; this is linguistic comedy, the *vis comica* of word-play –
puns, spoonerism, alliteration and assonance employed methodically, not just for a questionable joke (according to classical
standards) or a witticism, but for hundreds of pages. Not everyone
can understand such a performance.

Who has not heard of the Gauls, has not learnt at school half
a dozen stock phrases about Gaul and the Gauls? They were
strong and stupid, they buttered their hair, were overrun by the
Romans. . . . History cannot be cancelled out even when it is
humiliating; all we can do is find an excuse, and a good one.
France is Gaul; and yet it isn't Gaul, since there were the Romans,
the Barbarians, the Franks, so many invasions, so many wars –
including the last – and the Germans, the English, the Americans;
and then France is France once again, Gaul and not Gaul. Things
are what they are, and at the same time they are not what they are,
they always hide something different, something more. History or
story-telling? There is a gap, hardly perceptible it seems, but seen
from close up it is quite a sizeable crack that will have to be filled –
filled with words, words about history; metalanguage. There are
quantities of signifiers free of things signified, true history understood and misunderstood, signifiers ready for consumption. The
situation was vacant, but it had, none the less, to be located in
order to give France, the France of the Gauls and the Gaullists,
its absurd epic. With what enthusiasm it was accepted, this long-
awaited epic, this story that seems to have been written by children
but is so popular with the grown-ups, the young middle ranks,
knowledgeable, educated, well acquainted with words and things!
Does this mean that there is only one world for children and for
grown-ups, for infant prodigies and infantile adults?

Fill the gap between signifier and signified (and vice versa) with
a slight intellectual gesture that exactly sums up the paradox of the
disconnection and the unexpectedness of clearing it, and you have
found the absurd. It implies a relatively high 'cultural' standard,
a well-stocked, agile mind; for the shuttling from past to present
and from present to past, from the familiar (the quotidian) to the
unfamiliar, when expertly maintained by linguistic ambiguities
presupposes a fairly wide range of knowledge; the point of the

verbal paradox, the allusion, must be grasped in a complex of end-less reverberations (without reference), while images support and facilitate the process, anachronisms divided into signifier–signified elements. the verbal signifier reflected in the supporting image, and, inversely, the final signified being reality. You have thus an epic within everybody's reach, to hand, at home, on the hearth in the very midst of the family and everyday life.

Is this counterfeit history, this analogical sham made of linguistic tricks, a myth? Or is it an ideology? Perhaps we are rather overstating the case, for it is only Asterix the Gaul, and why should he not be named? France has found both a myth and an ideology, and in the process of pretending tragedy has vanished, there are no longer any victims; as to the enemy, we knock him out, he promptly recovers consciousness and we all laugh heartily. No passion, no eroticism, few women; absurdity is spontaneously generated, *cool* here (although it gesticulates, it is still *cool*), *hot* there; here fun and games without violence, else-where every possible violence (more or less simulated: eroticism, mass murders, Lucky Luke, Bond, Satanik).

Compare Bouvard and Pécuchet to this 'freely' flowing absurd: word-play is not thrust at you in every line, there are not even two puns to a page; how very tedious this funny book can be . . .

Flaubert created this genre, this category (disguising the death of 'classical' and 'romantic' categories of art and aesthetics as well as the death of linguistic aestheticism); he had not yet freed himself from referentials but he contributed to their destruction. The absurd was not yet in its prime, it had not yet achieved the comical dignity of pure writing, of leisure, of metalanguage and the mass-consumption of language.

There are other aspects to this linguistic consumption, such as televised games and competitions, crossword puzzles, but we are not really concerned with these. What is more to the point would be an analysis of *contrived games* (crossword puzzles, yes, but also the pools) and the artificial conjunction of eroticism and con-trivance, 'make-believe' commodities sold at a high price: betting machines that have acquired an immense popularity in Las Vegas and elsewhere, in which numbers are coupled with erotic signifiers to signify momentary almost oneirological satisfactions of desire. Our object is, in fact, to expose the non-quotidian as the quotidian in disguise, returning to the quotidian to hide it from itself; this operation is carried out to perfection by means of language consumption (or metalanguage consumption), more successfully even than by means of display consumption, which in any case it assists.

Thus before/for us daily consumption assumes its dual aspect and its basic ambiguity. Taken as a whole, quotidian and non-quotidian, it is material (sensorial, something to be taken, used, consumed, experienced) and theoretical (or ideological – images, symbols, signifiers, language and metalanguage being consumed); it is complete (tending towards a system of consumption based on the rationalized organization of everyday life) and incomplete (the system is for ever unfinished, disproved, threatened, unclosed and opening on to nothingness); it is satisfaction (of needs, this one or that one, the need for this or for that, therefore sooner or later it is saturation) and frustration (only air was consumed, so the desire re-emerges); it is constructive (choice of objects, ordering, filing, contrived freedom) and destructive (it vanishes in the centre of things, slides down the slopes of piled-up objects accumulated without love and for no purpose). The so-called society of consumption is both a society of affluence and a society of want, of squandering and of asceticism (of intellectuality, exactitude, coldness). The ambiguities proliferate, each term reflecting its opposite (its precise opposite, its contradiction, its mirror-image); signifying it and being signified by it, they stand surety for and substitute each other while each one reflects all the others. It is a pseudo-system, a system of substitutes, the system of non-systems, cohesion of incoherence. The breaking point may be approached but never quite attained: that is the limit.

4   Terrorism and Everyday Life

The concept of terrorism

Give unto Caesar that which is Caesar's and to literature what belongs to it; terrorism was first perceived by writers and critics – possibly because their ears and eyes are sharper than most, owing to their professional alertness and a cheerful spitefulness that passes for wit. Terrorism was in the air – like most things that are let loose and spread, signifiers, metalanguage, abstract forms in search of materialization and pure thought hungering for power – and these gentlemen had been aware for some time of certain pressures constricting their art (reputed to be the freest of activities, enjoying freedom of opinion, of conscience, of ideology), the most disturbing of which were intrinsic to the art itself. But for these easy-going intellectuals action only meant exertion and the fact of standing by one's opinions was a joke that should not be carried too far; so they did not inquire further – more especially since they were willingly relieved of the task by psychoanalysts and sociologists.*

The concept of a *terrorist society* is now more or less established; various stages in the development of this phenomenon can be distinguished:

a) Any society involving, on the one hand, poverty and want

---

* We are referring to J. Paulhan, M. Blanchot, R. Barthes, H. Marcuse, D. Riesman, etc.

and on the other a privileged class (possessing and administrating, exploiting, organizing and obtaining for its own ends as much social overtime as possible, either for ostentatious consumption or for accumulation, or indeed for both purposes at once) is maintained by the dual method of (ideological) *persuasion* and *compulsion* (punishment, laws and codes, courts, violence kept in store to prevent violence, overt violence, armed forces, police, etc.). A class society (and we know as yet no other) is a repressive society. We all know what part the Roman Catholic Church played in the repressive societies of Western Europe; as a state and rival to the political state the church provided 'spiritual' careers for its followers; thus it was soon in possession of a bureaucracy, a hierarchy, a (philosophical) ontology and a practical knowledge; it set the sacred against the profane, the spiritual against the temporal, directing its greatest efforts towards the 'spiritual' and spiritual power; subversive ideas and individuals were judged, condemned and handed over to the secular authorities to be dealt with. Oh most admirable contrivance, alas now sadly in need of repair!

A study of the foundations of a repressive society must be far reaching; only a superficial anarchist or Marxist interpretation can restrict the significance of this concept to the police force and to class legislation, for as things now stand the repressive nature of any society is more deeply rooted than that. Since the beginning of time groups, castes, classes and societies have always upheld as the truth and as 'principles' those things on which their survival depended – ideologically interpreted; but might it not be possible to establish a coherent society, whose foundations are not built on a rock or 'pedestal' and consolidated by basic repressions? There are those who too hastily admit this hypothesis; others who too readily refute it. The taboo of incest has been seen as the basis of society and culture, the cornerstone of the structure, but it would be more scientific and more exact to assert that every society has been faced with conflicting needs; the strength and power of each, its defensive and offensive capacity depended on the number of its members, but, in order to survive, the number had also to be limited by the natural yield of a given environment, the society's technological development and its productive capacity. Societies have solved the problem as best they could, some declining, others surviving or prospering; but survival methods have necessarily involved the control by one means or another of births within the society. Thus the basis of repression is *a controlled balance of sexuality and fecundation;* at one period repression would stress the limitation of births by enforcing celibacy on some members of the community, by the sacrificial offering of infants or by encouraging prostitution, homosexuality and onanism; at another, on the contrary, the reproduction of the population would be emphasized by dissociating sexuality from pleasure so that it became an act of fecundation, a social duty; there are evidently a number of variations and shadings between these two extremes, and other factors intervene; but *the field of repression covers biological and physiological experience, nature, childhood, education, pedagogy and birth,* it prescribes abstinence and asceticism and succeeds in imposing an ideology of hardship seen as virtuous and fulfilling. Thus it might be said that for certain periods, at least, repression spreads to the privileged classes, when their 'values' and strategies require that discipline and compulsion be practised in their own ranks.

This incessant conflict between repression and evasion, compulsion and adaptation *is the history of everyday life,* which we have as yet barely outlined (observing the paradox that the periods of most successful adaptation and greatest creativity were precisely those where ancient, brutally compulsive societies based on violence and oppression reigned).

Thus it is inexact to restrict an analysis of repression to economic conditions (one of the mistakes of economism) or to institutions and ideologies; both attitudes omit the important factor of everyday life, of the pressures and repressions at all levels, at all times and in every sphere of experience including sexual and emotional experience, private and family life, childhood, adolescence and maturity – in short, that which would seem to elude social repression because it is spontaneous and 'natural'.

b) *An over-repressive society* modifies the conditions of repression, its methods, means and foundations; with apparent innocence and by means of skilful compulsion it directs *adaptation* into the channels of 'purely' private experience – the family, the home – and portrays freedom as something spiritual and ideal that fits in perfectly with material oppression; repressive duties are, moreover, entrusted to intimate groups, to the family or the father, or better still, to the individual conscience. A good example of such an over-repressive society is that which was dominated by *Protestant* ideology; far more astute and more rational than Roman Catholicism in its theological and philosophical make-up, and dogmatically less repressive, Protestantism performed the repressive function of religion with greater subtlety; God and reason were the portion of each individual, everyone was his own mentor, responsible for the repression of his desires, the control of his instincts; the result was asceticism without an ascetic dogma, without anyone enforcing asceticism; the whipping boy and scapegoat being sexuality; but, repressed, condemned and *unadapted*, desire became the ferment of rebellion and revolt. We cannot overlook the historical link between Protestantism and capitalism; Protestantism provided the images and the language that capitalism, unobtrusively, adopted; when Roman Catholicism proved insufficient for the task Protestantism slipped into its shoes, intention replaced ritual and faith supplanted works; this religion furthered the generalization of industry and trade that appropriated its values by appearing to respect them (conscience, faith, personal contact with God). Thus we may define an over-repressive society as one that, in order to avoid overt conflicts, adopts a language and an attitude dissociated from conflicts, one that deadens or even annuls opposition; its outcome and materialization would be a certain type of (liberal) democracy where compulsions are neither perceived nor experienced as such; either they are recognized and justified, or they are explained away as the necessary conditions of (inner) freedom. Such a society holds violence in reserve and only makes use of it in emergencies; it relies more on the self-repression inherent in organized everyday life; repression becomes redundant in proportion to the performance of its duties by (individual or collective) *self-repression*. A society can proclaim that the Kingdom of Freedom is at hand when compulsion passes for spontaneity and *adaptation* no longer exists either in word or concept.

c) A *terrorist society* is the logical and structural outcome of an *over-repressive* society; compulsion and the illusion of freedom converge; unacknowledged compulsions besiege the lives of communities (and of their individual members) and organize them according to a general strategy; the distinction between *other-directed* and *inner-directed* conscience is abolished since what now plays the part of *inner* is the *other* disguised, integrated and justified; opposition is silenced either through being condemned as a perversion and thus invalidated, or by integration. According to our theory a society where violence and bloodshed reign is not a 'terrorist' society, for whether red or white, political terror is short-lived; it is a means used by a specific faction to establish and maintain dictatorship; political terror is localized, it cannot be imputed to the social 'body', and such a society is terrorized rather than terrorist. In a terrorist society terror is diffuse, violence is always latent, pressure is exerted from all sides on its members, who can only avoid it and shift its weight by a super-human effort; each member is a terrorist because he wants to be in power (if only briefly); thus there is no need for a dictator; each member betrays and chastises himself; terror cannot be located, for it comes from everywhere and from every specific thing; the 'system' (in so far as it can be called a 'system') has a hold on every member separately and submits every member to the whole, that is, to a strategy, a hidden end, objectives unknown to all but those in power, and that no one questions. But this does not mean that such a society can avoid change, for it may find itself in a state of crisis while doing all it can to avoid it; but when such upheavals occur they are officially interpreted and directed (or misdirected); it is conservative as a body, owing to a certain resilience (or lack of it) in its public services, institutions and structures; its 'values' need no explaining, they are accepted, they are compelling and any desire to understand or question them savours of sacrilege. In appearance at least a terrorist society is coherent and powerful, and there would be no answer to such terrorism if it did not exploit an ideology of Reason and of Liberty and thus involve irrationality with Reason, compulsion with Liberty, violence with so-called persuasive measures, in a word contradiction with an illusory coherence.

The argument that emerges from the preceding pages is that a terrorist society, that is, a society of maximum repression, cannot maintain itself for long; it aims at stability, consolidation, at preserving its conditions and at its own survival, but when it reaches its ends it explodes. It is based on the organization of everyday life (which is also its objective) of which terror is the outcome. Infringements from the everyday life it ordains are condemned as madness and perversion, for although everyday life is the rule it is free neither to set itself up as a principle, to organize itself nor even to appear as everyday life.

However, to uphold this theory we must do more than declare that happiness is not the accumulation of satisfactions and that a thousand pleasures do not make a single joy*; and to pronounce

---

* This seems the place to clear up a few misunderstandings and settle a couple of controversies. When ideas are 'in the air' they are also susceptible to practical analysis. The concept of a 'repressive society' derives from Malinovski, and we all know that Malinovski found no trace of censorship, repression or Oedipus-complex among the Trobriands, where, according to him, sexual experience and fecundity were socially controlled by other methods. Censorship and repression have, for him, definite and therefore restricted causes; if a repressive society exists it is because there is social repression; and therefore he takes Freud to task for having ratified and generalized certain localized circumstances (those of family life in a given Western society at the beginning of the twentieth century) and thus founded a scientific proposition and a general rule for social experience on a specific form of repression; an unfair criticism, on the whole, in view of Freud's faith in the liberating powers of science, namely psychoanalysis. Since Freud's day, however, an important psychoanalytical movement – perhaps the most important of those that lay claim to his theories – appears to have discarded this liberating function of the science and to see it only as the recognition and the sanctioning of compulsions; thus the incest taboo (or Oedipus-complex) is seen as a basic factor, both theoretical and practical, of social experience. Herbert Marcuse calls this tendency 'revisionist', and this Marxist-inspired psychoanalyst accuses psychoanalysis in general of being conducive to terrorism by salvaging perversions after defining them as neuroses and providing thus an ideological basis for outdated social pressures exerted in the name of norms and normality on the public 'consciousness' and 'unconscious'. Thus he defines repression and over-repression in psychoanalytical terms (the id, the ego, the super-ego, Eros and Thanatos, the pleasure principle and the reality principle) and in this way furthers the elaboration of the concept of repressive and over-repressive

this or that philosophy inadequate and guilty of confusing plenitude and saturation will not help either. Here our imaginary objector intervenes once again: 'Let us not make mountains out of molehills! People are happy, aren't they? What more can they want? Their elementary needs are catered for, and what does it matter if in the process their freedom is slightly restricted and a few unrealistic ambitions or subjective illusions must be given up? By improving living conditions all the old anxieties that still survive, notwithstanding satisfaction and even satiety, will finally be overcome. Your preoccupations are not the same as ours; we consider man's hunger and thirst, his basic needs, we want to give people food and drink, clothes and a place to lay their heads; our preoccupations are with want, suffering and death. Your aims are

---

societies; but he just falls short of the concept of terrorism because his critical analysis, remaining psychological, does not include the social (or 'sociological') and consequently the dual concept of *quotidian* and *modernity*. Marcuse and a number of others have also missed the concept of '*mondialité*' – and the correlative concept of actual or possible planetary *distinctions*.

Psychoanalysis in France has lately been split into rival factions or schools; for some the conflicting relationship between children and parents illustrated in the Oedipus-complex is still the central concept of psychoanalysis; for others it is the relation of the unconscious to language that takes first place. We would refute both theories and consider as basic the child's relation to society, or to everyday life; it is in social experience that the young 'human being' benefits from his weakness and compensates for his vulnerability; he has, from the outset, conflicting desires and aspirations (security, adventure, protection, independence) and, on the one hand, he *adapts* to the circumstances and his own social environment – more or less, depending on the circumstances and on his own disposition – while, on the other, he undergoes *compulsions*; thus in the family circle he has access to a daily life that either resolves or intensifies the conflict between bondage and experience (compulsion and adaptation); child and adolescent continue to develop until they finally get bogged down by maturity, sinking into the morass of adulthood. Language and speech, as well as parental pressures and individual emotional relationships, play an important though unequal part in this dialectic movement.

Second theory or hypothesis: the social community's relation to the soil is one of the elements in the make-up of repression. Such a relation presents a dual aspect; on the one hand the (limited) *natural resources* and on the other the *consecration* by the society of the soil to which it is attached, involving vast *sacrifices* (*sacrificial* cults). *Urban life* puts an end to such consecrations.

so lofty that they are out of reach; you want to enable people to live passionate, intense lives full of happiness and delight. We reject the "human" to assist man; you aspire to a world of super-humanity and poetry with the human as starting point, but without the concept of the Superman. Such an attitude is not only unreasonable, it is wicked! We consider it a criminal undertaking to kindle desire and to provoke unrest, to reinstate the values of the past, of the age of dearth – work, unity, "man". Our society may not have reached its final balance, but wouldn't it be better to assist it rather than to expose its shortcomings and aggravate discontent? It jogs along as best it can without knowing where it is going; maybe, but this form of progress has, none the less, by a stroke of luck, given quite substantial results; it has taught us to recognize the limits of the human condition. Let us accept them. Let us learn from philosophy that empirical man and real society are finite, not the philosopher's mistrust of reality, not philosophical discouragement. Oh yes, we know that we can rely on you, sociologists and other representatives of the social sciences, to draw conclusions from history that make history redundant! We abhor the complainers! They are nothing but deserters. They want progress, perhaps, but like those soldiers who cannot turn back because they know that in the rear there are other, faithful soldiers who will shoot them, so they advance blindly, unwillingly. You are deserters to unreality, and all we want is to put you out of action . . .'

This *terrorist* address has been attributed to our objector because it corresponds so exactly to arguments we have heard and read time and time again – though this is an abridged version . . .

As we said earlier, finding fault is not enough. We must establish the conditions from which terrorism arises, discover how and why a terrorist society explodes and especially we must find the *opening*, the way of escape, all of which must be done in the clearest possible terms.

There exist among our society's conflicting attitudes (analysed or analysable) some that appear to herald a solution; indeed, certain contradictions in the existing circumstances seem distinctly favourable to such hopes. On one hand, we see 'history', which continues willy-nilly notwithstanding its denial and rejection by some ideologists, drawing all highly industrialized societies towards an urban society where millions of men and women must live and congregate; such is the 'socialization of society' so dear to more or less Marxist-inspired reformers; the barriers burst and communications of all kinds, material, social, intellectual, become multiple and complex as a feature, if not the main feature, of 'mondialization'. On the other hand, the most unexpected phenomena of individualization take place in this massification, this planetary perspective where the individual seems to disappear, and they take place in everyday life. Nobody nowadays would deny a boy or girl of twenty or twenty-five the right to lead an independent life, leave the family, have – and if possible choose – a career, take lodgings and dispose of himself or herself freely; thus in this massification there exists a certain degree of individuation involving problems of rights, freedom of work, of leisure, of careers, of education, of housing; such extensions of *habeas corpus* are not achieved without difficulty, and they tend to take the form of claims, and to be formulated in ethical and legal terms; they are appropriated by the state for strategic purposes, but simultaneously recognized and ratified to a certain extent by it – as for instance in the case of the *housing problem* (an early and very incomplete manifestation, the first stirrings, one might say, of a freedom that will soon have to be reformulated as the *freedom of the City*).

Such aspirations that become demanding do not arrest the development of terrorism; housing rights – which could turn building into a public service – are far from being recognized as rights; the state, by intervening in this problem, has modified the practice but not the theory; it has produced new towns, whose main characteristics are immediately obvious: they are public dormitories for the recuperation – in more senses than one – of labourers and workers ejected from the city centre; and at the same time (the present) the shortage of lodgings is part of terrorism as it hangs, threatening, over the young (and not only the young); the housing problem still exacts its sacrifice of the best years of their lives from a social group whose members are mainly recruited among the young proletarians or 'lower' middle classes; these people must first 'settle' to earn the right to live, after which, if they are not completely exhausted, they can begin to think about living – only think about it, mind you, coming to 'Life' as they do through a long disheartening struggle; and they have survived. Through a thicket of pitfalls and hurdles these new freedoms must find their way, but in so far as they are demands and aspirations they are part of *civilization;* thus a certain number of cultural phenomena overcome obstacles and problems to emerge into our society. It would seem that a new contradiction has now come to light – and by no means a negligible one – between *culture* and *society* (our society). Are such cultural phenomena conducive to a degree of optimism and confidence in this society's future? A more careful scrutiny will show them to be more potentialities than facts, aspirations faintly tinted with assertiveness, and only an apologist or a politician could see them as accomplished facts; 'values' rather than facts, not even acknowledged as rights (except ethically, which is better than not at all, but does not go very far), there is no proof that they will not vanish, for if a crisis occurs or the consequences of 'massification' simply become overwhelming these faintly outlined rights will be swept away. Some 'values' which seemed to have settled into facts have already disappeared, at least for the present; but in social time is there anything that is not reversible, and in historical time is anything granted? Where is the transition, the split, the point of no return situated?

Thus it is no use relying on these cultural phenomena, for if they have a direction they do not show us how to reach the opening. Our arguments would be incomplete and carry very little weight if we did not show how these new values and rights are born and how they develop until social recognition becomes inevitable.

Writing and terrorism

The significance of the *written word* emerges from a critical analysis of *compulsion,* that characteristic feature of terrorist societies, where it is excessive and outweighs adaptation; compulsive and non-violent writing – or written matter – builds up terror. Ethnologists and historians (both ancient and modern) associate the significance of the written word either with the emergence of sedentary societies; or with the division of social labour into functions of unequal value, with the function of the scribe among the more valuable ones; or with the development of genealogical preoccupations that require written records. The discrepancies between these theories may be more apparent than real, for a sedentary society involves the consecration of the land; the exclusive possession of a territory by one group and the religious outcome of this possession are vindicated by mythical ancestors, the tribal heroes, demi-gods and gods. Apart from genealogical tables constituting memorials and a method by which a society recorded places and periods, a number of landmarks can be distinguished in primitive sign-writing; before the age of agriculture – or contemporaneously with it – territories were marked out, tracks were blazed and frontiers defined by hunters, pickers and nomadic herdsmen; signs and directions go hand-in-hand: a bush or a tree, a rock or a hillock may be used as signs under the stars that are themselves significant. Later there are signs that constitute a form of writing on the ground – a broken twig, a pile of stones, the tracing of a trail and a way of situating landscape or site (of the village or the town) in relation to the stars. Moreover such theories present only a minor interest, the main point being to note the imperative character of writing and inscription, its 'toughness'; writing makes law, is, in fact, law; it is compulsive because it imposes an attitude, it fixes (text and context), it is relentlessly recurrent (the past revived, memory), it is a witness (transmitting and teaching) and it establishes history for all eternity by what is everlasting.

We need hardly mention that writing is also the basis and the starting point of innumerable achievements; through rules it creates intelligibility; through recurrence it stimulates reflection and reasoning; because it is permanent and definitive it furthers accumulation (of knowledge, techniques) and social memory; as a condition of art and learning it promotes social organization and culture. With social labour and the division of labour – or based on these – it became an essential superstructure even before ideologies existed. To a certain extent the city began as writing on the ground; writing prescribed and signified the city's power, its administrative capacity, its political and military sway; writing imposed the law of the city on village and countryside. Later when the need was felt for a rehabilitation of speech, when there arose a demand for warmth and liveliness in the written text, writing was still an essential factor in theatrical and poetic history.

Besides constituting the basis of culture and, to a certain point, of society itself, writing was also an intellectual and social tool, cold and static, though to a greater or lesser degree according to the period; at times it reduced social communities to passivity, at others it served as a basis on which actively to elaborate a social structure, a city, a kingdom, an empire. But though civilizations may be upheld by and for the written word it simultaneously creates inertia through its very lastingness; it tends to outlive itself and that which is a condition of history tends at the same time to freeze it.

When Moses descended from Mount Sinai and set up before the Children of Israel the Tables of the Law written by the finger of God, he created the eternal Father; centuries were founded on his gesture and on its verbal commentary, the holy narrative that justified it. He was the founder and his mystification became the truth. These tables of principles owed their longevity to the holiness of their inscription, and the faithful would never doubt that they would last until the end of time. Moses was certainly indebted to a superior civilization for his understanding of the virtues attendant to the written word; before the artless Bedouin whom he was leading to their great historical fate he performed an action that was both magical and pre-eminently functional. Hard and cold, stone was the perfect symbol of the Writing's timelessness, of its permanence and (apparent) definitiveness, and thus of its trans-historicity. The Writing is anti-word; once God had written prior to time and for all time, he was silent, and his representatives would be reduced to interpreting and commenting on the Tables of the Law, while others would question their validity, thus giving rise to the conflict between speech and writing, between the Spirit and the Letter.

There is no society without writing if this word is taken in its widest sense – no society without signs, landmarks, tracks, directions; yet one can say that a giant stride was taken, and therefore a complete split and departure from the past occurred, when the written word was invented, when tables of laws, graphisms and inscriptions fixed actions and events, battles, victories and sovereign decisions for ever more in the store of human memory. History and sociology will settle dates: the city, written on mapped space and graduated time, transitions from laws of custom to stipulated laws (that is, from habit to conventional codes), the popularization of writing by printing, the *cumulative function* that written matter assumes in the modern world, emphasized by the reproduction of pictures (the infinite library, the absolute book, and finally writing appropriating all that is said, known, felt).

A history of writing (by and for society) would show that the written word is a necessary condition for all *institutions*, that there is no institution without writing. The written word as primal institutionalization enters social experience, fixing creation and activity by organizing them. It is the original and constant mechanism of substitution; the written word refers to 'something' else – custom, experience, event – and then becomes reference in its own right; written matter becomes a substitute for the referential in writing. Here the critical mind perceives the contradiction and displacement analysed above; indeed, it takes them at their emergence: *written matter tends to act as metalanguage, to discard context and referential;* prior to written matter there are actions connected to words. As metalanguage writing produces commentaries, exegeses, speech at one or two removes on one subject or another kept and preserved by inscription. Thus metalanguage prevails over speech; that is why scholasticism, byzantinism, talmudism and rhetoric play such an important part in societies based on the Scriptures. The second message grafted on to the first that is or purports to be the inscription of the original Word could be *critical*, and thus at every minute a dangerous and disturbing choice is made possible, a choice that is inherent to reflection and therefore to the history of thought; derived, the second message might deviate. Could those who were in possession of the written word and had acquired their authority from it, refrain from taking the necessary measures to prevent such deviations? A society that is founded on writing and written matter tends towards terrorism, for the ideology that interprets written traditions supplements persuasion with intimidation. However, the written word can never completely supplant real tradition, the word passing unmediated from mouth to ear; so that the controversy will never end between the Letter and the Spirit, with all it involves in the way of misinterpretations, heresies and distortions. A society based on Scriptures (that is to say, a society whose conditions of survival are justified and upheld by manifestations connected with the written word) is based on prescription, it ordains the details of practical experience, ritualizes costumes, eating habits and sexuality (by commandments and interdictions); it also tends to enforce its stipulations by threats and sanctions, for it is not content with proclaiming general interdictions and leaving the rest to its members' initiative. The enforcement of survival-conditions normally grows stricter as time goes by, but there is no question yet of organizing everyday life (though the tendency may be perceptible), because the critical Word, interpretation, and the formulation of further problems cannot be held in check by scripture or prescription (including what is expressed by objects: the structure of houses and towns, monuments, the meanderings of a road from the gates of a town to its centre, etc. which occupy not only space but also time); furthermore the written word preserves the nature of what is accomplished and must be justified before the assembled population; religions based on writing uphold political power, consecrate it and supply it with ideologies; but such religions can free neither power nor themselves from collective control, which remains, even for theologians of power, the source of supremacy (with the attached territory). It is this collective control that prevents priests, warriors and rulers from indulging their whims; even the most tyrannical and most cruel among them have to justify their actions by public works, monuments or festivals, and it is only when the threat vanishes with the community, when the Festival is a thing of the past and monuments and the city (as form) are decaying, when the meaning of such things is lost, that everyday life begins. Its *written* support is bureaucracy and bureaucratic methods of organization.

The recurrent nature of writing must not be overlooked. With written matter there is always the possibility of going back; your eyes, favoured by the nature of what they perceive, hold this page in a simultaneous vision; you leaf through a book and you return to the first page if you want to, and you can, after reading it once, read it again a second or even a third time. There is a change in the shape of time that becomes the conventional time of what you are reading so that you are no longer carried on its tide but in control, even if this time tends to shrivel up and grow cold under your eyes – or rather in your eyes. Here little-known correspondences obtrude between *intellect* and *society* (both a unity and a distinction between these terms). The operation of memorizing and that of message-receiving are projected on the page; a forward progression does not exclude an inverse progression starting from the present moment, a recurrent re-reading. A book creates the illusion of suspending the process of ageing, of subjecting time to knowledge so that it becomes completely linear and cumulative, and as a result temporality appears to be reduced to simultaneity, growth and decay to instantaneousness. This is and is not an illusion; if we make it the grounds for denying history, the past and the future, we are deluding ourselves, confusing the world with the book, or worse, with the library; yet for the reader, in front of whose eyes the signs detach themselves from the surrounding blank in a manner both predictable and predetermined, a pleasurable sensation of plenitude ensues; extrapolation creates illusion and philosophical error by seeing writing and written matter as models of society and the world and by 'ideologically' transforming the reader's circumstances and his delight into absolutes. The absolute book is relentlessly perused; 'it is written', its supreme author and reader is the Lord who created destiny, and there is thus nothing that is not predetermined. If God the Creator made man in his image, therefore free and active, God the Eternal Father chastises him; as Providence he controls every gesture, he has foreseen each lowliest worm. God stands for supreme recurrence: he sees all time at one glance from beginning to end and from end to beginning; in the name of memory history has been abolished; in the name of clarity reason – that fumbling quester for meaning – has been discarded.

Henceforth the gigantic outline of a memory- and information-machine stands on our horizon as the ultimate stage, both scientific and practical, of writing and recurrence. It inscribes and prescribes, and there is no reason why it should not be on the best of terms with the technologians' God, though it claims to replace him on the grounds that it 'incarnates' him in a complex network of circuits and valves. Is it mere coincidence that the mechanically minded, those who live in symbiosis with the machine, are also men of precision where writing is concerned and the authors of the book of absolute knowledge (called epistemology) – men who are, in short, Cybernanthropoi?

Written matter has a further peculiarity: mental operations, coding and decoding are an intrinsic part of it, but they are not included in the message. Such are the rules of the game and that is how forms operate; their clarity does not exclude risks and obscurities that are inherent in their very exactness and limpidity. Moreover – and this is more serious – the encoders and the real network through which the message passes are also concealed in such a way that their existence is ignored. The written word is before us – apparently given in its totality by 'being before us' as the philosophers say – and its innocent appearance exploits our innocence. Whence the power of printed and written matter over the innocent – and even over some that are not so innocent: it is accepted unanimously and is the meeting point of magic and reason; how could writing mislead? 'It is in the paper!' say the artless. 'I have before me a proof, a document,' say those who think they are not so artless. Metalanguage itself has this privilege of not revealing its 'nature' (or structure); it can be taken for a language, for a message, and although it is given as based on a code there is nothing to stop it from cheating and delivering codes that have been tricked or truncated by 'decoders' who take advantage of the situation and mislead on the quality of the goods – namely the code.

From this new angle, presented by a sociology of terrorism and written matter, bureaucracy's propensity to found its power on the written word leaves little doubt. The power of the written word knows no restraint, and bureaucratic skill, knowledge and rationality, founded as they are on written matter, infiltrate every detail of administration. The state replaces providence; bureaucracy, with the technical support of computers, supplants and incarnates the Lord; in this form of government where everyday life is totally organized nothing escapes or can escape organization; compulsions are seen as understanding and foresight; adaptation is *almost* unknown both as concept and as practice (save for an imperceptible residue); if 'humane' bureaucrats were to think of preserving the function of adaptation (which is highly improbable), their way of setting about it could only finish it off. Such is the terrorist society, where each individual trembles lest he ignore the Law but thinks only of turning it to his own advantage by laying the blame on someone else; a society where everyone feels guilty and is guilty – guilty of possessing a narrow margin of freedom and adaptability and of making use of it by stealth in a shallow underground darkness, alas, too easily pierced. The modern state-concerned, political bureaucracy rivals the old church in its detailed intervention, and is, in fact, a new church, a church with a new meaning but reaching the same ends: moral discipline and basic immorality, guilt, and duplicity before the law and those who enforce it; the surrounding darkness combated by many lights.

The multiplication and proliferation of offices by offices, or Parkinson's Law, only partially defines the process, namely the bureaucratic organization of everyday life. Terrorism reaches a point where bureaucracy binds the 'individual' hand and foot by total exploitation, besides making him do most of its work, filling in forms, answering questionnaires; bureaucracy bureaucratizes the population more efficiently than a dictatorship, integrates people by turning them into bureaucrats (thus training them for the bureaucratic administration of their own daily lives) and rationalizes 'private' life according to its own standards. Bureaucratic conscience is identified with social conscience, bureaucratic reason with pure reason and the bureaucratic mind with wisdom, so that persuasion turns into compulsion – which is an exact definition of terrorism. The only perspectives open to the (inner) gaze are the avenues of make-believe, the only possibility of (illusively) adapting to circumstances appears to be through the practice of violence and eroticism, that is, through consuming the symbols of violence and eroticism made available to the public.

Each bureaucracy maps out its own territory, stakes it out and signposts it; there is the treasury's territory, the territory of the administration and the juridical territory. It would be possible to make a semiological study of each territory as a sub-system depending on a *corpus* of rules, decrees and statutes, but such a study would present only a minor interest, for the totality (or body) of such territories is the rationally restricted territory of bureaucracy, a territory that shows pathological (schizoid) symptoms, not so much its own as reflections of a social pathology, the final merging of rationality and absurdity. Furthermore, these territories do not connect like the pieces of a jigsaw puzzle and there are gaps between them; these fragments of an ideal unified bureaucracy do not live together in harmony, yet they form an alliance against time, the arch-enemy, time that erodes regulations and assists the stratagems of carefully labelled 'objects' stacked in the bureaucratic territory which refuse to stay put. Bureaucracy prescribes schedules and proscribes that which eludes its prescriptions.

The relations between the most ancient of institutions (institutionalized religion) and the most modern, state-concerned and political, are rivalry and competition; the political bureaucracies distil their particular brand of philosophy and find themselves in the position of having to oppose the ecclesiastical bureaucracies' justificatory philosophy and ontology; at the same time these venerable and not so venerable institutions complement each other as their efforts converge. The first repress desire, the second take care of needs; the first establish order in the unconscious, the others in consciousness; the more ancient institutions have refined their displays and practices in accordance with the 'depth' they administer while maintaining a befitting detachment from worldly matters, whereas the others aim at what is on the surface, physical activities – consumption, everyday life; the 'spiritual' institutions direct the private life of each individual, their policy being to terrorize sexuality, while the rule of modern institutions spreads terror in everyday life. The result of this convergence is moral discipline, the insignia of terrorist societies; for ever cracking and filling in the cracks, this is the façade exhibited for the benefit of a well-governed everyday life; and in a well-defined and well-qualified society spiritual and civic discipline coincide with this moral discipline, which is the supreme signifier of the vast accumulation of scriptural signified.

Though we believe that a society should not oppose freedom of speech, this does not include every kind of speech nor every kind of freedom. Freedom of speech is not of equal importance with the freedom of work, education, health, housing and the city, and a declaration of the material rights of material man would be neither more nor less effective than the former declaration. Freedom of speech might possibly be placed on a par with the freedom of the city as a skyline of civilization, more than as a right claiming institutional recognition; moreover only critical and poetic speech can be considered in this context, and these forms of speech owe their acknowledgement to their own power; terrorism will always try to silence such voices and it is therefore up to them to find ears that will hear, cracks in the walls of discipline through which they can infiltrate. Furthermore, there can be no question of a special province for poetry, a province of poets or philosophers, of interpersonal relations; to accept such a status for speech and believe that it is a proof of acknowledgement is as good as condemning it to a ghetto, the ghetto of the intelligentsia accepted and justified in the name of the Word; one more ghetto to add to the others! Indeed, it is better to be persecuted than to be allowed the freedom of impotence. The science of the Word can only be elaborated theoretically in opposition to the science of writing, and not to that of language.

We are far from having brought the sociology of writing to a successful issue, or from having exhausted the critical analysis of its implications. The written word, or fixed sign, possesses a status and properties of its own; and this applies to music as well as to language. The isotope discovered by linguists (Greimas) is not a linguistic territory only, but a social territory (or territories) too; the isotope of written matter is the outcome of the isotope of words, of groups of words, sentences, meaning and system; this helps to elucidate its odd mode of existence – odd because we are confronted with the existence, both intellectual and social, of a form possessing formal properties (recurrence, amongst others). As the concept of *isotope* implies that of *heterotope* it involves a formal (structural) classification of intellectual and social territories into isotopes and heterotopes, related and intermingled, but also exclusive and dissociated. Such a classification can take written matter as its referential (which sets itself up precisely as an intellectual and social context and as a substitute for referentials); and this is not without significance for the analytical study of the urban territory (or urban territories). Moreover the formal and structural theory we are elaborating would present only a limited interest if it did not enable us to detect the movement that generates and connects these territories; in other words, we have reached the stage where our theory can include a formal classification of the structural relations in a historical and dialectical movement. So time claims its rights; for these territories do not fit exactly, do not constitute a perfect, coherent whole that can be frozen at any given moment; the separate parts of these intellectual and social territories do not exhaust their relationship in their formal juxtaposition and structural opposition, and that which links them together is neither a 'subject' nor a conscience (such philosophical hypotheses are no longer operant), but an action: Speech; Speech holds together the disconnected fragments of writing, and also of the social territory. Could the time of creation and history be the time of speech, of historical agents speaking at a given moment in given circumstances?

We have not yet nearly achieved the complete sequence:

activity
creations ⎫
products ⎭ organization

institution ⎰ active rationality
⎱ static rationality

rationality becoming static in bureaucracy after the pattern of Scripture and giving rise to a terrorist society.

Let us now take a look at Roland Barthes' book *Le Système de la mode*.* Is this an art book trying to be scholarly, or scientific scholarship directed towards an 'object'? We do not have to decide. The book is not about facts and things, dresses and fashions or fashionable women wearing dresses, actions and situations; it does not tell us what it means to be or not to be fashionable. No; Roland Barthes has other objectives, different methods and a different scientific strategy; his procedure starts by *reducing* the subject and eliminating part if not all the content. Throughout 300 pages on fashion no mention is made of the fact that it is women who wear 'fashionable' clothes, and if we are made aware of this fact it is by institutional examples – fashion photographs, covergirls. Body and bodies are withdrawn like the word in a semantic reduction while the analysis centres on talk about fashion, the written garb or writing about clothes, in other words the Fashion Magazine, the main section being based on two years in the life of a periodical. The author writes a masterly essay on fashion essays, settles into metalanguage with perfect lucidity† and writes a rhetorical treatise; he knows what he is doing and makes no secret of it, though without entirely revealing a mind that is too sharp for comfort. Thus he leaves to another science (sociology, perhaps, or economy or history) the task of dealing with 'reality' – the content, things (materials out of which clothes are made, techniques, economic conditions, etc.) and people (who and where fashionable women are). With the help of language he constructs an entity, a kind of extratemporal permanent essence, pure form defined by its purity: Fashion. Paradoxically enough it presides over the transitory and its formal purity is expressed in the acceleration of transition. What is Fashion? A form of utopia. If we imagine that fashionable women only exist in pictures and that the demi-goddesses pursue Fashion without ever 'being' part of it and only labour under the delusion that they 'make' it, Fashion would still be what it is. If we imagine the 'fashionable woman' as simply a

* Roland Barthes, *Le Système de la mode*, Paris, 1966.
† Cf. p. 38 f., p. 251.

reader of fashion magazines, the social existence of this essence would only be intensified. Its place is in make-believe and in reality, not at the frontiers that divide them but simultaneously and jointly in the two, in their connection and contiguity.* It is an Idea with ramifications and influences (on society, opinions, ideologies), set like a flag over a sector of intellectual and social experience where intellectual and social are as intricately conjoined as reality and make-believe. In short, it is an *institution* that has given shape to a 'reality' where compulsion and adaptation oppose each other and which has organized a creative and productive activity, fixing it in an essence by means of written matter, the fashion magazine's rhetoric. The author leaves to us the choice of a context, and proceeds – like the rhetoricians of old, who created an entity or essence, an Idea, to be used as example: eloquence; or like his own contemporaries who create Literature, the Law, Logic. We can but admire the ability with which such essences, situated in an intellectual or social territory or 'isotope', appropriate every signification, every signifier, to signify themselves! That is perhaps what is socially implied by 'being fashionable'. . . . A further cause for admiration is that what appears to be transitory precisely in so far as it is apparition, transparent and apparent, turns out to be stable, formal and exact (but only if the content is discarded as accidental and contingent, and left for others to ponder). A 'world' is revealed in the construction that discloses at the same time itself and this world, the 'world of fashion', no more artificial than law or philosophy. 'This power that enables man to contrive simplicity is the most social of all institutions,' writes Barthes – neither more nor less artificial than writing that exists as object and yet has no existence outside the seeing eye because its only existence is formal. What is artificial is not fashion but all that circumscribes it: the fashion trade. The elaboration of Barthes' theory is faultless, irrefutable. The hypothesis of a comparison between the pure form and the impurity of the content (reality) appears to be condemned *a priori* and challenged by the author's method of approach; it is not, we repeat,

* Cf. Barthes, op. cit., p. 248.

essential for the 'authenticity' of the disclosure/elaboration of a fashion system that real women should wear dresses and clothes; it is hardly necessary that real women, the readers of fashion magazines, should read the captions that accompany 'fashion photographs' – possibly real readers only perceive the connotation of the words that compose these accompanying captions; possibly all they read are items of practical information (the name of a couturier or a shop, the price of an article); all that matters is that it should be *written*. Barthes has taken the elimination of the Subject to the point of paradox. Fashion, he rightly assumes, eliminates simultaneously the body as physical subject and adaptation as social subject, and this is where it differs from the 'ready-made' and the 'ready-to-wear'; it discards its own content: woman, buyer and consumer, symbol of consumption and of trade (including her body).

Must we acknowledge such a 'system'? We can now proceed to *invert* it, like any systematic construct – including philosophy. In what sort of society does it take root, this closed system that has no value or meaning outside itself and that appropriates every meaning for its own personal use, what conditions (not *a priori* in the philosophical sense, but practical) does it require to exist and function? The unambiguous answer to this question is that it requires first (if not solely) a terrorist society. Not that fashion alone and independently causes terror to reign, but it is an integral–integrated part of terrorist societies, and it does inspire a certain kind of terror, a certainty of terror. To be or not to be fashionable is the modern version of Hamlet's problem. Fashion governs everyday life by excluding it, for everyday life cannot be fashionable and therefore is not; the demi-gods have not (or are supposed not to have) an everyday life; their life passes every day from wonder to wonder in the sphere of fashion; and yet everyday life is there, perpetually excluded. Such is the reign of terror, especially as the 'fashion' phenomenon spreads to all spheres, the intellect, art, 'culture'. . . . This system's knack of capturing everything within reach is unimpeachable; pressure without a specific pressure-group, it influences the whole of society and its field of action interferes with and intersects different fields with frontiers that are equally vague. The whole of society is assigned and consigned by a few systems (or sub-systems) that rival and complete the arch-system, metalanguage.

The prevalence of written matter favours the constitution and the institution of such entities by its peculiar orientation and its aptitude for accumulation. They exist both intellectually and socially, they are fictitious and real; and they determine social 'places', they are nodal points in social territories, the elements of a topology (or topics) of Modernity.

Fashion's main characteristic is its unconcern for *adaptation*; its objective is neither the human body nor social activity, but change and the obsolescence of things. If there is any adaptation at all it is purely accidental and confined to that no-man's-land between the 'ready-made' and 'couture': the 'ready-to-wear'. Thus practical rationality takes advantage of gaps, intervals and cracks or, one might say, of contradiction, to slip in unobserved – but not without difficulty. We have no intention of giving here a detailed history of clothing outside the system of fashion (materials, trade and its growth, the arrival on the scene of the ready-to-wear, its advantages and disadvantages), yet it constitutes an important chapter, none the less, in the critical study of everyday life.

Roland Barthes' inquiry into fashion and literature is a major contribution to the sociology of written matter, and he evidently had this sociology in mind. The concept, though stemming from literature, elucidates certain sociological problems, namely the place of the social and of the intellectual. Barthes dismisses sociology on behalf of semiology, but defines it none the less (possibly unawares) before discarding it for others to investigate; for this a reversal (inversion) of his procedure is required and the re-elaboration of the system (sub-system) that he built up semio-logically, justifying the institutionalization of an 'essence' or entity.

This essence, fashion, is in no way unique, and neither is litera-ture its only rival. Among the other essences are politics, econo-mics, philosophy, perhaps religion and science (or scientificness), but we cannot be too cautious, methodologically and conceptually (theoretically) in our diagnosis. The ticklish operation of making an ideology out of an incomplete activity or an 'essence' from a specialized discipline bears the name of *extrapolation;* for centuries religion tried to set itself up as a system and an essence (theology, theocracy) and failed; as a system it exploded and the fragments of various religions are scattered through history like a trail. 'Religiosity' might become an essence; indeed, there are those who would assist it. And why not? After all, it would be one way of accommodating religion alongside fashion in social topology or topics. Politics cannot be rightly (rationally) defined other than as a practice using ideological instruments to attain strategical ends in a class strategy; which does not constitute an essence, notwithstanding the powerful institutionalizations involved in this activity (state, political 'constitutions', etc.). Like religion, philosophy aspired to the status of a general system and as such it exploded; its fragments – also scattered throughout history – can still be salvaged so long as they are not taken for essences and are opposed to *praxis.*

As social and intellectual forms, essences have a remarkable air of extratemporality inherent in their significance and attributed to them; the faithful – theologians, philosophers, moralists – all lay claim to eternity. Fashion, in the modern sense, was born with fashion magazines and its reign dates from metalanguage. Built on change it changes ceaselessly and those who launch a fashion today are already preparing tomorrow's fashion (collections, shows); the demi-goddesses discard at night – already in the past – that which they bought in the morning, and fashion thrives on its own destruction. Yet for those who are outside fashion it has an air of eternity; outsiders cannot understand what was worn yesterday, ignoring as they do what will be worn tomorrow; yesterday's fashions are absurd, tomorrow's inconceivable but today is immortalized, it is existence (or non-existence). Writing, metalanguage, speech at one remove have the same properties of illusory eternity, apparent anhistoricity and the terror that is inherent in these. The necessary conditions for the existence of essences can now be identified (though none is sufficient by itself) as an activity, an organization and an institution based on metalanguage and written matter. From this point of view art and culture can also be included among the essences of sub-systems, for they require the same conditions; before being concepts they existed actively in works of art, but since then one might suppose that art and culture exist 'in themselves', outside works of art and not in them; such a misapprehension is due to the misuse of language, the use of metalanguage and the illusions inherent in 'one remove'.

Metaphysical illusions have often been denounced by critical analysis. The philosopher starts by classifying trees – which is a worthy occupation; then he makes pear-trees and apple-trees stand for The Pear-tree and The Apple-tree and finally these for The Tree or The Idea of The Tree; after which he endows the Idea (the classification made system and essence) with the power to generate real trees, pear-trees and apple-trees. Thus there are works of art, works of culture (under conditions that must be discerned, with functions, forms and structures that can be analysed); from works of art the mind passes to concepts, and then art and culture are seen as the justification of works of art and culture; and finally organized, institutionalized 'Culture' is endowed with the power to produce cultural works. From the end of the nineteenth century 'Art for Art's sake' implied a conception of art as an entity, as something above works of art and their conditions of existence. 'Art for Art's sake' is art about art, metalanguage, speech at one remove, the work of art already retreating before aesthetics, aestheticism substituted as metalanguage to works of art, while art becomes an entity sufficient unto itself. Here the philosophical illusion is reproduced on a larger scale, in an institutional experience and under conditions that threaten creation, where cultural goods are distributed for avid consumption but wearing the masks of entities called 'Culture' and 'Art'.

It is moreover quite possible that highly influential experts fully exploiting metalinguistic methods should succeed in constituting and instituting as essences the Religious, the Philosophical, the Juridical, the Political, the Economic and even the Logical or the Urban and Urbanism. Thus they will attempt to substitute essences for the real relations of ordinary experience, *reducing* the latter to formal definitions. Such an undertaking should be denounced before it is too late, by demonstrating its pointlessness; these ideologies – practical activities set up as autocratic provinces – would inevitably clash; indeed, they are already suffering from the effects of such impacts, some being now past repair, while for others *the irreducible is taking its revenge* and initiating a counter-attack. The attempt to erect economics as an essence is the most pernicious of these undertakings; instead of seeing industrial production and its organization as a means to an end (social, and consequently urban life) they are taken for the end and, as such, intitutionalized; thus the doctrine of *economism* emerges, posturing as science and the scientifically acceptable essence of Marxist thought, whereas it is nothing but an ideology.

In an earlier section of this book we tried to discover what the philosophical outlook of modern society was. We asked: 'Since this society has been incapable of extracting from its vast philosophical heritage and from its own history that image of Man which, through uncertainty, gropings and controversy, has always been the philosopher's objective; since philosophy is no longer a system but a reality; and since specific philosophical projects are elaborated and not a humanly projected philosophy, which philosophical influence or projection shall we discover here and now?' The hypothesis of a practical neo-Hegelianism is not unreasonable: specialized sub-systems encompassed in a tentative total systematization at state level; thus the relative failure of revolutionary Marxist theories would be counter-balanced (provisionally and finally) by a certain back-sliding, and this not only in the sphere of a philosophical reflection searching for systematization, but in 'reality', namely in social experience governed by ideology. And yet such an hypothesis cannot stand up to a critical analysis, for Hegelianism – or neo-Hegelianism – involves a conception of reality as persuasive rather than as compulsive power; though it is true that the presumed coincidence of reality and rationality virtually implies the coincidence of compulsion and persuasion. But is it fair to make Hegel responsible for terrorist societies, for the absence of adaptation set up as principle and system and compulsion exalted on behalf of a strategically subordinated understanding?

The idea of a neo-Platonic universe, governed in imagination and in reality from on high by entities that are simultaneously forms and powers, seems more apt. Self-government, the division of activities into social and intellectual, and the institutionalization of activity and ability as such determined by their own ends tend, when they converge, to constitute just such a 'universe'; whence the cosmic image mentioned earlier of constellations, planets and stars spilling their various influxes on the soil of everyday life, fixing its heavens and yet incapable of blocking the horizon. This vision of a 'universe' coming to a standstill (amid the swirling, milling mists of fleetingness) is worthy of our attention. All societies possessing a distinct, complex hierarchy (and therefore based on *writing* and written matter) have probably always inclined towards such a form; the summit of a half-fictitious, half-real intellectual and social ladder can only be fixed to a star that is both fictitious (intellectually) and real (socially); but what is different in our society is that the stars have changed, that we no longer have the same sky or the same horizon. Formerly the influx of the stars produced styles and works of art, but our stars shine on everyday life, our sun is black and it spreads terror. Among the stars presiding over the fate of everyday life we list once again Fashion (or fashionability), Technology and Science (or scientificness).

In the last few years we have tried literally to institutionalize adolescents. We are not concerned with enabling them to lead a specific life with adequate activities – though here and there well-intentioned people have given-this a thought (with no perceptible results however) – for what counts is to integrate the adolescent in trade and consumption by offering him a parallel everyday life. We tend to set up an essence, Youthfulness, with commercializable attributes and properties, pertaining to a privileged section of society – or at least one presumed such – thus vindicating the production and consumption of specific objects (clothes, for instance, epitomized and symbolized by 'jeans'). This entity sets an aura of innocence on consumption in general and an aura of decency and 'niceness' on adolescent consumption. Thus the star of Youth joins the highest and brightest in our heavens. The *corpus* required for a study of this system might be drawn entirely from *Salut les Copains*. Youthfulness contributes in its own way to terror, that is, in its special sphere of influence – which extends, growing fainter and fainter, right through society from end to end; indeed, who is not afraid of seeming young no longer, of no longer being young? Who does not contrast maturity and innocence, the adult and the adolescent? Who does not make the choice between youth and wisdom, a parallel and a primordial everyday life, unfulfilment and resignation? Thus everyone is confronted in his daily life with the heart-breaking choice between non-freedom or non-adaptation.

Youthfulness with its operational environment (organization and institution), the hypostasis of real youth, enables these adolescents to appropriate existing symbolizations, to consume symbols of happiness, eroticism, power and the cosmos by means of expressly elaborated metalanguages such as songs, newspaper articles, publicity – to which the consumption of real goods is added; thus a parallel everyday life is established. The adolescent expresses such a situation in his own way, stresses it and compensates for it in the trances and ecstasies (simulated or sincere) of dancing. So metalanguage plays its part to the end: encyclopedic compendium of this world, aestheticizing point of honour, disenchanted shadow seeing itself as substance and enchantment, aromaless world's aroma, etc. That which is signified by these vacant signifiers thus appropriated is youth itself, the essence of youth: youthfulness. Here is another pleonasm or tautology: youthfulness, signified by signifiers that signified something else, synonymous of joy, pleasure, fulfilment because it sanctions the consumption of the symbols for such states. Youth is a proof of the joy of being young, of being young because one is young; youth has a social standing by virtue of youthfulness. But what is left for those who do not gravitate in the orbit of youthfulness? To simulate youthfulness that simulates fulfilment, charm, happiness, completeness. The inevitable outcome of such tuned-up, geared-down dizziness is a feeling of incalculable discomfort and unrest, a sense of frustration that cannot easily be distinguished from satiety, a craving for make-believe, compensations, and evasions into unreality.

In this loveless everyday life eroticism is a substitute for love.
Though it seems difficult that sexuality should be conceived, constituted and instituted as an entity (therefore as a 'sub-system'
presided over in this presidential régime by an essence), everything
tends to indicate that such a procedure is being attempted, that
such an essence is in the process of formation. It is implicit in the
Eros cult whose symptoms transpire here and there, an occult,
popular cult that involves officiating, human sacrifice and anti-
phrases usually associated with officialized creeds, and of course
its High Priest, the divine Marquis. The proliferation of writings
on such themes as sex, sexuality, sexual intercourse and its more
or less normal outlets proves the case, as does the use of such
themes to promote publicity and trade. Sexuality, set up as an
essence, appropriates the symbols of desire; but desire does not
thrive under imposed conditions, so, faced with such irreducibility,
this undertaking is doomed to failure; the anomie of desire, its
social–extrasocial nature, resists social and intellectual systematizations attempting to reduce it to a distinct, classified need
satisfied as such. Desire stifles in everyday life, but it dies in a
specialized context; to organize desire its signifiers must be captured and signified, it must be stimulated by signs, by the sight or
rather the action of undressing, forms of torment that recall those
of desire. But desire refuses to be signified, because it creates its
own signs as it arises – or simply does not arise; signs or symbols
of desire can only provoke a parody of desire that is never more
than a pretence of the real thing.

Sexuality, reduced to a crystallized social and intellectual
essence, achieves the final spoliation of everyday life and that is
its contribution to terrorism; but then desire takes refuge in quotidianness, where it is reborn at random in the surprise of an encounter, in a quarrel. Methods similar to those used to control
natural forces cannot be applied to desire, for desire responds to
adaptation, not to compulsion; if one tries to provoke it by compulsive methods it takes refuge in make-believe, and it is precisely
in its escape-routes that exploiters are ambushed. A make-believe
everyday life doubles that of experience and it is here that desire
finds its imaginary permanence, an imaginary satiety; after which

psychologists and analysts recall it to itself – if they can. *Desire ignores recurrence* as it ignores accumulation; it emerges from speech but not from writing unless it has been led astray, and returns a changeling; it has nothing in common with intellectual operations, any more than with social activities.

So although the systematizing of Eros proves a failure there is still hope for a strange cult, and a kind of entity can be distinguished, neither quite fictitious nor quite real, quite intellectual nor quite social: the entity known as Femininity. This is the outcome of the fact (previously discussed, but which has its place in the present analysis) that:

a) women, as consumers (apparently), direct bureaucratic society's controlled consumption; or, in other words, the control of needs is directed towards Femininity as it is towards Youthfulness;

b) women are symbols of this society; objects of advertising strategies, they are also advertising subjects, nakedness, smiles, living display units . . .;

c) women are also superior consumer goods and trade value in so far as they are physical realities (a good figure is all that is required to obtain wealth and fame). So that the use of female bodies and undress helps to establish and justify the advertising ideology on which the ideology of consumption is based. The act of consuming acquires a certain diversity if it is presented not solely from the point of view of the object and its destruction through consumption, but also from that of the female figure and all it stands for; taken as a symbol of the consumer's customary act, it is conducive to an (apparent) evasion of rhetoric and metalanguage; it distracts attention while substituting another act for that of the consumer (a woman cannot properly be consumed like an object), and this diversion contributes a consumable aestheticism inherent in what is known as 'culture'. As a star of the first magnitude Femininity occupies the centre of a constellation composed of special stars, amongst which can be discerned the Spontaneous, the Natural, the Cultured, the Happy and the Loving; in short all the characters created by Femininity and that circle in its orbit. Not exactly characters, or natures either; rather pseudo-natures, products of culture, pure forms draped in artifacts. A certain mistrust of nature as a product leads to the hypothesis that this is a subterfuge employed by automization to creep in unobserved; Nature can only be another name for desire, which cannot be captured by words. We know only too well (having learnt the hard way) that automatism makes its appearance disguised as 'pure' spontaneity – a fact which distressed certain poets, making them long for death. Writing and the recurrence of writing create an illusion of pure spontaneity, freedom and profundity; but beneath and through apparent spontaneity the organization of everyday life is conducted. Femininity might successfully govern the everyday lives of Cybernanthropoi, where desire would be only a fiction – not a game but a role and a function; however, for the critical mind woman's significance in everyday life is too great to be confined to Femininity. If chance exists, if the individual can back the individual, it is in this field that the game is played, that the stake is lost or won; moreover Femininity forbids real women access to their own lives, adaptation to their own lives, for it submits individuality and particularity (specific differences) to trapped generalities. The same applies to 'creativity', an essence invented by experts and that conveniently localizes individual or collective creative energy, a social 'place' situated in hobbies and 'do-it-yourself' (which denotes the general disrepair and neglect of creative energy).

Under the laser of critical analysis the visible outline of everyday life dissolves and its true shape emerges; but how can we choose between images that all contain metaphors or metonyms, Platonic heavens, tree of pleonasms, compendium of vicious circles? Each one expresses what the others express with an imperceptible difference: suprasensitive heavens, stars, constellations, signs of the Zodiac, social and intellectual places, regions of space and time ruled by essences; pleonasms: autonomized 'pure' forms, Idols proclaimed and acclaimed in the identification of self with self, self-sufficiency, self-signification (and therefore self-consumption, self-destruction); vicious circles: swivels, eddies, fictitious finalities, means set up as ends and becoming their own ends.

The presence of Idols gives a certain unity to this weird assortment, Idols whose outstanding advantage is that they are perfectly unremarkable (neither too ugly nor too beautiful, too vulgar nor too refined, neither too gifted nor without gifts), that they lead the same 'everyday' life as anybody else and that they present to everyone an image of his (everyday) life transfigured by the fact that it is not his but that of another (an Idol, therefore rich and famous). Thus it is absolutely fascinating to watch an Idol amid his satellites having a bath, kissing his children, driving his car or doing any one of those things that everybody does but as if nobody had ever done them before. And this is what such metaphors as the Heavens, the Pleonasm or the Circle (vicious, infernal) hint at but cannot define.

All this is held together by the power of words. Not words as such, specific signs, detachable signifiers that have no power; but by talk that has power, is included in the methods of power; by forms, by logic that have power, by mathematics that is efficient and by trade value that has tremendous power. This is indisputable. Speech has power, but what power? A new theory is coming into view.

The theory of forms (a revival)

We shall attempt to define the mode of existence, both social and intellectual, of forms. The first step is the *de-consecration of writing*, a profanation that follows, rather belatedly, and complements the de-consecration of the land and of woman; we see it as the logical outcome of urbanization and all the contradictions that consolidate and emphasize it. In the context of an agrarian society the consecration of the land and of woman and the value attributed to all that was rare and precious, were extended to the process of writing; writing was seen, furthermore, as the prop and pedestal of the Sacred; it stood for an example of creation when it was really only a model for institutions.

However, by understanding the general properties of written matter we should be able to set the limits of its range and implications and thus to de-consecrate it.

In olden days when the conflict (or conflicting unity) between the Sacred and the Accursed prevailed – resolved by the Profane and Profanation – the conflicting relation of Letter and Spirit was also predominant; Christianity did not dispel the ambiguity nor terminate the conflict by ascribing Letter and Scriptures to the Father, the Book's interpretation to the Son and the Word to the Spirit of whom no more is said once it has been named.

In the context of modern times the social text profanes itself; it discards natural cycles and cyclic time, affective and emotional terrors inspired by natural phenomena, the fear of the unknown. Writing is now a signifier charged with precepts immersing individuals and communities in this context, which projects social and intellectual order on the field. Industrial and urban rationality make it possible at last to understand this dual dialectical movement of the intellectual process and the social process; and in overcoming this schism the mind perceives how Scripture was divided from the Word, and, moreover, made this division one of its imperatives, by arousing doubts as to the Word's reliability; but at the same time this theory enables us to understand how writing serves as a new starting point for the Word; it offers a specific object to this 'subject' that sets itself in a critical relation to the object. Written matter is both condition and obstacle, cause of the subject and its ultimate reification. An additional contradiction enables it still to benefit from the outdated tradition of its consecration while assuming the characteristics and properties of rationality, of the linear and of the profane; this contradiction has been resolved by a critical operation based on an analysis of metalanguage; but such an operation requires certain conditions. The city can be defined (among other definitions) as the reading of a social text, that is, as a representative miscellany of society and the heritage of past generations, each of which has added a page; it is also the place of speech doubling the reading of written matter, interpreting, commenting on and questioning it. Formerly it bore the mark of religions and rites originating in the cultivation of the soil; it radiated from a central point, temple or sanctuary – sites that were invested with a particular aura of sanctity – and the city itself was invested (surrounded, encircled, but also endowed with powers) by the territory whose sacred character it emphasized, casting out evil into foreign lands. Urbanism, however, in its primitive form unwittingly sapped the foundations of the Sacred when it was subordinated to rationality, foresight and politics, so that it is now relegated to folk-lore. Reasons and causes, the de-consecration and the profanation of the social text in urban experience, led to the de-consecration and profanation of written matter – but not without a certain delay. On the other hand urban life did not disappear with the explosion of its former morphology; on the contrary, the explosion was accompanied, paradoxically, by an implosion; in one place city life may be concentrated and emphasized in the ruins of this morphology (ancient cities and districts), in another it tends to establish itself as a new form that still lacks morphological foundations, as an embryo, a virtuality and potentiality, but demanding a complete social experience and occupying a material (spatial) base. And we are back at the problem of existing forms and their mode of existing (social and intellectual), calling for a new rationality through the intricacies of reason.

Speech implies a presence (sometimes an absence, evasion or deceit, but relative to the presence), a presence whose referential (hidden or apparent, hiding or appearing) is Desire; speech cannot be intentionally cool, in itself it is 'hot'. Writing is absence (also presence, but in an indirect way only reached by inference), recurrent and cumulative, it possesses the attributes of an object (socially) and of memory (intellectually) and only acquires the warmth contributed by reading through the action of a specific reader, public reader, reciter or actor; it is essentially 'cool', it inscribes and prescribes, and the first of its prescriptions is the reading that gives it being; cool because it is compulsive, compulsive because it is cool, it assists desire in its flight; asexual in so far as it is written, indifferent and haughty in so far as it is the law, it is a thing that sanctifies separation. It inscribes the schism between reality and desire and between the intellectual operation and pulsions or impulses (one of the basic ingredients of terror).

Desire cannot ignore the past but it ignores recurrence; though it is perceived only with an effort as 'being' or 'not being' it both is and is not; it makes itself known and expresses itself; and desires itself if only for self-immolation through satisfaction, or to be frustrated; it is activity, actuality and actualization, it is presence. Writing, because it is precise, tends to be icily pristine, always equal to itself and therefore alien to desire; when speech, presence and desire are restored to it the ice is set on fire and that is the paradox of poetry (which the poet achieves, perhaps, by relating the disorder of words to the order of recurrence, a disorder that is none the less orderly, that cannot be defined as a lack of precision but that delivers writing from the snares of metalanguage, substituting desire to conventional – or non-existent – referentials – desire and the *time* of desire, that chosen referential created by poetry).

The poet does not abolish writing and the precision of writing, but by an apparently miraculous act he turns coolness into warmth, absence into presence, the dread of desire into desire, spatiality into temporality and recurrence into actualization. Thus when desire flows into writing, infusing it with its own vibrations, the writing expands, overflows and, bursting its barriers and flooding the embankments, spreads and communicates by means of what seemed to enclose and restrict it; when a tremor runs through written matter, when its limpidity is disturbed and acquires by this disturbance a different transparency whereby it loses its quality of object (intellectual and social), the consequences are incalculable; and it is just such a miracle – which has nothing irrational about it, which conforms to a self-imposed order – that contributes to the inexplicable charm of a simple love-poem made, apparently, of nothing but pure form, or rhetoric.

The conflicting relation of Speech and Writing cannot be reduced to the relation of matter and the written word any more than it can be reduced to that of spirit and letter, for it goes much deeper. Let it suffice to recall here that those who spoke without writing paid with their lives for this law-breaking epoch-making act; we think of Socrates, Christ, perhaps even Joan of Arc; and we remember that Nietzsche's Zarathustra appealed to Speech, Presence, Time and Desire not only in order to re-animate frozen writing but to oppose written matter and its accumulation from the beginnings of Western civilization. Did the poet hope to give a more limpid significance to the words of the tribe, or simply significance? Be that as it may, 'death was triumphant in that strange voice'.

A pure (formal) space defines the world of terror. If the proposition is reversed it preserves its meaning: terror defines a pure formal space, its own, the space of its power and its powers; time has been evicted from this unified space; the writing that fixes it has eliminated speech and desire, and in this literal space, isolated from action, presence and speech, so-called human actions and objects are catalogued, classed and tidied away, together with writings that are lined up on written matter.* The superior power that keeps them in such order is everyday life.

The *double existence of forms* understood in this way (intellectual and social) invites a further inquiry into this contradiction, masking an ambiguity that in turn conceals a dialectical (conflicting) movement. Moreover, if we can understand this dual aspect – or aspects – it should help us to grasp further relations such as that of reality and possibility, or of product and act (what the philosophers used to call the relation of object to subject). This is also the relation of form to content, for forms would exist as pure intellectual abstractions and as social objects if they could – but they cannot do so, they cannot exist deprived of content; this aspiration to a pure abstraction imposing its laws and its strictures is part of the power of forms, it endows them with the power to terrorize. Specific *contracts* exist characterized by their content; thus a marriage contract specifies and regulates the relation between two individuals of opposite sex according to a given social code (order), subordinating sexual relations to relations of property (patrimony, marriage portion, inheritance and its transfer, the division of property, etc.); a working contract regularizes the acquisition and sale of working energy; and so on. Nevertheless there is a general form of contract or agreement, a juridical form based on the civil code; and we observe that all contractual relations presuppose a discussion and definition in verbal form, by the contracting parties, of the contract's 'fairness', though nothing remains of such

---

* Thus terror is not the space of false conscience (*La Fausse conscience*, a thesis by J. Gabel, Paris) but of true conscience or of the conscience of reality, isolated from possibility, virtuality and shaping activity; terror is not simply pathological, it becomes normal.

preliminaries, the proof being in the writing, the official deed; and a contract is concluded by the signatures of both parties – the most significant form of writing.

Similarly there is no thought without an object, no reflection without content. Yet there exists a general form of thought based on classification, which is Logic. Let us summarize in a few terms the problem of the dialectical movement of form and content, too often overlooked to the advantage of 'pure' form, existing as such, intellectual as well as social. There is no form without content and, inversely, no content without form; reflection separates form from content thus supporting the form's natural inclination to exist as pure essence; and reflection itself constitutes a form that aspires to the status of universal essence (the philosopher's ambition and illusion). 'Pure' form, by its very purity, acquires an intelligible transparency, becomes operant, a medium of classification and action; but as such it cannot exist; as form it is no more than an abstraction, and what is perceived as existing is the unity (conflicting, dialectical) of form and content. Form isolated from its content (or referentials) is enforced by terrorism. Our radical analysis turns formalism, structuralism and functionalism against themselves, attacks obsessional classification with a classification of forms and exposes their general content, which is everyday life maintained by terror. We observe in a decreasingly abstract progression:

a) *logical forms*. Intellectual: the absolute principle of identity $A = A$, a meaningless term, a tautology, therefore intelligible, limpid and transparent because it is void of content. Social: the pleonasm (ends taken as means, entity made autonomous and void);

b) *mathematical forms*. Intellectual: enumeration and classification, order and standard, equality in distinction, totality and sub-totalities. Social: ordering, rational organization;

c) *linguistic forms*. Intellectual: coherence. Social: cohesion of relations, codifying;

d) *forms of exchange*. Intellectual: equivalences, standardizing, comparing (qualities and quantities, activities and products, needs and satisfactions). Social: trade value, consumer goods (whence it acquires logic and language and tends to constitute a 'world' based on its form);

e) *forms of contract*. Intellectual: reciprocity. Social: the juridical formalization of relations based on reciprocity, a codification that extends to the elaboration of abstract principles;

f) *forms of practico-sensorial objects*. Intellectual: balance perceived or conceived in the object. Social: the symmetry of objects (including hidden relations between things, between each thing and its setting, between the self and the double, etc.);

g) *urban forms*. Intellectual: simultaneity. Social: encounters (bringing together neighbouring products and activities) that intensify – by materializing and de-consecrating – the landscape, produced by labour and imposed as form upon nature in a given territory;

h) the *form of writing*. Intellectual: repetition. Social: accumulation.

We omit recurrence; conceived by some (ultimately by Nietzsche) as the form of existence.

If the form of writing occupies an inferior position to that of the city in this decreasingly abstract hierarchy of forms it is because our classification stipulates neither priority, logic, ontology nor historicity but goes from pure, translucid form to substantial content, a progression that involves a now familiar dialectical relation, that of form and content. Form in its absolute purity $(A = A)$ is absolutely unviable; the greatest paradox of reflection is first that such a form can be formulated and formalized with such precision and then that it should be effective. How and why? Where does this efficiency come from, this working ability of pure form? Without the slightest possible doubt from the fact that it makes analysis possible, that is to say, it allows for the division of 'reality' along its line of least resistance, its joints and disconnections, its levels and dimensions; we all know that analysis kills, has the fearsome power of death and life that disconnect and re-connect in different combinations the fragments and elements previously disconnected.

Thus the form is reunited to a variable, resisting, content on which it imposes order and constraint. But the content is irreducible, is in fact *the irreducible*. The complex process of (ana-lytic) knowledge and experience, encompassed within the process of form and content, encompasses that of reduction and the irre-ducible. In the last analysis (but is a last analysis necessary?) the content is desire seen neither as the desire to be nor as the desire not to be, to continue nor to end, to survive nor to expire, but as the desire for action and creation signified by all things and identi-fied by none, concealed in the signified and under signs, and there-fore revealed as the signifier without signified which gives life to others and can be found in Speech and in Time but neither in Space nor in Writing nor in any spatial signified.

Everyday life is part of the content, but ambiguously; on the one hand it derives from the efficiency of forms, is their result or re-sultant. Product and residue, such is the definition of everyday life; forms simultaneously organize it and are projected upon it, but their concerted efforts cannot reduce it; residual and irre-ducible, it eludes all attempts at institutionalization, it evades the grip of forms. Everyday life is, furthermore, the time of desire: extinction and rebirth. Repressive and terrorist societies cannot leave everyday life well alone but pursue it, fence it in, imprison it in its own territory. But they would have to suppress it to have done with it, and that is impossible because they need it.

We do not have to demonstrate that form cannot depend on it-self for existence; our main concern is to show that form aspires – in vain – to a 'substantial' existence, in fact, to essentiality. It is rationally demonstrated that 'pure' form, the form of logic, con-tract or writing, has no right to autonomy, although it has such pretensions; the 'purity' of a form involves its non-existence. Critical analysis must therefore prove the social existence of some-thing that has no apparent 'substantial' existence; and the answer is that forms depend on social conscience at the same time as they influence it; they cannot do without speech, though they drain speech to their own advantage, activity on behalf of the agent, and action on behalf of mediation. Thus an idea or theory emerges: Speech maintains, assembles and unifies isolated forms, not in a form – or a structure or a function – but in an action.

Speech is necessary but it is insufficient, for it requires a basis, a material substantial foundation. *Production* may be seen as answering such requirements – in its dual aspect, as production of work and of produce – and so can *everyday life* in so far as it is the result of actual production relations and of the residue of forms classified above.

Here our critical analysis links up with the peculiar phenomenon of the *integration–disintegration* of modern society. The members of this society (individuals and communities) as well as the whole body (in so far as a body exists), its culture and its institutions, are obsessed with the need to integrate and to be integrated – an obsession, we note, that is symptomatic neither of a considerable integrative capacity nor of a total incapacity to integrate. Specific integrations occur in their own time and place, but it is total integration that is required. By the subterfuge of organizing everyday life the working classes have been partially integrated with present-day society – which implies their disintegration as a class; and at the same time, as a consequence of this phenomenon, the whole society is in the process of disintegrating – its culture, its unity and its values. We have already seen that our society no longer constitutes a system (notwithstanding state power and armed force, the intensification of compulsion and terrorism) but only a lot of sub-systems, a conjunction of pleonasms threatened with mutual destruction or suicide. Thus it is not really surprising if obsessional integration and specific limited integrations (of publicity to trade, programming to everyday life) lead to a sort of generalized racialism stemming from the disability to integrate properly: everybody against everybody else; women, children, teenagers, proletarians, foreigners are in turn subjected to ostracism and resentment, becoming targets of undefined terrorisms while the whole is still held together by the keystone of speech and the foundations of everyday life.

The concept of a 'zero point', like those of terrorism and of writing, is derived from literary criticism; a coincidence that is not really surprising in view of the perspicacity of those among our foremost critics who undertook the 'radical' investigation, and also because literature is the natural intellectual vehicle and social basis of metalinguistic popularity, of the spread of written matter.

We shall appropriate for our own ends the stylistic concept elaborated by Roland Barthes* for his analysis of the transformations in literary writing. 'Zero point' can be defined as the neutralization and disappearance of symbols, the attenuation of pertinence (contrast) and the prevalence of associations of words and sentences, associations seen as evidence of 'what goes without saying'. The writing claims to state simply and coldly what is, when it only exposes a formal coherence. Zero point is a neutral state (not an act nor a situation) characterized by a pseudo-presence, that of a simple witness, and therefore a pseudo-absence.

There is a *zero point of language* (everyday speech), of *objects* (functional objects split up into elements and contrived by arranging and combining these elements), of *space* (space shown as display, even when it is laid out in lawns and planted with trees, the space taken over by traffic circulation, deserted spaces even in the heart of the city), of *need* (predictable, predicted, satisfied in advance by imaginary satisfaction), and there is also a zero point of *time:* time that is programmed, organized according to a pre-existing space on which it inscribes nothing, but by which it is prescribed. Zero point is a transparency interrupting communication and relationships just at the moment when everything seems communicable because everything seems both rational and real; and then there is nothing to communicate!

The social topology or topics of this landscape has undergone a change; it would be too much to say that darkness had descended, for it is only twilight and we can still distinguish an assortment of neutralized places, each as neutral as possible, but each one assigned to a specific function, from above or in the whirlwind of an entity; these are ghettos, hygienic ghettos withal, and functional too; there is the ghetto of creativity and hobbies (do-it-yourself, collecting, gardening), the ghetto of happiness and of freedom (holiday resorts and holiday camps), the ghetto of speech (small groups and their talk), there is a place for Femininity and one for Youthfulness, one for traffic circulation, one for trade and one for consumption; and there are places for communication.

* Cf. *Le Degré zero de l'écriture*, Paris, 1958.

But we must not overstress the dreariness of the scene, for real dialogues and real communication do take place; not, perhaps, where they are expected, not in the places specially designed for communication and dialogue; but they happen elsewhere, when speech arises from a brief encounter, usually lively, sometimes violent and always free from the neutralizing effects of the pre-determined site; in this 'elsewhere' something may be said and heard above the monotone of written matter that appropriates all the 'topics' and cancels them out. More or less everywhere there are *bodies* (social, constituted) that stop up the channels of communication while claiming to encourage it, appointing given places and times for it in everyday life; but once groups and classes succeed in meeting face to face, once they come to grips, a free dialogue explodes under the dialectical impetus.

Thus we have a society that is obsessed with dialogue, communication, participation, integration and coherence, all the things it lacks, all the things it misses. These are our topics, our problems; we imagine we are solving problems by naming topics, by endlessly, learnedly, obsessively discussing topics; we dissect loneliness, lack of communication, discontent. But there is nothing unusual about these subjects; what is unusual is loneliness in the midst of overcrowding, lack of communication in a proliferation of signs of communication; new and unusual also is the fact that the place of communication is always elsewhere, in substitution. Zero point is the lowest point of social experience, a point that can only be approached and never reached, the point of total cold; it is made up of partial zero points – space, time, objects, speech, needs. A kind of intellectual and social asceticism can be discerned at zero point under all the apparent affluence, the squandering and ostentation as well as under their opposites, economic rationality, resistance. Moreover it can be held responsible for the decline of the Festival, of style and works of art; or rather it is the sum of features and properties resulting from their decline. In fact zero point defines everyday life – except for desire that lives and survives in the quotidian.

Maybe our description of this 'freezing' landscape is misleading, for it has nothing in common with an ice-age scene; it is merely a picture of boredom. On the other hand we all know only too well the dangers inherent in the boredom eating away at the heart of modernity. We cannot close our eyes to the fact that whole nations are bored, while others are sinking into a boredom at zero point. We can say that people are satisfied, happy . . .; of course they are, for they have come to accept and even to like boredom at 'zero point'; they prefer it to the hazards of desire.

Our inquiry into the manner in which forms exist has led to an investigation of social *reality*. Ought we to reconsider and modify our concept of 'reality'? The existence and the effects of forms are unlike those of sensorial objects, technical objects, metaphysical substances or 'pure' abstractions; though they are abstract they are none the less intellectual and social *objects*, they require sensorial, material and practical foundations but cannot be identified with such vehicles. Thus *trade value* requires an object (a product) and a comparison between objects in order to appear and express its content which is productive collective labour and a comparison between labours. However, object and content without form have neither a specifically intellectual nor a specifically social reality. To a certain extent form defines a thing's significance; yet it possesses something both more and less, something different from what is signified; it constitutes an object's significance but also appropriates it, allows itself to be signified and absorbs the signifier. Thus trade idioms are made of pre-existing languages that they adapt to their own use. The concatenation of efficient causes and effects is not the whole of social 'reality'; classical causality and determinism must give way to another process of exposition and explication; but this is no excuse for rejecting causality or substituting a kind of irrealism for 'reality', for in both cases the analysis by-passes the problem of the existence and effects of forms. They are real but not in the terms of other types of reality; they are projected on the screen of everyday life without which they would have nothing to explore, define and organize; in this way the various rays constitute a single beam and light up a territory that would otherwise be plunged in darkness. Once again the metaphor expresses too much and not enough.

Our analysis has proceeded up to this point from the higher to the lower, from forms to reality and content, to the base that is also a basis. We shall now settle down in everyday life, but not without a backward look at our analytical trip. Let us try to put ourselves in the place of a person living his everyday life without any historical, sociological or economic knowledge and without a particularly curious or critical mind; from this viewpoint we cannot help noticing a phenomenon that requires a further analysis; this inmate of everyday life, whether male or female, a member of one social class or another, has no (or hardly any) intimation of all that we have disclosed and discussed; he takes for granted all that he observes, he accepts as the here and now everything he sees and perceives, all his experiences; he may find them neither just, justified nor justifiable, but that is how it is, things are what they are; unless he happens to be a pathological case or a case of anomie he will almost entirely ignore the depth of desire and the stars that rule over him, for he rarely raises or lowers his gaze, looking only around him at the surface that he takes for 'reality'. This everyday being lives a double illusion, that of limpidity and evidence ('that's how it is') and that of substantial reality ('it can't be any different'); thus *the illusion of immediacy in everyday life is defined.*

Terrorism maintains the illusion, the zero point of critical thought. It is the terrorist function of forms (and of institutions deriving from these forms) to maintain the illusions of transparency and reality and to disguise the forms that maintain reality. People living in everyday life refuse to believe their own experience and to take it into account; they are not obliged to behave in this way, nobody forces them, they force themselves – a typical feature of the terrorist society; only a very small minority draw conclusions from what they know. Everyday experience is not cumulative; though there is a tendency to endow elderly people with 'experience' all they have really acquired is cynicism and resignation.

Where experience is concerned everyday life is wasted, but it is highly appreciated as a limited practice, that of an individual existence doomed sooner or later to failure and resignation. Those who resist are promptly isolated, integrated, silenced or reconditioned, accused by some of lacking experience, by others of being wanting in wisdom. Objections are what is not expressed, for the world of terror, of 'pure' forms and 'pure' space is also the world of silence when metalanguages are exhausted and are ashamed of themselves.

We now have before us the outline of a discipline or *science* (if one is not afraid of words), a science that would expose the position of everyday life in relation to forms and institutions; that would disclose these relations implied in quotidianness, but implicit and obscure in the quotidian.* In everyday life when we think we see everything quite clearly we are most deluded; when we are convinced that we are plunged in darkness a chink of light has already pierced the shadows; the operation that will expose the double illusion requires the precision of an experienced surgeon. An inquiry into everyday situations presupposes a capacity for intervention, a possibility of change (reorganization) in everyday life that would not be dependent on a rationalizing, programming institution. To initiate such a *praxis* either a conceptual analysis or 'socio-analytical' experiences are necessary; as a generalized social practice it is part of the cultural revolution that is based on the abolition of terrorism – or at least on the possibility of a counter-terrorist intervention.

The opening

In so far as there can be demonstration in such matters we have demonstrated the *non-closing* of the circuit. There is no single absolute chosen system but only sub-systems separated by cracks, gaps and lacunae; forms do not converge, they have no grip on the content and cannot reduce it permanently; the *irreducible* crops

---

* Inquiries of this nature have already been undertaken by Georges Lapassade, René Lalou and the members of the Groupes de Recherche Institutionelle, and might be called *socio-analyses*, for they presuppose interventions into an actual situation, a community's everyday life. The socio-analytical intervention *dissociates* into place and time the bearings of the situation, combined as they are with false evidence; it *associates* experiences that were previously foreign to it, and then proceeds by induction and trans-

up again after each reduction. Though necessary for scientific procedures, only a relative, temporary reduction can be achieved, entailing further processes. Science is related to a *praxis*, involves a *praxis*, presupposes or precedes a *praxis;* everyday life, as a layer of unreality and an illusory transparency constitutes a frontier between darkness and light, the seen and the unseen; far from closing itself it is only a *plane*.

Now that the opening has been located all that remains is to direct our inquiry towards it, for it bears a familiar name: that of *urban life*, or urban society.

Urban society rises from the ashes of rural society and the traditional city. For many centuries peasant life and an agricultural reality predominated, encircling and besieging the city, setting its limits. But a new era of urban society is dawning where the experience values that originated in the distant past of agricultural traditions will at last outshine the trade values that now overshadow them; its conception and realization require a departure from former ideologies (outdated survivals, utopian elaborations). There are certain neighbourhoods in the one-time urban centres of cities, neighbourhoods that were once prosperous but are now usually inhabited by a different class of people from those who founded them, where urban life survives or attempts to survive; elsewhere it can be found, with intellectual or social overtones, trying to create a new 'centrality'; but only the partisans of that ideology known as 'economism' can see urban society as the outcome of industrial production and organization; only the supporters of bureaucratic rationalism conceive the new experience as distribution of a territory and its programming, and both outlooks threaten the development of this new-born hope. Conversely, only ideologists believe that urban society can be founded

---

duction. Thus anti-Stalinist opposition inside communist parties was, in its time, a remarkable case of socio-analysis, and some of its findings can be observed in later developments (sociological in particular, Marxist in general). The third volume of the *Critique de la vie quotidienne* will develop certain features of this account and will probably be constructed according to the following plan: first, unmediated everyday life, its variations and misapprehensions, then an elucidation of forms.

on groups emancipated already from labour and social class divisions and that there is such a thing as an urban 'system'; for such idealists the new society would be modelled on those of ancient Greece, but they forget that these were dependent on slavery. Urban society stems from encounters, it must exclude segregation and be distinguished by the fact that it affords the time and the place for individual and collective meetings, the coming-together of people from different classes, with different occupations and different patterns of existence. This urban society – which is already more than a dream – is based not on the abolition of class distinctions, but on the elimination of antagonisms that find their expression in segregation; it must involve differences and be defined by these differences. Time in the city and by the city will be independent of natural cycles but not submitted to the linear divisions of rationalized duration; it will be the time of unexpectedness, not a time without place but a time that dominates the place in which it occurs and through which it emerges. This will be the place and time of desire, above and beyond need, because in this sense urban life will involve the performance of numerous functions and will still be transfunctional. Though it will be the place of another time than that of formal spatiality, a place where speech prevails over writing and metalanguage, the city will none the less involve structures (spatial, formal); its practical existence will be practically defined (inscription and prescription) but this morphology will project (inscribe, prescribe) on the field relations whose social and intellectual reality will not be reduced to this projection. In the city speech will unify the scattered elements of social reality, functions and structures, disconnected space, compulsive time; the city will have its everyday life, but quotidianness will be banished; and terror, more in evidence here than elsewhere, will be more successfully opposed, either by violence (always latent) or by non-violence and persuasion; for the essence of the city will be a challenge to terror, a manner of counter-terrorism. The city's uninhibited self-expression and creativity (morphology, setting, shaped and moulded sites, adequate space and spaces) will restore *adaptation* so that it prevails over compulsion and sets a limit to make-believe, restricting the imagination to style and works of art, monuments, festivals, so that play and games will be given their former significance, a chance to realize their possibilities; urban society involves this tendency towards the revival of the Festival, and, paradoxically enough, such a revival leads to a revival of experience values, the experience of place and time, giving them priority over trade value. Urban society is not opposed to mass media, social intercourse, communication, intimations, but only to creative activity being turned into passivity, into the detached, vacant stare, into the consumption of shows and signs; it postulates an intensification of material and non-material exchange where quality is substituted for quantity, and endows the medium of communication with content and substance. Urban society will not turn everyday life into make-believe and will not be content with throwing a different light on quotidianness, but it will transform the quotidian in its own quotidian terms.

A short dialogue

'You have, as was to be expected, abandoned every trace of scientific direction and your would-be analytical essay has turned out to be a diatribe.'

'You were forewarned. Questions and criticism are only forbidden by scientificness, a discipline that figures, as we have seen, among the so-called "pure" forms and the semi-Platonic archetypes of this little world; whereas scientific knowledge stipulates action, criticism and theoretical opposition simultaneously, according to the procedure of our essay (where we have attempted to take stock, define a direction, widen horizons). Moreover a hypercritical outlook is better than a total lack of criticism, for it stimulates even conformists like you.'

'Your conclusion is a vindication of urban society couched in high-flown prophetic terms.'

'Not at all. There exists a realistic and far-sighted conception of urban possibilities that coincides neither with the history nor the science of urban development to date, nor with the ideology called urbanism; such a knowledge grows as its subject emerges from the embryonic state, and actively contributes to its progress.'

'Utopist!'

'And why not? For me this term has no pejorative connotations. Since I do not ratify compulsion, norms, rules and regulations; since I put all the emphasis on adaptation; since I refute "reality", and since for me what is possible is already partly real, I am indeed a utopian; you will observe that I do not say utopist; but a utopian, yes, a partisan of possibilities. But then are we not all utopians, apart from you?'

'I am not the only one, and "we" at least do not confuse investigation and committal, trial and indictment. According to you people are miserable, terrorized.'

'You haven't understood a thing, not a single thing! I never said that people were terrorized but that they were terrorists. I said that a lot of people were satisfied and that a terrible unease prevails none the less. This contrast that translates a contradiction is my subject, my problem.'

'We were looking forward to hearing some details on the different everyday lives of the various social classes – the bourgeoisie, working-class families. But on the way you forgot that there were classes, and it would seem that everyday life is the same for everybody. Have you abolished distinctions?'

'By no means; but our object in writing this book was not to describe everyday life according to each class and community; we had no intention of providing budgets – either of money or of time; such an inquiry is worthy of consideration, though it will be hard to carry out without indulging in sociological trivialities, anecdotes and inessential reports based on statistics and a great show of scientific or pseudo-scientific efficiency; if this sort of study is to receive the approbation of most experts it must abound in examples of stereotypes and patterns if not in those of incomes, strata and averages; it would have to stay on the surface of things – and when I say things I mean things. The strategy that aims at programming everyday life is generalized, it is a class strategy; some may indeed benefit from such a project and its realization, but others, the majority, will have to put up with it as best they can. At the top of the hierarchical ladder there are those (the demi-gods) who apparently transcend everyday life; at the bottom of the ladder, among the new poor, the vast majority bears the weight and supports the great pyramid, living in the paradox of "satisfaction–frustration" and enduring it when it has already become a contradiction. You can draw your conclusions . . .'

'Don't you think you are a bit leftist at times?'

'I beg your pardon. There are rightist ideologists and leftist ideologists, though admittedly ideological distinctions are not always made according to the strictest logic; right and left analyses never seem to coincide, whether they refer to history, technology or the so-called society of consumption. The term leftism is evoked when a leftist analysis refers to a so-called leftist ideology such as economism or technocratism. That is my answer. Now, just one word more on utopism. It is serious, disturbing, to question anything concerning everyday life; thus there are a number of infinitesimal alterations that would be possible in traffic circulation or in the motor-car itself, that experts consider out of the question because they would entail too great an output of capital, involve too many consequences. And what does this prove? That everyday life should be put to the question as a whole. *Homo sapiens, homo faber* and *homo ludens* end up as *homo quotidianus,* but on the way they have lost the very quality of *homo;* can the *quotidianus* properly be called a man? It is virtually an automaton, and to recover the quality and the properties of a human being it must outstrip the quotidian in the quotidian and in quotidian terms.'

Towards a Permanent Cultural Revolution

First findings

The main points of our analysis can be summed up as follows:

a) The Marxist theory was significant in that it gave a language, a concept and a direction to industrial production at its advent and disclosed the new creative energies inherent in this industry. Marx accomplished his historic mission, developing the ideas of the great British economists Smith and Ricardo, and those of Saint-Simon; he adopted the methods and concepts of Hegel's philosophy but redirected them against Hegelianism, and he redirected against the 'upside-down world' in general all that it had achieved; finally he stressed and clarified the fact that industry was capable of mastering nature and of transforming the actual material and social world.

b) It is now possible, a hundred years after the publication of the first volume of *Das Kapital* (1867), to take stock and sort out the achievements from the shortcomings in the Marxist doctrine. Once Marx had stressed the dual aspect of production (production of things and relations, production of works and produce) he went on to stress the production of produce – the essential, specific aspect of industrial production in a capitalist state; in this way it became possible (though that was not his intention) to give a unilateral interpretation to his theory and thence to science and to social reality. Moreover *urbanization* – a process that, though linked to industrialization, is distinct and specific – had barely started in Marx's time, so that he was unable to grasp its significance or its relation to industrialization, did not, and indeed could not, perceive that the *production of the city* was the end, the objective and the meaning of *industrial production*. Whence a further limitation imposed upon his theory and an added occasion for misinterpretation, since industry was thus seen to contain its own meaning, rationality and objectives. Society today has acquired the reputation of dynamism when in fact it is stagnating in the no-man's-land between industrialization and urbanization where industry and economic expansion still figure as objectives and the true goal is considered accidental and contingent.

In *Das Kapital* Marx dialectically (critically) analysed capitalist methods of production. He exposed (after Smith and Ricardo, but going deeper and further) the *form* of trade value and consumer goods as the cornerstone, the theoretical and historical basis of this method of production. Reverting to an earlier theory Marx denounced the dangers involved in the practically limitless expansion of trade value and money and their material power. Perceiving the 'world' of trade's form, logic and language he foresaw its power both for destruction and for creativity; on the one hand its serious consequences, its virtualities, on the other hand the social force that could restrain this threatening tyranny, control the market and its laws and subordinate the mastery of nature to man's *adaptation* of his own natural and social being.

c) Marx's warning went unheeded, especially by those political parties that used his theories as a password (on the one hand *economism* where organization, programming and industrial rationality prevailed, on the other *politism* with the stress on institutional and ideological activism, both under the aegis of a *philosophism* of history, or of material reality). The theory of exchange, of trade value and its laws, and of overcoming them, lost its clarity, deteriorating into a utopian leftism (that aimed at transcending the law of exchange and value by a total revolutionary action) or an opportunist rightism adopting most of the theories of economism; and from this point the concept of *adaptation* was completely discarded by Marx's followers. The working classes' main mission was now seen to be political (the modification of state institutions) or economic (expansion of production involving trade expansion), thus the necessity to curb trade expansion was ignored, as were the methods and the social and intellectual scope of such a curbing. In this way one of the crucial lessons to be learnt from Marx and *Das Kapital* fell on deaf ears and was lost to social conscience, ideology and theories.

d) The conditions of capitalist production have not altered; indeed they have been consolidated by the discredit into which Marxist theories have fallen and favoured by historical events that accelerated technological development at an incalculable cost to society – two world wars and a third already in sight; in one half of the world these conditions are now firmly established, while weighing heavily on the other half. Such a situation has caused a considerable misappropriation of creative energy; the working classes should (and could) have taken upon themselves the realization of possibilities inherent in industrial production, but they have not (as yet) carried out this mission; there have been motives and causes, substitutions, displacements, replacements and diversions. To understand this complex process new analytical methods and a new intellectual approach are required; for want of such an analysis it has been possible to believe in the presence of hidden unfathomable structures within our society and, indeed, within all societies; if, in fact, the process cannot be imputed to an 'agent', analysis discovers none the less a class strategy whereby creative activity is replaced by contemplative passivity, and by the voracious consumption of signs, displays, products and even works of art so long as they are those of past ages; this thankless consumption thrives on history, works of art and styles but refutes history and no longer understands works of art, ignoring or rejecting their terms. The *reductive* process was practised before being sanctified as an ideology; all contemporary ideologies are reductive, including those that are taken for effective sciences; they ratify a disabling *praxis* disguised by promises and illusions of a final fulfilment. Ideologies turn facts into laws and actual reduction into 'scientificness'.

e) Thus everyday life, the social territory and place of controlled

consumption, of terror-enforced passivity, is established and programmed; as a social territory it is easily identified, and under
analysis it reveals its latent irrationality beneath an apparent
rationality, incoherence beneath an ideology of coherence, and
sub-systems or disconnected territories linked together only by
speech. To the question: 'How can such a society function, why
doesn't it fall apart?' the answer is: 'By language and metalanguage, by speech kept alive under talk at one or two removes,
under floods of ink.' This territory seems firm enough, but it is
not impervious to earthquakes, not by any means! Marx never
considered economics as determinative, or as determinism, but he
saw capitalism as a mode of production where economics prevailed, and therefore that it was economics which had to be tackled;
nowadays everyday life has taken the place of economics, it is
everyday life that prevails as the outcome of a generalized class
strategy (economic, political, cultural). It is therefore everyday
life that must be tackled by broadcasting our policy, that of a
cultural revolution with economic and political implications.

f) The concept of revolution – even of total revolution – is still
valid; moreover a revolution cannot be other than *total*. If the
concept has become vague it is the fault of reductions, uncritically
accepted and dogmatized. When the idea of revolution is restored
to include all its implications, three planes can be distinguished:
1) *An economic plane* where revolutionary strategy makes its objective clear; the growth of industrial production and its planification are necessary but they are not all; the aim and direction (or
the orientation and finality) are thus defined: to achieve an affluent
economy and to increase industrial production, by total automation, in proportion to social needs (instead of to individual
programmed demands), these needs being identified with the
demands of a nascent urban society; but the automation of production must in no way involve the automation of the consumer,
for such a consequence is symptomatic of a generalized mystification. When revolutionary action is restricted to the economic
plane it gets bogged down and loses sight of its true objective.
2) *A political plane* where the objective of revolutionary strategy
has not changed in the past century – from this point of view there

is no cause to modify, revise or amplify Marx's theory – the *decay of the state* remains its aim and directive. Restricted to the political plane alone, revolution produces Stalinism, the state as Idol, means taken for ends. No state-concerned and political structure is entitled to the name of Marxism if these aims and directives are not expressly formulated and do not constitute its social practice both in terms of strategical objective and on the plane of technique; short of which it is impossible (theoretically, in theory) to speak of revolution, Marxist doctrine or strategy, or of action directed towards improving the world, existence and society. Moreover it is only too true that, when one approaches the higher regions of state power, dialectics seem to lose their rights, for it is as though power could overcome progress, all progress, and ignore contradictions instead of settling them. And yet progress continues, for it is history whose progress is acknowledged by power because power makes it.

3) *A cultural plane.* This avenue has been blocked by economistic, politicizing and philosophizing interpretations of Marx's doctrine. It had been assumed that once revolutionary action had undermined the economic basis and the political superstructures the rest would follow, that is ideologies, institutions, in one word culture; however the plane has re-acquired or acquired its specificness;* its significance was recognized when the revolution encountered obstacles and setbacks on the other planes. In the 1920s, shortly after coming to power, Lenin noted the urgent need for a 'cultural' transformation of the Soviet working classes, a transformation that would enable them to administer the country and its industry, master techniques and assimilate or even outstrip Western science and rationality. Today the elaboration of projects on the *cultural* plane is justified by the acknowledged

---

* We feel there is no call here to take sides for or against the cultural revolution in China. Is it Chinese society or the Chinese revolution that is returning to its source? Is this revolution – whether novel or renovated – opposing its own counter-terror to bureaucratic terrorism? Are play and the Festival being reinstated by this revolution? Or is it only mobilizing all available energy in the prospect of a new world war? What counts, what is significant, is the revival of a concept.

specificness of this plane. It would seem that it might only be possible to by-pass the state and its institutions, to redirect 'cultural' institutions towards non-terrorist objectives when an overt, if not an official cultural crisis arises, a crisis of ideologies, of the institutions themselves, when terror would be inadequate for the closing of the microcosm. And it could only be possible to evade the compulsions of economism, of economic rationality, programming and that limited form of rationality that cannot see its own limitations, in so far as such compulsions do not succeed in closing the circuit according to their programming, in systematizing the whole of society; whence the advantage both of cracks in the structure and of the unforeseen demands of a progressive, pressing 'reality', urban reality.

Together with the concept of *man* and of *humanism* (the humanism of competitive capitalism and of the liberal bourgeoisie) the concept of *creation* has fallen into discredit. One of the first and most essential conditions for the realization of a cultural revolution is that the concepts of art, creation, freedom, adaptation, style, experience values, human being, be restored and re-acquire their full significance; but such a condition can only be fulfilled after a ruthless criticism of productivist ideology, economic rationalism and economism, as well as of such myths and pseudo-concepts as participation, integration and creativity, including their practical application, has been performed. A cultural revolution requires a cultural strategy with rules that can be set down.

The philosophy of compulsion and the compulsion of philosophy

For two thousand years it had been the philosopher's role to understand the theoretical status of natural and social man in the universe and in his natural environment. The efforts of philosophy simultaneously supplied and symbolized the answer, while philosophy summed up the disconnected experiences and knowledge of various activities. The advent of industry completely changed the status of philosophy and of the philosopher; for this new *praxis* appeared on reflection to be the depositary of the creative energy proper to social man, that creative energy which was included in philosophy but submitted there to the limitations of speculative and contemplative thought, to philosophical systems. It had formerly been the philosopher's task to disclose and formulate the significance of relations and phenomena, but now industry gave things a new meaning; a new direction; the mastery of material reality, taking the place of a 'detached' knowledge of phenomena and laws, the part once played by philosophy now devolved to a transfigured knowledge. Philosophy has taken part in the conflict between the city and the countryside, in the acceptance of 'nature' as such, in the prevalence of agricultural production, in the cult of uniqueness and in the division of labour in a society where labour was unequal, etc.; was its function to end there? Is philosophy extinct? Has it become a legend? Most emphatically not. Critical reflection, one of the products of the philosophical tradition, rejects a positivist solution; philosophy is not a thing of the past, indeed, it is starting a new lease of life; no longer restricted to the elaboration of systems, it is perpetually contrasting the philosopher's image, his concept and his ideal of mankind with reality and experience; this involves a knowledge of the whole of philosophy, as quest and as goal, a knowledge of all the philosophers, of the historical context and conditions of the different philosophies, their conflicting relations and their general trend. The supreme aim of the new revolutionary doctrine is to re-interpret the philosophers who interpreted the universe, to learn from them the theoretical procedure of change, and to achieve by these means the theoretical revolution.

Thereby the tendency to elaborate (apparently) new philosophical systems is not without its dangers; a philosophical system cannot easily avoid, nowadays, incorporating well-worn, not to say worn-out theories, categories and problems, and, moreover, contributing to terrorism; for dogmatism is undoubtedly an aspect (and by no means the mildest) of generalized terrorism.

Certain words have made their appearance of late in the vocabulary of a would-be philosophical trend or a trend that merely dodges philosophical problems; such words acquire the value of what they signify: norms, compulsions, demands, imperatives, not to mention 'rigour' and, of course, the word 'system'. These words *reflect* the limited rationalism of bureaucracy, of technocratic ideology, of industrial programming (which ignores the new problems of urbanism on behalf of a single organization, that of industrial expansion, and high-handedly decides the partition of territories, the distribution of populations).

We are thus witnessing the making of a system, the philosophy of compulsion. Social determinisms are no longer seen as obstacles to be overcome, data to be mastered and adapted by responsible measures, but as basic, essential, specific, as compulsive elements to be noted and respected; and this for the political motives we have already had occasion to condemn. Philosophy, now serving as metalanguage for this class strategy, disguises and justifies it, not by presenting it as a generalized plan or the result of political intentions, but by cataloguing it among the necessary evils; it is only too easy to pass from the philosophy of finitude and finality to that of a total acceptance of things as they are, of life as it is – a sophism that contradicts philosophy.

Philosophical tradition involves restrictions of a negative order, forbidding the assertion of certain absurdities, the pronouncement of tautologies or of postulates lacking in coherence; in this respect it is, like logic, an incomplete but essential *discipline*. This tradition attacks the philosophy of acceptance by radical analysis, distancing, rebellion and liberty; it sets against the philosophy of finitude the philosophy of desire. From such conflicts the mind emerges refreshed and restored, free from philosophical metalanguage, and avoids the two pitfalls: the death of classical philosophy, and the continuation of ancient philosophy.

He who asserts that he can do without a philosophical language is making an untrue statement and, furthermore, this sophist is using precisely such a language to formulate his claim. It is however true that metalanguage (including the metalanguage of philosophy and philosophy as metalanguage) finally convicts itself. But the intervention or a new philosophy or a philosopher of genius inventing new terms or changing the names of things is not an answer to the problem; if a scatty notion exists surely it is that of transforming existence through the transformation of words! No sooner is it stated than this proposition convicts itself. At the height of metalanguage the speaker raises his speech to the *n*th degree (is there an ultimate degree?) for the absolute message, the *fiat lux* of our age; but all to no avail. The answer is everyday life, to rediscover everyday life – no longer to neglect and disown it, elude and evade it – but actively to rediscover it while contributing to its transfiguration; this undertaking involves the invention of a language – or, to be precise, an invention of language – for everyday life translated into language becomes a different everyday life by becoming clear; and the transfiguration of everyday life is the creation of something new, something that requires new words.

The philosophical discipline preserves its educational, didactic purpose. With the city and in the city, alongside monuments and festivals, philosophy was primarily *creation*. Apart from being landmarks in historical time the different philosophical traditions indicate a 'time–space' relation, a space subjected to time, marked by it, a space on which time is inscribed. Such themes are central to a culture restored by a new preoccupation with everyday life, its analysis and transformation; for among the main objectives of the cultural revolution are the reinstatement of works of art without any prejudice to product, and the restoration of time as the supreme gift (life time); philosophy cannot be excluded from culture, and in the new culture it will be given a new and different significance by restoring – as with time and creation – its *experiential value*.

A radical critique of aesthetics and aestheticism as metalanguage is justified by the philosophical approach to art; moreover aestheticism today parodies the transfiguration of everyday life by the use of unmediated techniques – techniques that omit art as the medium of adaptation: swinging, singing mobiles, panels whose colour changes at a movement or at a word, musical corridors, a promenade made to look like a stage setting – this sort of aestheticism does not keep the promises it makes; and the restoration of art will make short work of these 'modern' antics.

Our cultural revolution

We have tried to prove that the 'cultural revolution' is a concept; it is implicit in Marx, explicit in the works of Lenin and Trotsky, and has been revived in a specific context by Mao Tse-tung in China. It is linked as a concept with the Marxist doctrine: what are the relations between basis, structure and superstructures, between theory and practice, between ideology, knowledge and strategic action? Are such relations fixed or changing, structural or contingent?

We do not intend to set up the Chinese revolution as a model; its interest and its significance lie in the fact that it gave new life and definition to the concept by expressing it in a 'modern' idiom; but the same scheme could not apply both to a predominantly agricultural nation and to one that is highly industrialized; it could not be transplanted, for a transposition of this kind is only possible in the minds of theoreticians influenced by the peculiar practice to which we have already alluded (displacements, substitutions, replacements).

Our cultural revolution cannot be envisaged as aesthetic; it is not a revolution based on culture, neither is culture its aim or its motive; we cannot aspire to infuse social reality and experience with culture, when *our* culture is fragmentary, crumbling and dissolving into moralism, aestheticism and technical ideology; this state of affairs would be more obvious were it not for the clearly defined terrorist role of a 'culture' where only philosophy still stands, and only on the condition that it is given a direction. The objective and directive of our cultural revolution is to create a culture that is not an institution but a style of life; its basic distinction is the realization of philosophy in the spirit of philosophy. The logical outcome of a critical appraisal of culture, of the prestige and glamour attached to this term, and of its institutionalization, is a total acknowledgement of philosophy, of its theoretical and practical significance, its educational, experiential, intellectual and social importance. The philosophy we have in mind is Western philosophy from Plato to Hegel, and we are concerned neither with American pragmatism nor with Confucius and Buddha; for it is common knowledge that the culture of the United States has no solid philosophical backing; that in the USSR the official culture adopted a philosophy derived from Marxist theories that were intended for a practical realization; while the East has a philosophy of its own that we shall not presume to discuss. *The theoretical revolution which constitutes the first step towards a cultural revolution is based on philosophical experience.*

The revival of art and of the meaning of art has a practical not a 'cultural' aim; indeed, our cultural revolution has no purely 'cultural' aims, but directs culture towards experience, towards the transfiguration of everyday life. The revolution will transform existence, not merely the state and the distribution of property, for we do not take means for ends. This can also be stated as follows: 'Let everyday life become a work of art! Let every technical means be employed for the transformation of everyday life!' From an intellectual point of view the word 'creation' will no longer be restricted to works of art but will signify a self-conscious activity, self-conceiving, reproducing its own terms, adapting these terms and its own reality (body, desire, time, space), being its own creation; socially the term will stand for the activity of a collectivity assuming the responsibility of its own social function and destiny – in other words for *self-administration*. Superficial observers note the distance that separates Peking from Belgrade, or they might contrast self-administration and cultural revolution; but such political comparisons are invalid in the context of concept and significance; self-administration involves certain contradictions in its make-up, among which are 'cultural' contradictions; thus, far from rejecting the cultural revolution, this phenomenon constitutes one of its features; though it does not solve the problems raised by self-administration this fact makes their exact formulation possible.

Let us set forth some of the aspects or elements of the revolutionary process:

a) *Sexual reform and revolution.* The changes contemplated are not concerned only with 'male–female' relations, juridical and political equality between contracting and engaged parties, nor with de-feudalizing and democratizing the relations between the sexes; the reform should modify the (emotional and ideological) relations between sexuality and society. Repressive society and sexual terrorism must be liquidated and dispatched by all the theoretical and practical means available; sexual repression must no longer be the concern (indeed, the main concern) of institutions; it must be eradicated; the more so as repression and terror are not limited to the control of sexual activities, but extend to all the energies and potentialities of the human being. It is not a matter of abolishing all control of sexual activities; indeed, a complete absence of control might result in the disappearance or lessening of desire by turning it into an unmediated need; desire cannot exist without control, although the repression based on control kills desire or perverts it. Control should be in the hands of those concerned, not enforced by institutions, still less by the joint methods of ethics and terror.

b) *Urban reform and revolution*. There should be no misunderstandings at this point; urbanism will emerge from the revolution, not the revolution from urbanism; though, in fact, urban experience and in particular the struggle for the city (for its preservation and restoration, for the *freedom of the city*) provide the setting and objectives for a number of revolutionary actions. Until the rationality of industrial planification undergoes a radical change and industrial administration is reorganized, production will never be geared towards urban existence and the social requirements of urban society as such. The battle is therefore fought out on the field of production and it is there that strategy must set its objectives. A practical realization of urban society involves both a political programme (covering the whole of society, the entire territory) and an economic control.

Furthermore, an *urban reform* could assume today the role and the significance that were, for half a century, those of the *agricultural reform* (and that it still preserves in some places); the structure of neo-capitalist ownership, laws and ideologies would be shaken by this revolutionary reform. Neo-capitalism and the society of Controlled Consumption are not concerned with checking the decay of what is left of urban existence today, with inventing new developments, enabling them to become generalized or

with helping and encouraging the growth of a nascent urban society; while the very notion of play as a work of art, of the city as
play, would strain the imagination of even the most cultured
bourgeoisie who would therefore be quite incapable of providing
the necessary spatio-temporal conditions.

c) *The Festival rediscovered* and magnified by overcoming the
conflict between everyday life and festivity and enabling these
terms to harmonize in and through urban society, such is the final
clause of the revolutionary plan. This specification brings us back
to where we began, to the concept of *adaptation*, setting it in its
rightful position above the concepts of *mastery* (of material reality)
and of *praxis* in the usual acceptance of the term.

Saint-Just said that the concept of happiness was new to France
and to the world in general; the same could be said of the concept
of unhappiness, for to be aware of being unhappy presupposes that
something else is possible, a different condition from the unhappy
one. Perhaps today the conflict 'happiness–unhappiness' or
'awareness of a possible happiness–awareness of an actual unhappiness' has replaced the classical concept of Fate. And this
may be the secret of our general *malaise*.

Paris 1967